Pindura by Mateus Acioli

SOUNDS AND COLOURS BRAZIL

EDITOR-IN-CHIEF, DESIGNER
Russell Slater

EDITOR
Marlon Bishop

ASSISTANT EDITORS
Nick MacWilliam
Leo Nikolaidis

COVER ART
Zansky

ASSISTANT DESIGNER
Thellius Zamprogno

TRANSLATIONS
Emily Angharad Brown, Julia Duarte, Alina Karnics, Sam
Katterfield, Jurema Simoes, Russell Slater, Eloise Stevens

CD MASTERING
Mark Jasper at Sound Savers

THANKS
Matthew Bishop, Raul Cordúla, Marcelo Costa, Natacha
Fink de Andrade, Mauricio Fleury, Thiago França, Anthony
Godfrey, Glenda Jung, Leo Justi, Darien Lamen, Pio Lobato,
Maga Bo, Luciano Matos (El Cabong), David McLoughlin,
Junia Mortimer, Felipe Muanis, Otaner (La Cumbuca), Simone
Ribeiro, Lewis Robinson, João Cezar de Castro Rocha, Greg
Scruggs (MIA), Robert Urbanus, Wax Poetics Magazine and
a huge thanks to all our contributors and everyone else who
helped make this project happen.

SOUNDS AND COLOURS BRAZIL is published by
Sounds and Colours

WEBSITE
www.soundsandcolours.com

CONTACT
info@soundsandcolours.com

OBRIGADO

This book was made with the help of a number of fundraisers who pre-ordered the book, making it possible for us to print it without going bankrupt. It's absolutely certain that without these generous people this book wouldn't have been made. So, a huge thanks (*obrigado* in Portuguese) to these fine people:

Adam Garsh • Adam Kidd • Adeline Veyret • Alastair J Rawlence • Alec Herron • Alessandro Onori • Alex Shaw • Alexander Brief • Amaya Garcia • Ana Lucia Nishio de Sousa • Andrew Ashley • Ben Stein • Bruna Gala • Carl W Meier • Chris Albee • Christine Lofgren • Clemence Aberki • Dan Swerbilov • David Abramovich • Dirk Schade • Dylan Gross • Fernando Mora • Frank Hubbard • Frode Norstrand Olsen • Geoffrey Greene • Graham Lovatt • Gina Vergel • Habib Msallem • Ian Middleton • Jeffrey Browitt • Jessica Parsons • John Mazza • Karen Hersschens • Kosmas Chatzimichalis • Lauren Valdez • Le Foyer De Costil • Leslie Totten • Lewis Robinson • Lisa Jenkins • Ludovic Barnouin • Luiz Valente • Mark Bronchtein • Mary Catherine Smith • Matt Burnett • Matthew Slater • Meghan Dwyer • Mike Andrews • Moses Iten • Muriel Bazin • Neil Forgham • Nick MacWilliam • Oliver Arditi • Pallante Center for Italian Research • Paul Herbert • Paula Abreu • Paz Chauhan • Philippa Arthan • Renee Scruggs • Richard Jackson • Richard Watt • Robert Bresnan • Ryan Nash • Sam Fraser • Sean Higgins • Sean Leigh • Seth Archambault • Simon Brueggemann • Simon Roach • Slawomir Olszewski • Sophie Johnson • Spencer Low • Sytse Groenwold • Tammie Evans • Thomas David Nicholson • Thomas Harrison • Vincent Geijsel • Vincze Barbara • Will Lahti • William Roper • Wolfram Lange • WorldCupOfJoe.com

Special thanks: Michael Deane

CONTENTS

Greg Caz, Tom Crookston, Julia Furlan, Kariann Goldschmitt,
Pedro Gutierres, Pablo Miyazawa, Russell Slater, José Teles,
Allen Thayer and Steven Totten

INTRODUCTION

by Russell Slater

Something's bubbling in Brazil. A new identity is growing. The same spirit that saw Brazil captivate the world with names like Tom Jobim, Caetano Veloso, Hélio Oiticica, Glauber Rocha and Carmen Miranda in the 50s through to the 70s is perhaps upon us again. Whichever way you look at it, it's time we stopped talking about those icons as representing Brazilian culture. The picture has widened, it's been through a dictatorship, countless protests and political shifts, it's gone digital, it's got in touch with its African roots and fallen in love with its folklore. Just as Hélio Oiticica grew tired of the way that his idea of *tropicália* (of countering the invasion of Western popular imagery by cannibalizing it) had been misappropriated with some only interested in its "tropical-ness", so Brazil needs to be treated as much more than "samba, football and City of God" (as my old boss Juliano Zappia once said).

In fact, despite the fact that this book is imbued with our passion for Brazilian culture, we're not saying that everyone should run out and learn how to samba, throw a capoeira kick or cut some nasty shapes to a *funk carioca* beat. You can if you want, but you also need to look beyond that. There are so many resources and creative minds within Brazil that the answers to many of the problems artists in the Western world face have already been answered there. Criolo, mentioned in our article on São Paulo, first released his latest album as a free download before then releasing it physically and becoming one of Brazil's biggest musical sensations of recent years. Yet in the Western world, musicians still debate whether free downloading is good or bad. In Shannon Garland's article on digital culture you'll release that Brazil's music fans are already crowdfunding so that they can see their favourite artists. Read about *cordel* literature and you'll discover that before fanzines rose up with Western counterculture, Brazil had already been producing them for close to 70 years. There's a reason why Brazil has such a great reputation for street art. In a country where it's even harder to break into the mainstream, people have had to do-it-yourself and have done so willingly, with artists like Derlon Almeida creating completely unique works of art that reflect their Brazilian reality. Essentially, there's a lot to learn and cultural appropriation should not be the long and short of it.

Yet, I can't pretend we have any real notion of changing perceptions of Brazil. This is just a book after all. But I like to think that we made it with the right idea, that we should concentrate on things that we were excited by and that through their subject or through their author's perspective had some soul to them. We cast our net wide for contributors, who thanks to our budgetary constraints (have you noticed there's no adverts?) worked on fumes of passion alone. And this says a lot, because when you think about the amount of people who helped with this book (50+ contributors, 80+ fundraisers and the countless others who helped in some way) that's a whole lot of energy created by Brazilian culture and non-commercial engines in motion. This new Brazilian bubble has balls to back it up!

BRAZILIAN MUSIC: AN INTRODUCTION

by Marlon Bishop

Really, really good music is part of the codified Brazilian "brand" – along with aptitude at football, the tumbling surf and those fabric-efficient swimsuits. Cue whispering bossa nova guitar, a gentle flute and... action!

But hold up a moment. Most of Brazil is nowhere near a beach. Brazilians wear actual clothes. And Brazilian music is so much more than bossa nova. It's an afrobeat orchestra getting the dance floor sweaty in a São Paulo club. It's glitzed-up country music at a televised rodeo in the interior. It's mind-bending electronic experiments in a Rio basement. It's US pop radically remixed at a soundsystem rave in Belém. It's an accordion-driven dance party, a clangy indie rock song, a *Beat Street*-inspired hip-hop crew.

In short, music in Brazil is many things, and far more complex than the stereotypes suggest.

In this book, we hope to give a glimpse into the immense musical creativity happening in Brazil right now. Despite the cranky complaints of some critics that Brazil isn't living up to its former musical glory, we firmly believe that Brazil is experiencing an artistic moment like none other in its history. Look around and you'll see *novo-MPB* stars who combine Brazil's great singer-songwriting tradition with contemporary indie sounds. You'll see young musicians renovating the golden-age styles of the Amazon. You'll see São Paulo rappers who channel the energy behind *tropicália*'s protest songs into cries of social justice for the poor. If you are willing to keep your ears open, you'll hear a Brazil that is constantly re-inventing itself, a Brazil that's drawing on the nation's powerful traditions while at the same time barrelling boldly into the unknown.

Behind the music are big changes that have been re-shaping Brazilian life over the last decade. The nation's economic boom has empowered a new middle-class eager to express themselves, and new digital tools to do it with. The Internet has given Brazilians access to sounds from around the world as never before, and social media has given artists new channels for sharing ideas.

In the pages that follow, we've tried to shine a light on the many musical currents electrifying Brazil today through articles by a truly fantastic collection of writers. Since you can't understand the present without the past, we also pay homage to Brazil's rich musical history in a section looking at twenty hugely influential Brazilian albums. In the end, we hope to have helped unpack the different ways music is capturing this so-called "Brazilian decade" – this moment so messy, exciting, confusing and vibrant all at once. Vamos embora, gente!

SETTING THE SCENE: RIO DE JANEIRO

by Russell Slater

"The samba is there [in Rio], it's inescapable, but it doesn't reign supreme, at least in the alternative universe." – Otaner, La Cumbuca

There was a time when Rio ruled the roost. It was the nation's capital, home to the big television networks, the movie industry and the major record labels. It was the birthplace of samba and bossa nova, and the destination for any new musician looking to make it, arriving to join those who already had. Its carnival was the biggest and brightest; a glorious showcase of what being Brazilian was all about. In short, it was the cultural and entertainment hub of the country. These days São Paulo has taken that crown – it's the new destination for aspiring artists, musicians and film-makers – and you could argue that the increasing popularity of carnivals in Salvador and Recife are even taking away its status as the first choice destination for those wanting to experience that most fabled of Brazilian parties.

Today, Rio is a city with an identity crisis. Its image – beaches, great architecture, easygoing lifestyle and the redemptive glare of Christ looking over the whole thing – is great for tourism (surely São Paulo will never take away that crown) but the samba and bossa nova that's so often associated with that image no longer takes centre stage. In underground clubs and record shops, on the streets during carnival and in recording studios up and down the city there's a new generation of musicians going beyond the picture postcards to reveal that this city's image is far more multidimensional than it's often given credit for.

One common saying about Rio is that once you pass through the tunnels from the plush surroundings of Copacabana, Urca and Ipanema in the city's Zona Sul, passing under the hills and ending up in the working-class neighbourhoods of the north, it's like entering another world; and so it is with music. Head through the tunnels passing from samba, carnival and bossa nova and you'll find a surprisingly diverse alternative music scene in Rio, full of brass bands, experimental noise and rockers trying to find that *carioca* groove.

It's Time For Plan B

The neighbourhood of Lapa, a short walk from Rio's financial centre, is the throbbing heart of Rio's party culture. Come nightfall the streets around Lapa's famous arches are packed with people, there to drink *caipirinhas* and experience the carnivalesque atmosphere. The neighbourhood is known best for its atmospheric *botecos*, its impromptu samba jams, and its many dance clubs. Yet just five minutes walk from the arches, tucked up a side street, is Plano B, a record store that has become a hub for Rio's new experimental music scene.

Felipe, of the group Chinese Cookie Poets, a cornerstone of the scene, describes Plano B as "a five square metre hot oven." In 2004, in cramped surroundings, the shop started organizing improvisation sessions every Friday night. Attendance was often confined to just a handful of people, but the simple fact that Rio's avant-garde musicians had a place to meet had a big effect. According to Felipe, genres from free jazz and avant pop to IDM and noise rock mingled at the sessions. "Just by being there and seeing other people sharing the same musical interests was like discovering the lost island," says Felipe.

Slowly word got out and a network of open-minded musicians began to coalesce around the shop, which also began featuring international touring artists. In 2011, a new night called Quintavant started in Botafogo's Audio Rebel club and splintered into an additional venue at Comuna (also in Botafogo). This meant that the scene finally had venues that could accommodate a full band, something which was never possible at Plano B. This move from mostly electronic gigs at Plano B to full bands at Quintavant is one of the reasons why this scene is so diverse. The range of styles includes the heavy doom of Bemônio, Chinese Cookie Poets' arrhythmic rock, Duplexx's glitchy IDM, Sobre A Máquina's Throbbing Gristle-esque noise assault and the *Tropicália*-tinted improv of Negro Leo. This is a scene united by a spirit of experimentation.

  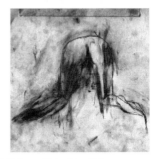

Chinese Cookie Poets, *Worm Love* (2012); Bemônio, *Santo* (2013); Sobre a Máquina, *Sobre a Máquina* (2012)

The scene was galvanized further by the emergence of Novas Frequências in 2011, an avant-garde music festival set-up by Chico Dub. The festival increased the profile of the movement and helped grow networks between like-minded Brazilian and international musicians. In the notes accompanying Chico Dub's compilation *Hy Brazil Vol 2: New Experimental Music From Brazil 2013*, he writes that "Sobre A Máquina, Bemônio, DEDO and Chinese Cookie Poets [who all featured on the compilation] are part of something very exciting that has been happening lately in Rio de Janeiro."

Despite the lack of venues in Rio for the scene and the relatively small audience – the Quintavant nights pull in up to 200 people, a good amount though not much for a city the size of Rio – the scene has been able to grow via attention garnered on the Internet. Releases by Bemônio, Chinese Cookie Poets and Sobre a Máquina all featured on the "Best of 2012" lists of many well-respected journalists and bloggers. O Globo picked up on the scene in late 2012, with journalist Silvio Essinger declaring that "the musical vanguard is gaining force in Rio", citing "the consolidation of venues, regular visits by international names, a growing interaction between the musicians and Internet buzz" as reasons for this success.

Bring On The Fanfare

While the experimental scene in Rio works on finding space for its sonic adventures, another group of bands are feeding off Rio's carnival traditions and bringing a new audience to the city's famous *blocos*. Brass bands are popping up all over the world – CQMD in France, the Youngblood Brass Band in the US and Hackney Colliery Band in the UK are just a few examples – and nowhere in Brazil is this trend getting more love than in Rio. Taking the name *fanfarra* from the European tradition of fanfare groups, Rio's bands are orchestras of brass and percussion that are primarily assembled to make music on the street. This is exactly where Orquestra Voadora, one of the break-out successes of the scene, started out. The group began as a carnival *bloco* in 2008, differentiating themselves from typical groups not just by their instrumentation but also by their repertoire,

Orquestra Voadora

which would feature covers of international pop songs alongside classic sambas and *marchinhas*.

Such was the popularity of the Orquestra Voadora *blocos* that by 2012 they were able to pull in an audience of 80,000 for their main carnival show. They also toured Europe that same year, and in 2013 released their first album *Ferro Velho*, which features covers of Fela

Kuti, Stevie Wonder and Rage Against the Machine alongside songs from the Brazilian music canon. By freeing up their repertoire to include pop songs and by offering a different sound, Orquestra Voadora have been able to offer an alternative carnival experience for young *cariocas*, and it certainly seems to be catching on. Other *fanfarra* groups in the city include Cinebloco, who interpret music from film soundtracks, Os Siderais, Go East Orkestar and Sinfônica Ambulante, from nearby Niteroi.

For these bands, samba is just one of the musical foundations, alongside rock, funk afrobeat and *forró*. This trend for big bands that appeal to a modern audience could be seen as starting with Orquestra Imperial, a *carioca* group that started life in 2002 with the idea of creating an old-school *samba de gafieira* (ballroom samba) orchestra, but featuring musicians and singers from the Rio pop scene. Some of the artists who have collaborated with the group include Seu Jorge, Ed Motta, Elza Soares and Fernanda Abreu. But when former Los Hermanos singer Rodrigo Amarante became a regular member, the group really began to attract a strong indie audience. They've since released two albums (2007's *Carnaval Só Ano Que Vem* and 2012's *Fazendo As Pazes Com o Swing*) which both focus on carnival-ready samba, though with the variations and occasional experimentation you'd expect from such a diverse range of collaborators.

One City Under A Groove

Orquestra Imperial was created by Alexandre Kassin and Berna Ceppas, two musicians who helped define a new alternative rock/pop scene in Rio since the 90s that has continued to this day. Kassin's group at the time, Acabou La Tequila, as well as Mulheres Que Dizem Sim (featuring Domenico Lancellotti and Pedro Sá – more on them later) created a new fusion of rock and pop with a certain Brazilian swing.

"In Rio it's the unique way you divide the tempo, it's the city's groove. Everyone has it inside their head," is how Kassin described this swing in a recent interview. Kassin has produced and played on countless records that contain this particular *carioca* groove [where *carioca* is the name used to describe something or someone from Rio de Janeiro]. Together with Moreno Veloso and Domenico Lancellotti, Kassin released three albums for the US record label Luaka Bop. It was known as the "The +2's" because each album would focus on the songs of one of the musicians with the other two as backing band, leading to the recording names of *Kassin +2*, *Moreno +2* and *Domenico +2*. Recently Kassin has been playing in Jorge Mautner's band (creating a link to the older *Tropicália* generation), as well as getting involved in diverse projects such as scoring the anime cartoon *Michiko to Hatchin*, producing major stars like Vanessa da Mata and Mallu Magalhães, and finally releasing his first solo record in 2011, *Sonhando Devagar*. Lancellotti has also been busy with many projects, such as Taksi, a recent collaboration with João Brasil which promises to fuse electronic and pop music in all the right places.

Caetano Veloso dipped into this talent pool for three of his most recent records, 2006's *Cê*, 2009's *Zii e Zie* and 2012's *Abraçaço*. Searching for a more experimental sound, Caetano reached out to his son, Moreno Veloso, for help. Moreno recommended some of his friends as up for the task of offering a new, angular setting for Caetano's music. The group, who became known as Banda Cê, includes Pedro Sá on guitar, Ricardo Dias Gomes on bass and Marcelo Callardo on drums, the last two of which are both members of Do Amor, a younger band who have also become a big part of this scene. They followed up their well-received debut album with the more introspective *Piracema* in 2013.

Moreno is not the only famous son to earn success of his own in Rio these days. Bem Gil, son of Gilberto, has a group called Tono who caused a ripple in 2010 thanks to their song "Samba do Blackberry", an upbeat number that took the samba cliché of lamenting a lost lover for inspiration. Here the protagonist wasn't losing his lover to another man, but to her new Blackberry. The song ends with the payoff line: "Ela me trocara por um Blackberry" ("She exchanged me for a Blackberry").

The Rio rock/pop sound, infused with what Kassin called the "city's groove" and which could be translated as a certain joie de vivre, is all over the music of Tono. It's also present in the similarly upbeat Fino Colectivo and Alvinho Lancellotti's excellent 2012 album *O Tempo Faz a Gente Ter Esses Encantos*. It can also be sensed in the folkier sounds of Cícero (for fans of Beirut) or the layered electronic excursions of SILVA, an artist originally from the state of Espírito Santo but now making a name for himself in Rio.

Seeing The Unscene

Rio is a complicated place – it's the capital that's not a capital, a city renowned both for friendliness and violence, etc., etc. – and this applies to the music too. Ricardo Dias Gomes, of Do Amor and Caetano Veloso's Banda Cê, says that "in Rio, people don't define

GIVE UPP THE FUNK

The infectious beat of *funk carioca* makes hips shake at even the chicest club in Rio, but the powers that be have always had a conflicted relationship with the city's most popular sound, and recent events have often left *funkeiros* with unusually quiet weekends. For the last five years, the letters "UPP" have been on every *carioca*'s lips. The acronym stands for "police pacification units", a government program to forcefully invade favelas and kick out the drug gangs.

While its record is mixed, UPP has had one indisputable impact: shutting down *bailes*, as the open-air *favela funk* parties are known. When the cops come in for good, they inevitably pull the plug on the sound system for any "community *baile*" that was financed by the local narcotraffickers. The rub is that it also means the end of a free party for hundreds, if not thousands, of local youth who have nothing to do with the drug trade and just want to have a good time in their own neighbourhood, as well as lost business for all the residents who benefit from the activity on *baile* night. Already, cancelled *bailes* have led to conflicts with police, from rocks and bottles to Molotov cocktails and gunshots.

At the heart of the matter are conflicting laws and regulations that highlight the public ambivalence about *funk*. Supporting the crackdown is Resolution 013, signed in 2007 by the architect of the UPP policy. As a statewide ordinance, it sets an unreasonably high and completely nonsensical threshold for cultural events in an environment like a favela. The Technology and Society Center at the Fundação Getúlio Vargas Law School, which has been working with the Association of Funk Professionals and Allies (APAFunk) to disentangle the legal barriers to *bailes*, dug through the resolution and discovered a morass of bureaucratic red tape that runs counter-intuitive to the spirit of the *bailes*. In most cases, they draw their patrons from the neighbourhood, who care more about whether or not the sound system works, if the DJs and MCs are any good, and how much beer there is on hand.

Unfortunately, Resolution 013 is selectively wielded by the UPP and largely depends on the personality of the captain in that favela, leading to a kind of capriciousness depressingly similar to the era of the narcotraffickers, when the boss' word was law. MC Leonardo, President of APAFunk, isn't opposed to police in favelas, much to the contrary, but his main concern is that "culture has been thrown into the hands of the police." DJ Sany Pitbull, who represented the Rio cultural delegation to London during the 2012 Olympics, echoes him: "Funk isn't a police matter, it's a cultural matter."

Moreover, this mantra is not just rhetoric, it's the law. In September 2009 the state legislature of Rio de Janeiro – which does not have authority over Resolution 013 – repealed a law designed to crack down on *bailes* and raves and approved the Lei Funk é Cultura (Funk is Culture Law), making *funk* an official expression of popular cultural heritage in the state of Rio. More than just a symbolic gesture, this is now a legal way to fight back against police repression. In a country that doles out lots of public money, it also means that *funk* projects are now eligible for culture funds to produce albums and cut music videos.

Cultural victories aside, the legal battles continue. APAFunk has taken steps to press its case politically, thanks in part to this unlikely fusion of *funkeiros* and law students. MC Leonardo warns that without changes, the end result would be "shutting down the largest cultural encounter in the city." While APAFunk is still a minnow in the largely apolitical ocean of *funk*, it's a significant step for a music culture that has long been considered purely hedonistic.

by Greg Scruggs

themselves by a style but have an open mind to experiment." That sentiment is backed up by Otaner, from the excellent Rio-focused blog La Cumbuca: "It's not possible to say that there exists a "musical scene" in Rio, because this would mean that there existed a group of artists that all shared the same characteristics."

It's true. Though historically Rio's musical identity has been easily summed up by the homegrown genres of samba, bossa nova and, more recently, *funk carioca*, its current musical output is almost impossible to pin down. Aside from the bands and trends identified above, there are Rio artists, such as these, who don't fit into any scene:

BNegão's fusions of hip-hop, Afro-Brazilian music and rock; Lê Almeida's Pavement-fawning garage rock; the tropical pop experiments of Gabriel Muzak; Digital Dubs' reggae soundsystem parties; Dorgas' psychedelic musings; US expat Maga Bo's rhythmic tropical bass; the hard electronic beats of Leo Justi and his more eclectic compadre Omulu; the alternative hip-hop of Cartel MCs, DJ Saddam and DJ Erik Skratch; and the undefinable Wladimir Gasper, who we are sure you'll be hearing a lot more from in the future.

There's no doubt that when you visit Rio you can easily find a club playing samba, a bar flowing with bossa nova melodies or even a party in the hills playing the hardest of *funk carioca* beats (you could even hear some saccharine pop/*baile funk* crossover fare in the clubs of Ipanema if you want). But if you dig a little deeper, there is a rich and diverse alternative scene that shows Rio for the cosmopolitan, hyper-social city that it is. Just follow the grooves, winding through the city much like its twisting tunnels, and you'll find there's something for everyone.

NA LAPA

A YOUNG SAMBA COMPOSER RECOUNTS THE AWAKENING OF RIO'S MOST MUSICAL OF NEIGHBOURHOODS

by Alfredo Del-Penho
translated by Russell Slater

Although samba is such an important part of Rio's cultural identity, it's gone through long periods in which it was ignored by the media and absent from the city's event listings. But samba was never gone; just waiting to come back to life.

During those dark days it was only thanks to underground musical gatherings that the genre kept alive not just in Rio but all over Brazil. The *roda de samba*, a kind of samba jam session around a table, has been a common practice since the music began in the early 20th century. The *roda* (circle, in Portuguese) has always been an easy way to bring new people into the music by encouraging composers, singers and musicians to mingle. Anybody can participate, whether or not you have musical training. The get-togethers happened in informal places, like people's homes. During the *roda*, it was common not only to play samba standards, but to try out new compositions and even create new songs spontaneously, on the spot. The *roda* encourages games of improvisation – for example, altering the lyrics of songs to talk about things happening during the night.

Over time the format of the *roda de samba* was copied by professional musicians in venues, clubs and samba schools. It became a show, but it kept certain traces of the *roda's* informality. For example, there was no pre-established set list, and the musicians could drink and eat during the performance. Most importantly, there wasn't a traditional front-facing stage, allowing the musicians to interact more with the audience, who gathered around them in a circle and often sang along.

In the mid-90s, the neighbourhood of Lapa in Rio de Janeiro certainly wasn't the place it is today. It wasn't a hotspot for investors, nor a place the city government promoted to tourists. In truth, it wasn't even seen as a potential hub of entertainment. Near downtown, Lapa was a low-rent and rundown neighbourhood known as a zone for prostitution and various other sketchy activities. But during this period, the samba and *choro* musicians that had doors closed in their faces in the more affluent Zona Sul neighbourhood found shelter in Lapa.

Soon, thanks to the influx of musicians, the bars Arco da Velha, Semente and Emporium 100 – all pioneers of samba in the 90s – were packed every night of the week with thousands of people eager to hear live music. This would have been unthinkable just a few years earlier. It didn't take long before plucky entrepreneurs saw what was happening and moved to the neighbourhood. Soon, countless clubs sprung up to replicate the samba dens, such as Carioca da Gema, Rio Scenarium and Sacrilégio – all of which are still active today. In the new samba clubs the tables, where the *rodas* took place, were replaced by stages, but the informal style and audience interaction remained hallmarks of the samba being made in Lapa.

Thanks to the introduction of live music, in just ten years, the formerly bohemian neighbourhood had become one of the major tourist attractions for the city. It's almost unthinkable now to visit Rio without spending at least one night in Lapa. The rebirth meant great things for the musicians, who were able to make good money and play a regular schedule of shows, with groups often playing on the same night, in the same club, every week. The traditional dance halls, like Clube dos Democráticos, Estudantina and the old Dancing Eldorado (which was turned into the Rio Cultural Centre), began to host samba again, bringing renewed interest in the salon-style samba dance known as *samba de gafieira*.

Many musicians and singers passed through Lapa during this new phase, from traditional performers with huge recording careers to young artists who were just getting started, inspired by the thrill of Lapa's nightlife. Of the regular singers, the stand-outs were Teresa Cristina, Eduardo Gallotti, Pedro Miranda, Moyseis Marques e Casuarina, Anjos da Lua and Sururu na Roda. These artists shared many traits that were prominent in the samba shows of the new Lapa – mainly the decision to make-up the set list during the show, according to the demands of the audience. Another characteristic was the regard they held for the composers, no matter whether the song was a samba classic or brand new. Almost always at the end of a show you would hear cheers of "Salve Geraldo Pereira!" or "Salve Cartola!", plaudits for the people who wrote the music.

Samba shows – which could last up to four hours, with just short breaks in-between hour-long sets – demanded an enormous amount of attention from the performers as to what was happening both on and off the stage. I would watch friends play the music without fault, even when changing style, tempo and genre on the fly. At the same time they would be engaging the audience, getting them to listen and dance and making sure they returned the following week. This was made possible by the performers' vast knowledge of both the traditional samba repertoire and the new repertoire that was taking shape: largely unrecorded songs composed by the new Lapa generation, as well as new works by storied composers who became involved with the revival, such as Wilson Moreira, Hermínio Bello de Carvalho, Elton Medeiros and Délcio Carvalho.

The exchange of experiences and recordings, as well as the work of researchers like

Paulo Cesar de Andrade, Nonato, Luis Fernando Vieira and Cristina Buarque, ensured that there was real understanding within the scene of the many subgenres of samba. As such, the Lapa singers could do weekly shows without pre-determined set lists, and still not have to repeat songs. You could hear samba variants like *samba sincopado*, *samba de partido alto*, *samba de roda*, *samba de breque*, *samba enredo* and *samba maxixado*, in a seemingly endless supply of songs. The real sense of community in Lapa allowed this kind of knowledge to flow freely between its members.

Once Lapa had become a known force, record labels signed some of the most important figures from the revival, who were still largely unknown to the public outside of Rio. The labels marketed these artists with images of the neighbourhood's famous Lapa arches and bohemian lifestyle. When Teresa Cristina recorded a double album of Paulinho da Viola songs for the Deck Disc record label, Lapa's voice was suddenly heard throughout Brazil. The success was immediate. Gradually other performers connected to the neighbourhood began recording albums, expanding their careers nationally and winning plenty of recognition along the way.

Almost 15 years have passed since my first visit to Lapa for a *roda de samba*. In this time I have seen samba clubs open and close and new urban developments appear and disappear. The neighbourhood has changed and Lapa has come to embrace much more than the samba and *choro* that kick-started its rebirth. Eclectic venues such as Fundição Progresso and Circo Voador have brought shows from every genre to the neighbourhood – artists ranging from Caetano Veloso to Forroçacana. Today the neighbourhood itself is an attraction. The tables and chairs from the bars stretch out onto the pavement and people fill the streets, especially on Friday nights. The number of samba clubs has decreased, and the *roda* regulars as well, but the samba that was being made in Lapa has since grown into many other clubs around Brazil and the world, constantly growing and spreading the joy of the Brazilian people.

For more than eight years in Lapa I played with a group called Orquestra Republicana. Together we recorded a song called "Noite À Lapa" ("Night In Lapa"), a samba I composed. This is how I remember those nights in Lapa:

Noite à Lapa (Alfredo Del-Penho)

Eu que não nasci na Lapa	*I, who was not born in Lapa*
Vi a Lapa antiga renascer	*Saw the old Lapa reborn*
Vi o Samba acontecer	*Saw the samba unfold*
Tanta gente eu vi voltar onde a lua pinta os arcos	*Saw scores of people return*
Ah, dá gosto olhar: A vida é a vida à noite aqui na Lapa	*To where the arches are painted by the moon*
E a gente generosa encontra os mais novos que	*Ah, what a sight! Life here in Lapa is the life of the night*
aprendem por lá	*Where big-hearted souls teach the young all they know*
E a Lapa segue em frente tendo quem tocar	*And Lapa strives on, embracing all those who perform*
A Lapa que sorri com a paz de quem cantou a vida	*Smiling with the peace of he who has sung his whole life*
inteira e faz se ouvir: A Lapa	*and is now finally heard: Lapa*

BATE-BOLA

DISCOVERING ONE OF RIO DE JANEIRO'S LESSER KNOWN, BUT MOST COLOURFUL, CARNIVAL CELEBRATIONS

words and photos by Damian Platt

Everyone has their own carnival.

Oswaldo Cruz, in the suburbs, feels like another country after Rio's Zona Sul and its gringos, sameness, endless beer advertising and throngs of inebriated *paulistas* in fancy dress. Here the streets are quiet and empty, nay deserted. It's mid-carnival and the only signs of the "greatest" party on earth are the bleary-eyed revellers making their way home. But at the station there is a group of men dressed in the brightest multicoloured outfits, unlike any costume I have ever seen.

They look like visitors from another planet.

The costumes are designed to make the men appear bigger than they are. They are

carrying poles that appear like medieval staffs, and attached to the poles are balls, mini-footballs, that they bounce off the ground. The *bate-bola* (also known as *clóvis*) are groups, mainly youth, who get together for carnival, and tour the city together. The name *clóvis*, apparently comes from a mispronunciation of "clown", the word used by the English in the early 20th century when they first came across the multicoloured characters at carnival time.

I'm in Oswaldo Cruz to visit Anderson and his bate-bola *turma* (group) called "Fascinação". The residential street where he lives is closed and anything but quiet. A gigantic sound system is churning out loud *funk*. The friendly and voluminous Anderson, nicknamed "Buddha", is under siege in his house, colourful uniforms decorating the walls.

The slogan for this year's costume is "Quem ta duro já sabe, não se envolve!" which is printed over images of 100 *real* notes. It's a blatant provocation, typical of the *zoeira*, the way Rio youth wind each other up. "If you're broke then you already know – don't get involved!" To wear a bate-bola costume is an expensive investment. A portion of each month's wages is saved and paid into an account, to pay for the outfit: printed leggings, T-shirts, gloves, pouches, gear that goes underneath the full costumes which are all gaudy colours and phantasmagoric detail.

The Fascinação group have Wolverine printed on their undershirts and Magneto on the front of the elaborate costume. The *turma* also has other t-shirts that have the slogan: "O único passo entre a realidade e o sonho é a atitude e isso nós temos de sobra" ("The only step between reality and dreaming is attitude and this we have in excess").

Some tough looking guys on motorbikes arrive wearing multicoloured leggings and identical box fresh Nikes. They're wearing their masks, pulled back, and therefore sport luminous semi-afros. A group of girls dressed in maids' outfits hang out across the road. The guys on bikes disappear and reappear half an hour later. They are in the company of a fully dressed bate-bola who is simply enormous and gets off his bike to bowl down the street, swaying, swinging his full body weight side to side and beating his ball to the ground – CRACK, wack, CRACK!

It's provocative, and because you can't see his face – a mixture of play and menace – a clear expression of the thin line between fun and danger, the point where the two merge and one can very quickly become the other: energy, adrenaline and aggression. The rocking side to side, the dancing and the lurid colours and masks resemble a tribal ritual.

The evening moves on and I realize that the visitors are other bate-bola *turmas*, come to pay a visit to Fascinação. They sway and swagger up and down the street, first faces covered, then with masks pulled back to reveal the grins behind as they compliment friends and relatives. As each one arrives, the crowd in the street parts in front of them as they surge through – CRACK-WACK – skipping and beating the asphalt.

Fascinação are typical *carioca* timekeepers and therefore it's well past the 7pm time they were supposed to leave. At 9pm preparations are still underway as the front of Buddha's yard fills with people getting dressed. Kids and friends are kicked out, and only the bate-bola are allowed. Outside the street has filled up, with girlfriends, neighbours, friends and sisters. Finally we can see flags emblazoned with 100 *real* notes above the wall. Dozens of firecrackers are set off and the neighbourhood lights up, smoke filling the road. The music is full blast.

Then the doors are opened and Fascinação and its soldiers of fun spill out across the road bouncing, flags clutched, swinging their poles and *bola* like gladiators of kitsch. They make two or three ascents and descents of the street before pulling back their masks and mingling with their supporters. There are mini bate-bolas in tiny costumes, and plenty of people taking photos. Mothers, sisters and girlfriends make final adjustments to their outfits. They're off.

On the way back to the south of the city by van, some teenage passengers break the monotony of the long journey by making wisecracks and targeting pedestrians with a water pistol. But they reserve special admiration for any bate-bola, who they spot from afar. I ask them what they think of the bate-bola. One of them responds immediately: It's the best thing there is. He frowns. But this year, he says with a sigh, "I couldn't afford it".

"Quem ta duro já sabe, não se envolve!"

THE JOY OF JONGO

HOW ONE COMMUNITY IS CULTIVATING AN AFRO-BRAZILIAN TRADITION IN THE MOUNTAINS OF RIO DE JANEIRO

by Eloise Stevens

An elderly man, white scarf wrapped tightly against the Rio de Janeiro mountain chill, is sitting amidst a swarm of people, eagerly vying for his attention. He responds slowly but assuredly, his wizened face often cracking open into a wide smile, perfect teeth gleaming from his mouth. Just as he launches into another anecdote, his daughter, Elizabeth, helps him to his feet and ushers him into the mud hut chapel before him, from which clusters of candles spill their light into the velvety darkness. Hundreds of people pour in, nudging one another for a glimpse. There, before the altar bedecked with saints and shells, Tio Mané takes a deep bow, and asks for the blessing of his ancestors.

He walks out to a large clearing, his entourage following behind him. A huge bonfire is ablaze in the clearing's centre, and they quickly form a wide circle around it. Tio Mané and his daughter make their way into the middle, the flames flickering slivers

photo by Ana Pinta

of light onto their solemn faces. The piercing wail of a woman's voice is catapulted into the circle, immediately punctuated by the response of the drums. The pair begin to dance, swooping in to meet each other, then out again. His movements are as lithe and fluid as a deer's. Soon the whole circle is chanting, ricocheting their replies off the leading woman's calls, driving forth the dance that will go on long past sunrise.

As the patriarch of the Quilombo de São José, Tio Mané holds the responsibility of opening this dance, the *jongo*. And tonight's jongo is arguably the most important dance of the whole year, the raison d'être of the Festa de Cultura Negra (Black Culture Festival). Thousands of people have travelled here, high up in the mountains of Rio de Janeiro state to celebrate this festival, established to commemorate the day of the abolition of slavery on May 13th, 1888. The festival may be a relatively recent venture but the veneration of the day is a long-established tradition. As for jongo itself, its seeds were sown long before when Africans first set foot on Brazilian soil in 1580.

These Africans, originating from diverse Bantu tribes in Angola and the Congo, brought with them a wide variety of the Bantu dance traditions. Forced to work together on the coffee plantations in the Valley of Paraíba in Rio de Janeiro state, the distinct characteristics of each of their dances became amalgamated, and a new Brazilian variety was born: the jongo. As in the Bahian *samba de roda*, the participants of jongo form a circle while one couple, such as Tio Mané and Elizabeth, dances in the centre. It is a dance of the *umbigada*, or "belly strike", a gesture which consists of the couple coming together to strike their bellybuttons one against the other, and which is traditionally a celebration of fertility. Although the plantation owners suppressed many aspects of African culture, they allowed jongo to be performed on certain saint days, believing that it increased the fertility of the slaves and would render them more offspring to work on the plantations.

Though the dance may not have increased the fertility of the slaves it definitely increased their cunning, as the dances became spaces in which the slaves could communicate privately, away from the ears of the plantation owners. For many of the jongo chants, though seemingly poetic, are actually encrypted metaphors. Furthermore, the majority follow a call and response pattern, allowing *jongueiros* to communicate openly under a canny guise. It is speculated that slaves were able to plan their escapes in these *rodas de jongo* (jongo circles), and consequently communities of escaped slaves, or *quilombos* as they are known in Portuguese, sprung up all over Brazil. These became spaces where the slaves could practise their traditions more freely, and are now recognized as a vital part of Brazilian patrimony. Naturally, each *quilombo* devised certain ways of carrying out their traditions, and slowly began to develop their own distinct identity. As such, there are fifteen different communities which dance jongo, each with their own particular characteristics.

Unlike other *quilombos*, the Quilombo de São José was not formed by escaped slaves. It was founded after abolition when the plantation owners allowed their former slaves to remain living on the land, but their form of jongo is no more repressed as a result.

Here, just as in the days of slavery, jongo has been typically danced to celebrate certain saint days, which often correspond to a particular African deity. Due to its religious nature, only the most respected members of the community were able to dance jongo. Nowadays, although it is still a crucial means of venerating the ancestors, jongo is no longer restricted to saint days, and can be danced by all members of the community, young and old. A great bonfire is lit, which is the physical and spiritual centrepiece of the celebration. The three drums used to beat out the rhythms, the *tambu*, the *candongueiro* and the *caxambu*, are laid by the fire to warm them, which finely tunes the instruments. Once the dance has begun, not only does the fire serve the practical purpose of providing light and warmth throughout the night, but its smoke also rises up to the heavens, paying due homage to the watchful ancestors.

Yet if jongo is the heritage of these rather isolated and marginalized communities, why do so many people attend the Festa de Cultura Negra? The dance, it seems, with the help of cultural organizations such as the Companhia de Aruanda and the Jongo da Serrinha, which work to teach and promote jongo in Rio de Janeiro, has gained a great deal of popularity in the last five years. According to Rodrigo Nunes, a historian at the Companhia de Aruanda, "many people from many different places have begun to learn jongo, to write books, theses, record CDs and make films, and the Festa de Cultura Negra has become the main point of reference for many of these people, not solely as a means to see the dance and the ceremony in action, but as a means of connecting with their heritage and ancestors."

This is perhaps the most powerful appeal of the dance, and one that was formerly made more explicit when the festival was called Homenagem aos Pretos Velhos, literally "Homage to the Black Ancestors". Brazilians are very conscious of the great mix of ethnicities that make up their diverse physical appearances, and as such often feel a great affinity to their Afro-Brazilian heritage. This affinity is further consolidated in the chants that accompany the dancing of jongo, which are often dedicated to the ancestors and their imagined homelands. For example:

"*Eu nasci n'Angola,*
Angola que me criou,
eu sou filho de Moçambique,
meu Deus de Ceú,
eu sou negro sim sinhô."

"*I was born in Angola,*
Angola raised me,
I am a child of Mozambique,
I am black, yes I am."

Yet it is not just ancestral affiliation that is attracting more and more people to learn jongo each year. The dance is a delight in itself. The form of the *roda*, in which participants form a ring to clap and chant while taking turns to dance within the circle, means that everybody can participate, even if they do not want to dance. Dance does however play a vital part of Brazilian culture, and jongo is not just relatively easy, but also incredibly expressive. "Everybody puts a bit of themselves into the dance. You just have to let your body dance for you, feel the rhythm of the music and let your body respond," says Nunes. And of course, there's the flirtatious nature of the dance. Although jongo is no longer strictly a dance of fertility, it very much appears as one of courtship. The *umbigada* may no longer be a literal "belly strike", but the dance still obliges the couple to swoop in to greet each other, arms raised, making it the perfect space for the exchange of furtive glances.

Its fun and lively appeal coupled with the historical importance of jongo are likely to continue attracting more participants and researchers. Nunes is very optimistic about the future of the dance. "With all these people beginning to take more and more interest in jongo, I think that it will soon become as important and as well-known as samba throughout Brazil," he says. That may be a long shot, but in Rio de Janeiro, *rodas de jongo* are slowly making their way into the centre of the city, performed under the Lapa Arches and in the lofty vaults of the entertainment venue Trapiche Gamboa, two traditional samba hotspots.

It is even possible that jongo's legacy might spread beyond the borders of its national turf as lesser-known Brazilian rhythms gain attention abroad. The US DJ and producer Maga Bo, for example, has recently released an album entitled *Quilombo do Futuro*, which incorporates jongo in "Balanço da Canoa", and which is getting played at so-called "global bass" parties the world over.

These events and recordings, no matter how underground, are fundamental to the survival, not just of the dance itself, but of the Quilombo de São José. For as more people visit the *quilombo* to learn about the dance, so too they bring a small income to the community and learn about the way of life of its inhabitants. Since the *quilombo*'s establishment, the inhabitants have worked the land, growing coffee, beans and potatoes to lead a self-sustaining lifestyle. Yet they do not own the rights to the land they have lived on and cultivated for over 200 years. The festival has attracted the attention, not just of the general public, but of NGOs and social movements who have dedicated themselves to helping the *quilombolas* fight for ownership of their land. The process is a long and gruelling one however, and may take a further ten years to be completed, according to Nunes.

Furthermore, on July 4th, 2013 construction crews entered the territory, uprooting trees and destroying local agriculture in order to build a road between the municipalities of Valença and Barra do Piraí. Awareness has been raised within the jongo community, with plans to involve the IPHAN (Institute of National Historical and Artistic Patrimony) and the Environmental Delegacy to put a crucial stop to these actions. The survival of jongo depends on the survival of the Quilombo de São José, just as the *quilombo* depends on the dance. Not only is jongo an invaluable symbol of the community's identity but it is a fundamental part of their livelihood, as important as the crop harvest itself. Neither jongo nor *quilombo* can afford even the slightest of knock-backs. Yet Tio Mané retains a staunch and dignified optimism, demonstrating a resilience worthy of his 93 years: "As long as we plant our crops, we will dance our jongo." In the name of vital Brazilian heritage, we can only hope that all lovers of jongo will fight for this statement to remain a reality.

SETTING THE SCENE: SÃO PAULO

by Russell Slater

"São Paulo is a hard city. A concrete jungle. However, it is a city that breathes culture. Things happen here. The access to movies, albums, shows and books is intense, and it ends up being reflected in the culture." – Marcelo Costa (Scream & Yell)

São Paulo doesn't possess an identity in the way that Rio de Janeiro, Salvador or Recife does, which is all the more surprising given that the city is the undoubted musical hub of the country. In fact, other than Brazilian hip-hop, there are few genres that you could deem as being quintessentially *paulistano* (as São Paulo natives are known), and up until the 90s there were very few artists that could be seen as godfathers of a São Paulo music scene. Excluding Os Mutantes, who had a big impact on Brazilian rock but whose creative fulcrum Arnaldo Baptista eventually became ridiculed for being "crazy", you could say the first real São Paulo music icon was Arnaldo Antunes. He is a singer, poet and author whose work has refused to sit still, shifting between pop, rock, spoken word and the avant-garde, often with collaborators who steer his craft in new directions.

Antunes, whose career started in 1984 with the iconic rock band Titãs, describes São Paulo as being comparable to London or New York, "a metropolis with many cultures, a city of cities." He sees this aspect, the mixing of cultures to be a big influence on his work: "The idea of fragmentation, of collage." This multiculturalism comes from São Paulo's history as an entry point for immigrants from overseas and migrants from other parts of Brazil, which still continues to this day thanks to the city's formidable economy - São Paulo alone has a higher GDP than Israel, Portugal or Ireland.

A more recent musical ambassador for São Paulo is Céu, whose first album came out in 2005. She has always used her lyrics and music to tell her personal stories while simultaneously evoking the claustrophobic urban nature of the city. She continues Antunes' point about the scale of the city: "In São Paulo there are so many people from all over Brazil, from the north, the northeast, the south, so I think it's natural to make this collage, using all these different styles. It would be strange to do just one specific thing as if I was from Recife or from samba culture. I am not from this, I am from a huge city that has a lot of different languages. I think that's why my style of music has a lot of different sounds, because it's natural for me."

Despite producing such different music, both Antunes and Céu would most likely be categorized as MPB, a generic term for music that flits between genres, styles and influences but carries the common thread of being devoted to songcraft rather than based on a particular rhythm. Many artists from São Paulo – thanks to their musical collages – fall within the MPB bracket.

Pushing The Boundaries of Pop

Céu's success (international tours, critical adulation, Latin Grammy nominations, etc.) has led to a surge in strong female singers coming from São Paulo. Some were instantly forgotten, but several have managed to create their own identity. Karina Buhr, previously of the *Pernambucan* group Comadre Fulozinha, is currently mixing rock, pop and sardonic wit with the help of two of Brazil's finest guitarists (Edgar Scandurra and Fernando Catatau); Cibelle has consistently reinvented herself from electronic chanteuse to acoustic troubadour or kitsch pop star while living between SP, London, Berlin and New York; Luisa Maita is on the way towards a perfect samba-MPB blend, much as her famous *paulistano* father Amado did in the 70s; Barbara Eugenia, on the other hand, fashions her songs with a retro Lee Hazlewood/Serge Gainsbourg flavour. But perhaps the most interesting of all the new female *sampa* singers is Tulipa Ruiz.

Tulipa, who released her debut album *Efêmera* in her early-30s, arrived in the São Paulo music scene from her small-town upbringing in Minas Gerais as a fully-formed personality. Her ability to create vignettes of everyday life that carry with them a sense of joy and catharsis are Lennon-esque in their simplicity and impressionism. At the same time she plays with melodies in a way that neither sounds Brazilian nor Western in their approach. On her second album, *Tudo Tanto*, she collaborated with Lulu Santos and Hurtmold, retrospectively the kings of *brega* pop and Brazilian post-rock, illustrating how she is able to create pop songs while still being musically adventurous. Best of all though are her lyrics. Her song "Dois Cafés" is a perfect snapshot of São Paulo life, with lyrics saying: "The bank, the asphalt, the motorbike, the pneumatic drill / Car exhaust invades the entire house."

Of course it's not just women making pop music in São Paulo. Marcelo Jeneci has become a hugely influential producer, arranger and songwriter, working with artists such as Antunes, Tulipa, Vanessa da Mata and Kassin, as well as recording a critically-acclaimed debut album as a solo artist in 2010. Marcelo Camelo is another influential singer/songwriter from SP, though he's best-known for being a former member of the band Los Hermanos. It's safe to say that without Los Hermanos, the São Paulo music scene would be very different. They had a big hit with "Anna Júlia", their first single in 1999, and never looked back, establishing themselves as the quintessential São Paulo indie rock band, and can be seen as the last underground group from the city to really crossover into the mainstream. Their influence can be heard in SP-based acts like Tatá Aeroplano, Apanhador Só, Jair Naves and Wado.

Proving that MPB could literally stand for anything is the fact that Passo Torto also exist within this genre. A four-piece band comprised of Rômulo Froes, Kiko Dinucci, Rodrigo Campos and Marcelo Cabral, Passo Torto could be seen as a São Paulo supergroup, such is the reputation of all of these musicians. Their sound is free of drums, just guitar, bass and voice, sometimes recalling the traditional *voz e violão* of João Gilberto, while at others, the heavy distortion of Tom Waits' cubist funk.

All Begins With Exu

Much of the country's Afro-Brazilian consciousness is seen as coming from the northeast of the country, from Bahian artists like Gilberto Gil and Carlinhos Brown, from the carnivals of Recife or Salvador, and from afro-syncretic religions like *candomblé*. However, there is an increasing presence of African roots in music coming out of São Paulo. Kiko Dinucci, guitarist for the band Passo Torto, is one of those. His research into the subject led him to make the documentary *Dança das Cabaças - Exu no Brasil* and write songs that expressed his interest in *candomblé* for his group Kiko Dinucci e Bando AfroMacarrônico, and later for Metá-Metá. This group, which consists of a core of Dinucci on guitar, Thiago França on saxophone and the vocals of Juçara Marçal can be seen as continuing the tradition of Vinicius de Moraes and Baden Powell's Afro-Sambas, especially on tracks like "Obá Iná." The song's explosive chorus sings of Xangô, the king of fire, with the mention of his name serving as a musical bolt of lightning striking the earth.

Hip-hop artist Rodrigo Brandão is another devotee of *candomblé*, integrating his belief into songs such as "Rainha do Mar" ("Queen of the Sea"), an ode to the water goddess Iemanjá. A hugely different artist and *candomblé* devotee is DJ Tudo, who makes field recordings of Afro-Brazilian religious practices, releasing them through his Mundo Melhor record label and later integrating samples into his Afro-Brazilian funk-jazz collective DJ Tudo e Sua Gente de Todo Lugar, who are well on their way to becoming a popular fixture on the European festival circuit.

Other artists to explore African roots include Gui Amabis, whose *Memórias Luso/Africanas* album was a heavy and moving tribute to the various ethnic groups that combined to make Brazil's cultural DNA. This extraordinary album featured vocals from the likes of Criolo, Tulipa Ruiz, Lucas Santtana, Céu and Siba, which really makes you wonder why so few people have discovered it. Another album that deserves to be better-known is *Bahia Fantástica* from Rodrigo Campos, which again explored Afro-Brazilian stories on songs like "Ribeirão", a heartfelt tale about the enslaved Africans who lived in Bahia.

Tulipa Ruiz, *Tudo Tanto* (2012); Ekundayo, *Ekundayo* (2012); Criolo, *Nó Na Orelha* (2011)

Who are the São Paulo Underground?

One of the best albums of 2012 was recorded in the El Rocha studio, located in the artist-friendly neighbourhood of Pinheiros. Ekundayo was the name given to both the album (a multilingual, percussion-heavy jazz/hip-hop opus) and the band, which included the vocal talents of Rodrigo Brandão, Lurdez da Luz and revered US poet/rapper Mike Ladd, and the instrumental skills of Pernambucan percussionist Nana Vasconcelos, NY-based bassist Scotty Hard and the trio of Guilherme Granado, Mauricio Takara and Rob Mazurek. Those last three are better known internationally as São Paulo Underground. They have released four albums to date which continually push sonic boundaries, mixing rock, free jazz, electronics and percussive noise-scapes that occasionally burst into serene melodies that bring some accessibility to their musical experiments.

Both Granado and Takara also play in Hurtmold, a band that emerged out of the punk/hardcore scene in the 90s to become a progressive-minded band that refused to be pinned down by genre. Granado told me that they grew out of the punk scene because they "didn't want to play loud, screaming shit all the time." They "wanted to try two drums, try different instruments." Takara, Granado and the other members of Hurtmold also play in a huge variety of bands – Bodes e Elefantes, M. Takara 3, Response Pirituba and Chankas, to name just a few – that explore electronic music, free improvisation and hard rhythms.

Is Hip-Hop The Future?

If you know anything about contemporary Brazilian music, you will know that there has been one great omission to this article so far and that is the presence of Criolo, undoubtedly the most exciting new artist to emerge from Brazil, and hence São Paulo, in some time. In truth, he's not alone – Brazilian hip-hop is in great shape with rappers like Emicida, Rael, Ogi and Sombra all part of an exciting rap scene that is fusing Brazilian traditions with the urban landscape.

Yet it's Criolo who stands out for representing many of the things that are great about the music scene in São Paulo. Hailing from the huge but impoverished neighbourhood of Grajauex, Criolo combines tough hip-hop beats, black consciousness, a love for traditional Brazilian rhythms, live instrumentation and a pop sensibility. He also has an ability to connect with the public across class lines, thanks to the sweeping poetic statements of songs such as "Não Existe Amor em SP" ("Love Doesn't Exist in SP").

If Criolo is able to continue his success and continue releasing records that are anywhere near as good as his breakout success Nó Na Orelha in 2011 then São Paulo will most certainly have their own musical icon for years to come, someone who is able to translate the city's landscapes and multiculturalism into emotions and rhythms that we can all understand. As Criolo so beautifully put it in "Não Existe Amor em SP", São Paulo is a "mystical labyrinth." It's artists like him who are able to show us that if we keep searching through that maze there are many amazing things to be found.

NOTHING BUT AN SP THANG

A SÃO PAULO STREET CULTURE ICON TELLS
THE STORY OF HOW HIS HOMETOWN AND
HIP-HOP FELL IN LOVE AT FIRST BEAT

by Rodrigo Brandão

My first contact with hip-hop came in the mid-80s through the movie *Beat Street*. It was also the first time mom and dad allowed me to get on the bus to go out by myself – for a Friday afternoon showing at a run-down old theatre in Osasco, a factory town on the outskirts of then far-from-trendy São Paulo.

For my schoolmates and I, like pretty much everyone else in attendance, everything in the film was brand new – we didn't know shit about the four elements, break beats or even where the Bronx was. It was all about that crazy new dance they were doing. Instantly, we tried to copy the moves on the screen. Maybe this story wouldn't pass a B-Boy purist's test, but that's no shame around here. All the hip-hop originals in Brazil started the exact same way.

Wild Style, the real deal when it comes to old school hip-hop flicks, wasn't available for Brazilian audiences until its DVD release in 2004. That's just one example of how hard it was to get any proper information about hip-hop during the early years of beats, rhymes and graffiti in the land of samba, carnival and football. The lack of sources might have been the end of it in some other nations, but in Brazil, it ended up making it grow in some unexpected, original ways.

Make no mistake – although cats from Rio De Janeiro, Belo Horizonte or Recife might fairly claim that they discovered hip-hop at the same time – São Paulo has been the undeniable capital of the culture since day one. Maybe it's because it's the largest urban centre in all of South America, São Paulo provided the habitat to let it grow. Maybe the old cliché that parallels SP to New York and Rio to Los Angeles as like-minded cities has some truth to it. Or perhaps it was something else: the fact that, except for São Paulo, every part of Brazil has an ancient rhythm attached to its local cultural identity. It's possible that this lack of roots caused the country's least-postcard-friendly city to be open to this crazy new style from far away.

No matter the reason, even the proudest MCs, DJs, b-boys and graffiti writers from around the country wanted to get to know the legendary São Bento subway station, that most iconic temple of hip-hop in Brazil. Located downtown, the station was the perfect spot for gathering people from every ghetto neighbourhood, because it wasn't too far out for anybody. Guys had to travel about an hour to get there, no matter if you lived in the north, south, east or west side of town, so it was fair for all.

Since a bunch of dudes worked as office boys in those days, doing small jobs like paying bills for their bosses or getting somebody's signature on contracts, it was normal to have a small group rocking a cipher during the week once in a while. But the main thing was going on every Saturday. That's when you'd see hundreds of Adidas-suited dancers going crazy round an old family stereo that roughly looked like a boombox, playing terrible sounding cassettes that somebody recorded off the radio.

Back then computers were rare and the Internet wasn't even a concept yet. But on top of that, the country was coming out of over 20 years of military dictatorship. During that long, dark period in Brazil's history, it was harder than hard to access what was going on around the globe in real time, so every time somebody managed to get their hands on anything related to hip-hop – be it a record, an article or even a picture, they would take it to São Bento to share the precious artefact with the community.

Through this ritual, the first generation started to expand their knowledge of the culture, but they also added some local flavour without even meaning to. Capoeira, the Afro-Brazilian body expression that is a mix of fighting and dancing, has been popular for ages among Brazilians, and it has some similarities to what the Rock Steady Crew did in *Flashdance*, another movie that became influential for Brazilian b-boys. It was only a matter of time before they linked the two dances and morphed the style of b-boying into something subtly Brazilian.

It was the same thing with rap. Samplers, drum machines, mixers – none of those tools were around, and most guys didn't even understand where the beats came from. It was all so new and fresh and they just wanted to do it. That's when our musical heritage took over. It's a deep-rooted tradition that you can see on any corner – a bunch of friends around a bar table, drinking, doing a *batucada* (percussion jam) and singing samba standards. So the aspiring MCs did hip-hop the same way, banging on trash cans with their bare hands to fill in for instrumentals while somebody else dropped rhymes. Forget rap battles or freestyling. Those only started happening a few generations later, during the late 90s. Back in the day cats had to hold the rhythm for each other, so competition wasn't the main ingredient as it was in the States. It was all about coming together.

Many now-legendary figures of the scene were there from the start: Brazilian Zulu Nation king Nino Brown (crowned by Afrika Bambaataa himself in a 2002 ceremony), iconic dancer Marcelinho Back Spin, proto-street celebrity Nelson Triunfo (he has the largest afro ever, earning him the nickname "Tree Man"), the late visionary JR Blau and Rappin' Hood (the master of blending samba and hip-hop aesthetics), to name just a few.

But the first stars to make hip-hop in green and yellow were Thaîde & DJ Hum, the Brazilian parallel to Eric B. & Rakim. In 1988, when the pioneer local rap album came out, a compilation called *Hip-Hop Cultura de Rua* (Hip-Hop Culture Of The Street), it was their single "Corpo Fechado" that became the real subterranean hit. Nowadays it's considered the indisputable number one classic track. As a kid who wasn't an active part of those early chapters in history, that was the first rap I learned the lyrics to in my life.

Of the São Bento crew, the only ones to achieve true global recognition are the twin brothers Gustavo and Otávio Pandolfo, the street art wizards collectively known as Os Gêmeos. Their artwork has evolved from its initial emulation of traditional New York throw-up style to such a higher level that it can't be described strictly as graffiti, but hip-hop is definitely where their roots are, and that essence remains untouched in their art.

Even though anything they spray is worth a lot of money, the brothers have found a way to stay hungry. We're friends, but since those cats are big international travellers, sometimes it's not that easy to keep up. I often realize they're back in town only when I see a load of fresh pieces go up in São Paulo overnight. No matter how many galleries are waiting for some new exhibitions, Os Gêmeos just keep bombing the city.

While Gustavo and Otávio went off to conquer the world, Brazil was left firmly in the hands

BRAZILIAN SAMPLES THAT MADE HIP-HOP HISTORY

"Fuckin' [Dilla's] the first person to sample a Brazilian record," hip-hop photographer B+ says. "The first dude [in hip-hop] to be feeling that shit." B+ is right about Dilla making Brazilian grooves safe for the masses, but he wasn't the first DJ or producer outside of Brazil to flip a Brazilian beat. The earliest and most egregious sampling of a Brazilian artist was when Rod Stewart jacked Jorge Ben's "Taj Mahal" groove for "Da' Ya' Think I'm Sexy?" Before Brazilian songs were getting reworked for hip-hop, dance music DJs were playing the originals and remixing them into fresh productions, most notably in the rare groove and jazz dance scene of 80s London. Here's a few of the most prominent samples from the hip-hop world:

Arthur Verocai – Like the second coming of David Axelrod, producers jumped to sample Verocai's hens-teeth rare solo album, assuming they could find a copy. 9th Wonder flipped "Caboclo" for Little Brother's 2005 "We Got Now," holding on to the brass-tastic "Na Boca do Sol" for Ludacris' 2008 track "Do the Right Thang" with Spike Lee and Common. For its relatively short (known) existence, the album racked up numerous placements, including MF Doom and Bow Wow featuring Snoop Dogg.

Jorge Ben – In addition to the cheap and sexy appropriation of Ben's slice of samba funk "Taj Mahal," another track from *Africa Brasil* anchored an obscure 1990 track by MC Jewel with DJ Screen sampling "Ponta de Lança Africano (Umbabarauma)". Back when the Black Eyed Peas were underground, they liberally sampled Jorge

Ben on their first album, like when they used Jorge Ben's funky acoustic strumming and Trio Mocoto's organic rhythm section from their classic "Comanche" for the 90s indie joint "Falling Up."

Tom Zé – To be honest, it's surprising more producers haven't sampled Zé, especially the album profiled here... but there is that one track he did that has a really funky/chunky guitar riff – "Jimmy Renda-se" that CeeLo rocked to great effect on Amerie's 2006 single, "Take Control."

Tim Maia – It's about time the rest of the world started getting hip to Tim Maia. Maybe we'll soon hear some US hip-hop tracks built off of his massive and massively funky catalogue. It's no surprise that the originals of the Brazilian rap scene recognized a kindred spirit in Tim Maia's brash, black and bold style. First generation Brazilian crews (Filosofia da Rua and Sampa Crew, for example) sampled from Tim Maia's catalogue in the same way that DJs in the US pilfered the James Brown catalogue. "Ela Partiu" gets some extra boom-bap as the base for Racionais MC's rhymes on "O Homem na Estrada".

Marcos Valle – "I got some money," Marcos says about his compensation for Jay-Z's devastating use in "Thank You" of a bombastic horn intro from his 1970 tune "Ele e Ela." Kanye took a couple of bars of moody piano from "Bodas de Sangue" for "New God Flow." The Madvillian album is infested with Brazilian samples, the product of Madlib's prior trip to Brazil as part of the *Brasilintime* project. Madlib flipped Osmar Milito's performance of Valle's swinging piano percussive samba-pop, "America Latina" for the rhythmic base of "Raid."

by Allen Thayer

of a man who could be described as rap's Pelé. Imagine if Tupac was slick enough to stay alive and had the heavyweight aura of Dr. Dre, the lyrical gifts of Nas, and lived in the Third World. Ladies and gentlemen, meet the one and only Mano Brown.

Brown is the ultimate ghetto super-hero. He imprinted Brazil with the idea that rap's job was to give a political voice to those on every periphery – people outside society both geographically and financially speaking. He single-handedly took hip-hop in Brazil to the hardcore path it went down and remains on today, even with the more pop-oriented take from younger generations.

Mano Brown is the leader of Racionais MC's, the most legendary rap act to ever rise from this land. Although they've been prominent since the early 90s, they've never stopped being on top of the game and haven't changed the line-up to this day. Brown's cinematic storytelling skills and poetic/prophetic tone really came out, starting with Racionais' third record, *Raio-X Brasil* (1993). A couple of years after, when Ice-T was in town, the Brazilian version of Yo! MTV Raps took him to shoot a show visiting Mano Brown in his 'hood. Already, the man was a legend in São Paulo.

When *Sobrevivendo No Inferno* hit the streets at the end of 1997, there was an instant fever from the bottom to the top of the country. The album was pushed by the video for "Diário De Um Detento," a track featuring seven minutes of straight verses detailing the infamous Carandiru prison massacre, when police invaded the largest jail in town allegedly to stop a riot and ended up murdering 111 inmates. That's just according to official sources; everybody in the streets said it was at least three times that number. It was the most unlikely track to become a hit single, but it was impossible to avoid it.

It was literally everywhere.

Half a decade later, the highly-anticipated follow-up was released. CD piracy was at its heyday and record industry execs were in despair, so they couldn't believe what happened when Racionais put out *Nada Como Um Dia Após O Outro Dia*, a double album. With Mano Brown at his creative peak, dropping one street anthem after another, they topped even the most optimistic sales forecasts. At that point, the crew had developed their style to the fullest and were recognized as the masters of the *rap nacional* aesthetics of rhyming and producing.

It wasn't always like that. At the beginning, they were just young guys who loved Public Enemy. So much that the first time Flavor Flav & S1W hit São Paulo during their *Tour Of A Black Planet* in 1991, a young Mano Brown dared to sneak through the security block and reach Chuck D to ask for an opening spot at the show. Chuck gave it to them, back when Racionais was considered way too radical for the stage even by the local promoters who brought Public Enemy, who were pretty Black Panther-ish themselves.

Edi Rock, Racionais' other lyricist and former frontman, told me that inside story years later. Back during that October night, I was just one of the kids in the huge crowd who felt the impact of the two-track-only appearance of Racionais that Chuck D secured for the group, completed by rapper Ice Blue and DJ KL Jay. As a teenager, I don't think I realized it in the moment, but looking back, that was one of the most important moments in my life. It was the moment when I realized that not only did I love hip-hop (thanks to the Beastie Boys and Run DMC), but that I was hip-hop. After that day I decided to take up the lifestyle and run with it.

Both acts killed and I remember walking for miles and miles through São Paulo in a *Warriors*-type journey back home (minus the fighting though), and realizing how much the art form of hip-hop spoke to my soul. It was its freshness, because you could make music just using the records I had always loved collecting instead of having to be a trained musician. And I loved to write. I felt like I could do this.

Rodrigo Brandão

It took me a few more years before I managed to pick up a mic and get on stage, but thanks to the pioneers like Thaîde and Mano Brown, street poetry is still my everyday.

THE FELABRATION HAS BEGUN

HOW A NATION FELL UNDER THE SPELL OF AFROBEAT

by Russell Slater

"I was totally fucked up, almost giving up because I couldn't pay my bills. You know how it goes for musicians?"

When I met Mauricio Fleury in his São Paulo studio he had no qualms in stressing how tough life had become in 2007, a time when he was seriously reflecting if music was his future. Soon though, things began to change. The stewardship of a Nigerian drumming legend, an offer of a production job and his meeting with a number of like-minded musicians resulted in the formation of Bixiga 70, a 10-piece Brazilian afrobeat group. And they weren't the only ones to embrace Nigeria's percussive dance music, brought to the world's attention by Fela Kuti in the 1970s. A year previously, Abayomy Afrobeat Orchestra started life in Rio de Janeiro, soon to be joined by Belo Horizonte's Iconili. Brazilian afrobeat had come alive.

It Began In Africa

Any story involving Brazil and afrobeat must start with Gilberto Gil. In 1977 Gil had been invited to perform at FESTAC, the self-appointed World Black & African Festival of Arts and Culture that was having its second edition in Lagos, Nigeria. Kuti was one of Nigeria's and Africa's biggest stars at the time, but wanted nothing to do with the festival due to his ongoing battle against the government. Instead, he ended up staging an "alternative" FESTAC in his Kalakuta Republic home with the invited musicians, including Gil, Stevie Wonder and members of Sun Ra's Arkestra. Gil told me in an interview that he "had an immediate identification with [the music] because our formation in Brazil has a lot to do with Africa, and especially from that area, from Nigeria and the Gulf of Guinea area." After this experience, Gil's music carried with it a strong influence of highlife and jùjú, styles that informed afrobeat, though not necessarily afrobeat itself, which was a harder and more adventurous sound that wouldn't have fit into Gil's pop career at the time.

For many people, Kuti was a figure similar to Bob Marley, a strong icon that believed in finding a new black identity that would free black people from the shadows of colonialism and slavery. When I spoke to Carlos Moore, Fela's official biographer and a close friend (who also happens to live in Brazil these days), he told me that the most important thing to come from Fela's music was "a feeling of nonconformity and rebellion against social and racial injustices", characteristics that you could easily relate to his Jamaican counterpart. Yet, while Marley's fame reached fever pitch leading up to his death in 1981 and has continued to grow since, it took longer for Kuti's music to be internationally recognized. If anything, his reputation as an anti-authoritarian polygamist came before his music, which was mostly self-released and which – owing to its long track times and political content – was far less radio-friendly than Marley's. Things change, however, and Fela's reputation has grown immeasurably in recent years.

While reissues, documentaries, musicals and biographies have all helped raise Fela's profile worldwide, the story of how this current explosion of interest in afrobeat in Brazil came about is a complex one. First off, it's worth noting that after Nigeria, Brazil has the largest concentration of black people in the world (over 50% of Brazil's nearly 200 million people are estimated to have African ancestry), with Salvador in particular having deep roots to the Yoruba people of Nigeria. Then, there have been a number of occurrences in the past 5-6 years which have all raised awareness in the style: the publishing of Carlos Moore's Fela biography in Portuguese, concerts by Fela's sons Femi Kuti and Seun Kuti in Brazil, the beginning of a number of afrobeat parties in Rio and São Paulo (such as Festa Fela and Fela Day) and the discovery of afrobeat records via the Internet, to name a few. But one of the biggest catalysts of all has been the influence of two afrobeat icons, Tony Allen and Oghene Kologbo, who have both had a big impact on the new crop of afrobeat bands in Brazil.

Two Fateful Encounters Give Afrobeat A Brazilian Twist

Tony Allen, who was Fela's drummer and musical director, is perhaps the main reason why Bixiga 70 exist. It was he who eventually helped Mauricio Fleury out of the musical vacuum he found himself back in 2007. It was that year that Mauricio had been invited to participate in the Red Bull Music Academy in Toronto. Allen was also invited and the two instantly made a connection, Mauricio saying of the encounter, "we just got together and really had fun playing." Suddenly Mauricio's musical ideas began to make more sense. "[He] made me re-evaluate lots of stuff that I had been working on. My head turned very much to this afro thing".

This idea for a new direction would soon find a way to become reality. Bruno Morais, a well-respected artist and producer, asked Mauricio to help out with a recording in a studio in Bixiga, a neighbourhood in the centre of São Paulo. During the recording, Mauricio got on so well with the musicians there that, as he told me, he "couldn't leave." "I would just come here [to the studio] and say 'what shall we do?', 'let's do a new song', trying to be here all the time." One day he got together with drummer Décio 7 to finally work out how to incorporate this new "afro thing", that Tony Allen had got him thinking about, into his music. The idea was to give afrobeat a Brazilian twist. "It was not just like 'take this Tony Allen beat'," says Mauricio, "it had to [reference afrobeat] but it was a mix, it was like a Brazilian kind of disco." After a full day in the studio they were no closer – "we were playing for like 6 or 7 hours and it didn't work" recalls Mauricio, who had pushed Décio hard in finding this new rhythm – but on the second day they got it. They had what Mauricio calls "an original beat." Invigorated, Décio offered to contact all of his musician friends and put together a big band to play this new "afro" music they had begun to get a feel for. They played their first gig at 2010's Festa Fela (an annual party in São Paulo celebrating afrobeat), where they appeared as Banda Malaika. It was later that they christened themselves Bixiga 70, paying reference to their neighbourhood and Fela's Africa 70 group.

Festa Fela poster by MZK

By this time Abayomy Afrobeat Orchestra had already formed in Rio do Janeiro, playing their first concert together in October 2009 as part of Fela Day, a separate celebration of afrobeat. Tony Allen had also been a big influence on Abayomy's music, though their meeting with the legendary drummer was far more contrived. Seeing that Allen had been invited to play a festival in São Paulo, they set up a fundraising campaign using Queremos (a kind of Brazilian Kickstarter focused on micro-financing concerts) to get their idol to play Rio. The campaign was successful, and not only did Allen play in Rio but Abayomy managed to record with him too, resulting in their cover of Jorge Ben's "Meus Filhos" which came out on 10" in 2013.

Abayomy, who include 13 members, see their music as being a strong mix of African and Brazilian influences. Their drummer, Thomas Harres, told me that one of the main characteristics of the band is "to unite the weight of afrobeat with hints of *candomblé* and touches of *umbanda* and *jurema*." For him, afrobeat has special values that don't exist in other styles. "It deals with spiritual, political, behavioural and racial matters, and most importantly the fight against colonialism, responsible for the extinction of popular and regional cultures in Brazil and the world in general," says Harres. Whereas Bixiga 70 make purely instrumental music, Abayomy use vocals to spread their message. Rio rapper BNegão is one of the singers they've worked with.

Abayomy also played and recorded with Oghene Kologbo, a Nigerian guitarist who was a vital member of Fela's band during the 70s. Oghene came to Brazil as a member of Tony Allen's band in 2012 and was blown away when he heard Abayomy in concert. His plan was to perform in Brazil and leave, but that's not how it worked out, as Oghene recalls: "I changed my mind and extended my stay from 4 days to 7 weeks because I heard them trying to play afrobeat in their style and I liked the connection, so I stayed to do some workshops with them." He joined Abayomy for their Fela Day concert in Rio in 2012 before travelling to Belo Horizonte for another Fela Day celebration and a meeting with the third band in our Brazilian afrobeat triumvirate.

Iconili, with 11 members, come from Belo Horizonte, a Brazilian city that is seen as less multicultural as Rio or São Paulo, with far more ties to rock and pop music. Perhaps this explains why the group began with a different sound. "We were looking to shape our music with a base of psychedelic rock and contemporary jazz", the group told me by email. This early sound got a good reception in BH but there was something missing. "Always we wanted to see everyone dancing and vibrating with our sound", they told me. It was during this time that they first encountered the music of Fela Kuti and this soon filtered into their shows. "We started to include songs with an afrobeat groove and we saw that the people were already dancing more and getting more excited by the band." Their sound, which they see as "mixing Afro-Brazilian rhyhms, *brega*, Ethiopian music, carnival *marchas* and other styles" is the furthest away from Fela's original sound of the three bands mentioned in this article.

As with Bixiga 70 and Abayomy, Iconili were also heavily influenced by two US-based afrobeat-influenced groups, Antibalas and Budos Band, who Mauricio sees as making "a collage with afrobeat and influences they had from their musical background: soul, hip-hop". He sees Bixiga 70 as continuing this theme: "the whole idea of afrobeat is blending traditional and urban music styles, it's already a hybrid, so that's how we see afrobeat, as a process of mixing styles." Undoubtedly, the additional influence of Ethiopian music in the work of Budos Band can be heard in Iconili's sound.

Even bands that don't use the afrobeat big band formation have been influenced by the music. Thiago França who plays sax and flute in a huge variety of São Paulo-based groups, told me that "afrobeat influenced us a lot in Sambanzo and Metá-Metá [two of

Bixiga 70, *Bixiga 70* (2011); Abayomy Afrobeat Orchestra, *Abayomy* (2012); Iconili, *Tupi Novo Mundo* (2013)

his groups] but not in an obvious way. There was the song's non-radio-length. This may sound silly, but if you are used to listening to 3-minute tracks, afrobeat can come as a shock. We also saw how we could get away from classic intro-theme-solo-theme-end structure, we could do things in whatever order we'd like. But the thing that influenced us the most was Tony Allen's beats. His polyrhythmic patterns and dislocated accents really opened our minds to construct new grooves."

It's this fact that the Brazilian bands are not copying the music but using elements of it to create new styles and rhythms that has made this nascent scene so compelling. The ever-enthusiastic Oghene is in no doubt that the Brazilian bands are furthering the sound of afrobeat. "Yeah", he told me, "I can see the afrobeat music continuation in Brazil. And even more when the musicians add *maracatu* and samba to give Brazilian flavour

Illustration by MZK

to afrobeat music. Then I will say 'yeah, yeah' Brazil's going far with the afrobeat!"

A Growing Global Tribe

Film-maker Pedro Rajão has now begun to make a documentary about afrobeat, named *Anikulapo*, for a Brazilian audience. He's already filmed the Brazilian segment and is now planning a trip to Nigeria to discover the origins of the style. I asked him why now is the right time to make this documentary. He told me that "afrobeat was born from a rich and vibrant political situation, it's ethno-cultural and musical and, like Brazil it's a force of blackness and so many other colours. I would say that the 'arrival' of Fela's music [in Brazil] is far too late." He says that "the figure and the music of Fela needs to be known better here. As much as Bob Marley."

Whether Fela's 'hits' "Monkey Banana", "Coffin for Head of State" or "ITT (International Thief Thief)" will ever be as well-known as "No Woman, No Cry" or "Buffalo Soldier" is unlikely, but what does seem certain is that those who find his music will continue to be inspired to create their own groups that accentuate the raw power of percussion and horns, Tony Allen's grooves and Fela's cries against suffering and corruption. As Brazilian bands mix these elements with their own backgrounds and musical education, you can be sure that the reputation of afrobeat worldwide will only increase, and that one of Fela's predictions, that of a "global tribe", isn't so far off after all.

UNHAPPY HILLBILLIES & TEN-GALLON HATS

BRAZIL'S MOST POPULAR MUSIC IS ... COUNTRY?

by Alexander S. Dent

There's no better way to understand Brazilian "country" music than to visit one of the largest rodeos in the world, situated in the town of Barretos in the northern part of São Paulo state. Buck the trend and instead of showing up at what locals call "The Peon Party" around nine or ten in the evening, as most people do, and get there for lunch. ("Peon" is the old school Brazilian term for cowboy).

The big stadium will be empty but off to the side there'll be a traditional cooking competition where teams face off to prepare a meal the way the cowboys used to when they were moving herds: steak, rice and beans cooked over an open fire, using iron tools and pans. One of the categories that the different cooking teams are evaluated upon is "hygiene," and pointing out the humour in this to the event's organizer won't get you any laughs. He'll still let you sample the wares, though, and while you're doing that you'll be serenaded by yet another competition, for the best pair of singing country brothers.

What you're hearing is called *música caipira*, roughly translating as "hillbilly music". One brother sings the melody while the other sings harmony. One will also play a nylon string guitar and provide the rhythm while the other plays the consummate instrument of Brazilian rural music, the *viola caipira*, a ten-string guitar similar to a twelve-string guitar, but smaller, missing its lowest pair of strings and with a strident sound that allows it to be heard over the rest of the music. It plays the melody while the brothers sing of the sadness of having to leave the countryside for the city, of bird songs, of waterfalls or of working in the fields.

They say that when the *viola* is played properly, it sounds like sobbing, and the grief in the music might remind you just a touch of the country brother teams of the great days of American country radio (The Blue Sky Boys or The Lone Star Cowboys of the 30s and 40s). In Brazil, the great practitioners of bygone days were Zé Carreiro & Carreirinho (Joe the Wagon-Driver & The Little Driver) or Tião Carreiro & Pardinho (Uncle Wagon-Driver & The Dark One). In *caipira* music, the present is always lacking when compared to the good ol' days, as you can hear in one of the genre's most famous songs, "As Tristezas do Jeca" (The Sadness of Armadillo Joe), written back in 1918 by a police scribe, dentist and music store owner named Angelino de Oliveira:

"I was born off in those hills
In a hut, cradled by the ground. ...

With this viola
I sing, and cry, truthfully
And each tune is like a piece of longing. ...

I want to tell you
Of my suffering and my pain.
I am like the song-bird,
Who can only sing of sadness
From his branch."

Once the competition ends and your belly's full, you'll have some time to kill, because it's not until after dinner that the main rodeo events begin. They centre around cattle competitions, including some events particular only to this area, like a form of bronco riding that lacks a saddle but uses reins, called *Cutiano*-style. The main rodeo event is the bull riding, and here, Brazil is the equal of countries like the United States, Canada, Australia and Mexico on the global rodeo circuit. Brazil consistently produces superb bull-riders. Indeed, the only five-time world bull-riding champion is Adriano Morães, of Cachoeira Paulista, São Paulo. Retired now, he was so good in his day that when The Professional Bull Rider's Association polled their members for whose statue should adorn their headquarters in Colorado, his name was the hands-down favourite. Eat your heart out, Texas.

After the livestock events have ended, punctuated by a short exhibition football match to make sure you remember that you're still in Brazil, the crowds start to thicken, packing the stadium in ten gallon hats, boots and big buckles, preparing for what will be the evening's main event: a show by a mainstream country duo performing *música sertaneja*. Translating as "music of the backlands," the music grew out of *música caipira* but it is backed by electric guitars and drum kits, and the brothers aren't singing about how sad they are for having to leave the countryside; this stuff is all about broken hearts.

Sertanejo is more plaintive and raw than *música caipira*, and it's also much more orchestrated. It is one of the best-selling musical genres in Brazil, if not the best. Since the early 90s, *música sertaneja* has been at the top of all licit and illicit music sales, online views, downloads and ticket sales in the nation. And it shows no signs of slowing down. Its stars sell huge numbers of records and play to tremendous crowds, and though their largest draws are in the central-southern region (consisting of the states of São Paulo, Minas Gerais, Goiás, Paraná, Mato Grosso and Mato Grosso do Sul), you'll hear these duos from the jungles of the Amazon all the way to the cattle-lands of the south.

The *viola* is no longer the primary instrument since Fender Telecasters and even saxophones handle the solos, but masculine foibles and grief are still at the heart of the performance. In the typical *sertanejo* song, a vulnerable pair of males, known as a *dupla*, bemoan the loss of a once-perfect love. And here is an important irony of modern Brazilian country: while the masculinity of the bull rider is stoic and strong, the masculinity on display in these songs is anything but. These men are completely dependent on their women, and are utterly lost without them. "She left me and I want to die, oh me, oh my" is the message. Great practitioners include Chitãozinho & Xororó, who take their names from the songbirds that form the title of an old Brazilian country tune. Their first hit was called "Fio de Cabelo" ("A Strand of Hair") and focused on a grief-stricken protagonist who had found a sign of his past love on his jacket. She has long since departed, but that hair remains:

"And today made me sadder still.
I found a little piece of her,
A hair on my jacket. ...

I remembered all that passed between us:
The vivid love,
That long strand of her hair,
Once stuck in our sweat."

Another famous *dupla* is Zezé di Camargo & Luciano, who became the subjects of a biographical film that broke Brazilian box-office records in 2008. This duo's first hit, "É o Amor" ("It's Love") provides a great example of how *sertanejo* lyrics present romance as disorienting and disempowering:

"You are my sweet love
My happiness
My fairy tale
My fantasy
The peace that I need to survive
I'm your lover, my soul's transparent
A raving lunatic, inconsequential
A case that's tough to understand...
It's love that messes with my head and makes me this way

That makes me think of you and forget myself
That makes me forget that life is for living
It's love that arrives
Like a bulls-eye, at my heart
That bowls over the strong base of my passion
And that makes me understand that life is
Nothing without you."

Yet, as popular as *sertanejo* is in Brazil, this is not music that has travelled abroad. There are both linguistic and musical reasons for this. The music's emphasis on Portuguese leaves those who don't speak it out in the dark, particularly because its slower tempos aren't fun to dance to in a "Latin" sort of way. But even more importantly, this stuff has not travelled outside Brazil because of its embarrassing content: weepy males, bemoaning the loss of a love. This is not what foreigners think of when they think "Brazil". The national press plays along with the embarrassment by chastising each new wave of commercial country for having lost its "roots".

The explosion of commercial country has led to a revival of traditional *caipira* music. Viola schools are springing up all over the place, many led by talented solo performers like Roberto Corrêa, Ivan Vilela and Paulo Freire, who draw on old rural traditions with elements of jazz and classical technique. There is also a revival of traditional *dupla* performance headed by brothers Zé Mulato & Cassiano. The revivalists are often harsh critics of commercial country music, which they claim has sold-out the soul of *caipira* music. To understand how they sound when they are complaining about *sertanejo*, think about what contemporary practitioners of bluegrass or old time music might say about Shania Twain or Garth Brooks.

At the same time a new craze has taken over Brazil called *sertenejo universitário*. Its famous practitioners include *duplas* like Victor & Leo and Fernando & Sorocaba, and more recently, solo performers like Gusttavo Lima, Luan Santana and Michel Teló. In this latest wave, the tempos are more upbeat, and the songs are allowed to celebrate casual sex and drinking. Indeed, so catchy was one of these offerings, "Ai Se Eu Te Pego" by Michel Teló, that it became an international hit in the summer of 2012. But the point is that the dirge-like songs still predominate, and even in more upbeat tunes about college hook-ups, the male narrator of the song is still no seduction machine. In this respect consider the hit by João Neto & Frederico, two brothers from Goiás, who voice a disempowered narrator;

"I have no money.
I'm not famous.
I've got no car,
I got a ride here.

My credit card
Has been blocked
Because I blew through
My limit."

Far from the confident narrator of samba, this character is celebrating what he lacks to his female interlocutor. So, even in the flashy update to Brazilian country, the male narrator is still tragic, not unlike his weepy progenitors who wore their hearts on their sleeves. Some things never change. Although, of course, they don't make them like they used to either.

THE MODERN PILGRIMS

PERNAMBUCO PRODUCES MORE
TALENT THAN IT CAN CONSUME

by Lulina Abduzida

Singer/songwriter Lulina discusses why she left her home state of Pernambuco for the urban jungle of São Paulo, and why she's just one of many to do so.

Of all the clichés you hear when you're a *pernambucano* in São Paulo, the most frequent always questions why you swapped the beach for a grey city. The obvious answer is the same reason as why *paulistanos* don't exchange their city for a northeastern beach: São Paulo is where the work is. But it's emotional factors that seems to decide whether you stay or return to your home town and in the case of most *pernambucanos*, they end up staying.

"Here come the *pernambritânicos*", say some of my *paulistano* friends, referring to a connection that some see between Recife (the capital of Pernambuco) and London because of a similarity in new cultural trends, and perhaps it's this connection that causes many *pernambucanos* to fall in love with São Paulo. The lively culture, an interest in the avant-garde and a strong sense of creative freedom are just some of the similarities between Recife and the world's biggest cities. However there is a noteworthy difference: *Pernambucanos* have a huge attachment to, and are fiercely proud of, their cultural traditions; *frevo, maracatu, caboclinho, ciranda, baião* and *coco* to name a few. This parochialism is an advantage when creating art, in that it encourages a spirit of independence and lightness, as well as one of the greatest qualities of the northeast, originality.

Pernambuco is so culturally resonant that local musicians do not need to look beyond their own backyard for creative references; these come from within. Historically this has been a disadvantage as it has discouraged innovation, with non-regional sounds struggling to earn media attention or receiving offers to play the big shows. All the talk of pride in the state's rich traditions resulted in the public turning their nose up to modern movements, particularly as these movements used new, unfamiliar sounds and featured their own distinct personalities. Igor Gazatti, who's been involved in Recife's independent music scene for the past 15 years and who currently plays in Kingsize, thinks that this situation has now improved: "people are more open to listening to indie bands without the prejudice that existed before. There was a time when if it didn't have a little drum it was wrong," referring to a period of time when music from Pernambuco always had to have a reference to its traditions and specifically its drumming groups, its *batuques*.

Pernambuco produces more talent than it can consume, with many artists still unable to support themselves within the scarce live circuit that feeds all new cultural events and productions. Traditional musicians take the biggest slice of the cake while new generations are squeezed between the annual events sponsored by the government and the city, with paychecks that often take months to be cleared. "If you want to extend your career you have to leave, to come to this 'side'. Otherwise, the artist becomes a repetition of himself, having to create millions of projects to play in the same place and this is not healthy for a career," says China, singer, songwriter and, since he moved to São Paulo, TV presenter. "The main reason I moved to São Paulo was a bid to try and expand my career. In Recife, I was already playing in all the venues. There's not a large live music circuit in the northeast," he says.

Whether for the need of professional growth or to identify oneself with the São Paulo rhythm, the *pernambucanos* take the road to SP every year and are welcomed by an audience interested in discovering new things. That was what charmed me most in this city that I adopted as my second home: the public thirst for something new. There is appreciation for anything that is sincere and authentic, regardless of fads or technical skill. But despite this great reception, it's a tough climate. The horizon, enclosed by buildings, can be inspiring or dispiriting for those accustomed to sea breezes or quiet walks around the block – which in São Paulo becomes a Saint Silvester Road Race, where everyone is constantly in a hurry. In my case, the loneliness of the early years and the emotionally testing learning process were inspirations for many experimental homemade discs, paving the way for independently-produced shows, and later, to a record label and bigger shows. "I think the mass rush of the city is almost an incentive for you to run too. You have to work. It's a tough city when you arrive, but it becomes a surrogate mother, full of hugs, after you find your place within it," concludes China, who has lived in São Paulo for three years.

Not everyone adapts, however, and some choose to cut short their journey; like Rogerman, who played in Eddie and Bonsucesso Samba Clube, hugely successful bands in Recife and São Paulo respectively. "In 2009, I decided to live in the city [São Paulo]. In 2010, I returned to Pernambuco. Later, in 2012, I spent three months living in the city to work in the production of Virada Cultural [a statewide São Paulo festival]. My relationship is to come and go, never to leave forever and never to stay forever. Someday that may change, and I will want to stay for a long time, since it is the city where I have spent the second most amount of my life," explains Rogerman. The list of Pernambucan musicians who have stayed in SP is huge: Siba, Karina Buhr (who is from Bahia, but grew up in Pernambuco), Lirinha, Fábio Trummer (from Eddie), the boys from Mombojó, and many more. These bands straddle different generations of musicians, working and mingling with *paulistanos, cearenses, mineiros, gaúchos, curitibanos, goianos, baianos, cariocas* and others that come to São Paulo with the same expectation: to find their place in the drizzle. It's not easy, but difficulties often become catalysts for creativity. It's a city that creates a clash of emotions, generating an endless array of questions about the meaning of rushing everywhere, the cost of the São Paulo lifestyle, the consequence of so much competition and ambition on your spirit; in São Paulo, there are no lack of factors that can take the musician outside of their comfort zone.

I've lived in this city for ten years, having left Recife during the "drumming dictatorship". I consider São Paulo the city of my artistic birth as it was here that I received the greatest support and motivation to become a singer and songwriter. Yet despite the fact that my music has had good exposure and been well-received, in these ten years I have never played at any cultural event in Pernambuco. Only once have I played an indie festival in Recife, organized by the class of young musicians who were there before I moved to SP, who today have a space to put on ever-more experimental and "cool" events in the city. The difficulty of playing in my own city spawned jokes and pranks, like the unfinished song "Exilada de Olinda" ("Exiled from Olinda"), that the São Paulo singer/songwriter Rômulo Froes suggested composing with me – he was another that had difficulties playing there. I think because of this side of Pernambuco, I became as *paulistana* as Rômulo.

Lulina (photo by Habacuque Lima)

But here I am still, admiring and loving my state from a distance, full of pride for the talents that keep springing up there, in music, in film, in everything that can be called art – even when that love is not reciprocated.

SETTING THE SCENE: BELO HORIZONTE

by Katia Abreu
translated by Alina Karnics

Belo Horizonte misleads you. Christian values, traditional morals and good manners are all held dear by the city's mainly Catholic families. But all it takes is one long night out in the city to discover a radicalized-youth willing to break the rules and question the city's old-fashioned ways.

Belo Horizonte seduces you. It's the Brazilian capital city of the *boteco* (a common name for Brazilian corner bars that sell drinks and snacks and historically have a Bohemian reputation). In fact, the city has the highest number of bars per capita in the country. Inside them, one can always find good conversation, alongside good *mineiro* food and drink. It's there, in the *botecos*, that Belo Horizonte pulls you in.

It's between the *cachaças* and *torresmos* (toasted pigskins) that much of the *mineira* music has flourished. Whoever visits the bars of the bohemian stronghold Santa Tereza (especially Bar do Bolão, open 24 hours a day) can see photographs of famous clients proudly hanging from the walls, including Sepultura, Skank and Pato Fu – the top bands that emerged in the city in the 80s and 90s. Hanging alongside are mythic figures like Lô Borges, Milton Nascimento and Beto Guedes, responsible for the most famous artistic movement of the city in the 60s and 70s: Clube da Esquina.

Clube de Esquina laid the foundations of what would become known by many as *música mineira*: ornate lyrics and melodies, intricate arrangements and harmonies and a tireless search for pop perfection while never leaving experimentalism behind. But taking a look at the variety that makes up the rich musical scene of Belo Horizonte today, I'd say that Clube de Esquina's real legacy isn't so much stylistic, but something more intangible, an emotional quality. What's really impressive about the current Belo Horizonte scene is not that they're creating new genres or movements; it's in their contagious will to

45

collaborate and discover new, diverse human and artistic possibilities.

Kindness and Mobilization

Maybe the best synthesis of the Belo Horizonte spirit at the start of the 21st century is Graveola e o Lixo Polifônico. Since their formation in 2004, the group have impressed the public and critics alike with songs marked by politically-charged lyrics and references to Brazilian musical icons such as Gilberto Gil, Jorge Ben and Itamar Assumpção. Their sound is a mix of Latin rhythms, rock, blues and other wide-ranging styles. The band is as comfortable playing alongside avant-garde artists like Kristoff Silva as it is with indie rockers like Dead Lover's Twisted Heart and Fusile. They have played both in the fancy surrounds of Palácio das Artes (filled with 1,700 fans for the recording of their first DVD) and in the middle of protests fighting for social justice. For example – they released their third album, *Eu Preciso de Um Liquidificador* (I Need A Blender), in 2011 at the Dandara occupation on the outskirts of Belo Horizonte, to an audience of activists and poor squatters fighting to resist their community's eviction by the government.

Audience during Graveola's Dandara performance; Graveola at Dandara (photos by Junia Mortimer)

Indeed, the mixture of art and politics is fundamental to understanding BH today especially manifesting itself in how public space is increasingly being used in new and interesting ways. Several initiatives, like Festival Conexão BH (a cultural festival formerly patronized by a phone company and now realized through partnerships of local artists and producers) and the S.E.N.S.A.C.I.O.N.A.L. festival (organized by the band Pequena Morte as an exchange between local, national and international artists) offer free shows and other cultural activities in the squares and parks of the city each year.

In 2010, an attempt by the local government to ban musical events in Praça da Estação on the grounds that the noise bothered nearby residents had the exact opposite effect than was intended. The area is now transformed into an urban beach every summer with thousands of people enjoying the sun in their swimming gear. It's also now being used for carnival rehearsals. This is especially significant – carnival in BH used to be lame, an opportunity to escape from the city and see the distant ocean of Rio de Janeiro. But now, carnival is guaranteed fun for both locals and tourists who fill the streets throughout the city's neighbourhoods.

This scene has an interesting relationship with the city institutions. On the one hand, it's because of programmes like Música Minas, a project of the State Secretary of Culture, that various artists have been able to play shows around the country and even abroad, and it's the local government's aid that has made the organization of so many public events possible. On the other hand, this system, which involves asking the government for "permission" to use the city, means that cultural events are seen by the authorities as a privilege, rather than as a fundamental right of the people. It's this kind of attitude on the part of the city that has led young people to respond with a potent mixture of politics and the arts in places mentioned above, such as Praça da Estação and Dandara.

Other Landscapes

The constant meshing of diverse influences to create something new appears to be in the DNA of Belo Horizonte's scene. If in the streets this results in the uniting of politics and art, then indoors there is a different discussion, one of aesthetic intersections.

Playing at places like A Obra, a legendary underground rock club, wasn't the ideal scenery for experimental bands such as Constantina, Iconili and Dibigode. This lack of good venues for unconventional artists led to the creation of the project Pequenas Sessões (Little Sessions). Starting as occasional events in which members of Constantina would bring like-minded indie bands to the city to play, Pequenas Sessões has evolved to become a full-fledged festival with seven editions already behind them. Not limiting itself to specific genres or regions, the festival's motto is "free and independent music." They offer shows in small theatres or cultural spaces, where contact between the public and the artists is more intimate, often working with artists who project visuals on top of the performances.

Events organized in places like Mercado das Borboletas, Espaço Centroequatro and C.A.S.A follow the same premise of opening opportunities to young musicians. Often, they bring together a mixture of live music and DJs, which helps generate new audiences. There are also clubs like Casa de Shows Granfinos, which have a long-standing association with independent artists across Brazil (and even internationally) without losing sight of the variety of local talents: from the hip-hop of Flávio Renegado to the indie folk of Transmissor and the next-gen samba of Aline Calixto.

Belo Horizonte charms you. By the diversity and the vitality it generates constantly. And Belo Horizonte surprises you at every new visit. You can end your night eating a simple "pão moiado" (bread soaked in tomato sauce) in Bolão or going to a crazy, improvised jam session organized by one of the artists mentioned in this article, in the house of a new friend that you've just met. And, because of that, Belo Horizonte wins your heart in the end.

SOCCER, SAMBA, SOUNDCLOUD

MYSPACE BEFORE MYSPACE, DO-IT-TOGETHER TOURING AND CROWDFUNDED CONCERTS – WHEN IT COMES TO DIGITAL CULTURE, BRAZIL IS AHEAD OF THE CURVE

by Shannon Garland

Quick quiz: which catchy tune and accompanying dance went viral on YouTube in 2012, prompting versions in dozens of languages, topping charts internationally, becoming a football goal victory dance and sending the otherwise obscure singer to worldwide fame? Answer: Brazil's Michel Teló, with the maddeningly infectious "Ai Se Eu Te Pego". As of July 2013, the video has been streamed over 500 million times online, beating out the equivalent US summer hit (Carly Rae Jepsen's "Call Me Maybe") and putting it on the list of Top 10 most-viewed YouTube videos of all time. As far as the 2012 rankings, Teló was outdone by Korea's Psy, with "Gangnam Style" (another correct answer), only toward the end of the year. And unlike Psy, Teló didn't have any of America's tweeting celebrities, popular gossip blogs and national talk show hosts to help him out. But what Teló did have proved nearly as powerful: fellow Brazilians on the Internet.

Brazilian Digital Culture, From the People to the Politicians

Brazil is a nation of highly sociable people, and new Internet platforms, particularly social networking sites, are quickly and massively adopted there. Even with millions logging in at Internet cafés, Brazilians often overtake network membership and Internet usage rates in countries where far more people have home Internet access – Brazil currently ranks as the number two country for both Facebook and Twitter accounts. Brazilians are quick to create blogs, Orkut groups, satiric Tumblr and sincere Facebook pages, to crowdfund projects through Catarse, or to organize public rallies through Twitter.

But it seems the most innovative ways Brazilians have used the Internet revolve around culture, and music specifically. For the past century music has played a big role in the way Brazil has defined itself as a state and dealt with questions of culture, economy and identity. It's only fitting that for the past decade Brazil has also been on the cutting edge of new digital means for producing and consuming music.

The spheres of digital technologies and music were officially brought together with the 2003 appointment of cultural icon Gilberto Gil as Minister of Culture. Gil had seen media as fundamental to cultural renovation and political change since his days as a *tropicalist* artist in the 1960s. So he not only shared Brazilians' excitement about new digital communication possibilities, but also tried to radically shift their role within both government and Brazilian society as a whole.

Gil launched what he called an "anthropological do-in" on the national body, where digital technology would be deployed like a "shiatsu massage" on sore points of cultural diffusion. This would help release social tensions and create a more democratic circulation of art. In practical terms, the national government adopted open source software and Creative Commons licenses (the first country in the world to do so). The Ministry of Culture also launched the Pontos de Cultura (Cultural Points) program, which helped equip poor communities with digital studios for accessing art from distant lands and dispatching their own creations, via the Internet, to the rest of Brazil and the world.

Gil's leadership made the role of digital technologies in redefining ideas of intellectual property, economy and art a permanent fixture in national discussion. And Brazilians seem to produce a new, creative way for using these tools every day.

Trama Virtual: Better and Before Myspace, with an In-House "Emo"

April 1st, 2013 marked the end of an era for Brazilian independent music. It was the date that the music networking site Trama Virtual went offline. Founded sans press release in 2004 by the Trama music label as a way to publish music it couldn't otherwise take on, the site quickly became an online music hub, eventually hosting more than 200,000 songs by nearly 79,000 artists from all musical genres and corners of Brazil. Inaugurated before Myspace had gained much traction as social network – let alone as a music site – before Facebook was public and before YouTube and Twitter existed, Trama Virtual combined the virtues of social networking, music hosting and blog coverage into one.

Anyone could join Trama Virtual as a user, and any musician could create a profile and upload tracks, videos and other info, all for free. But the site also employed a staff of music geeks – even including a resident "emo guy"– to curate the vast amount of music available. Staff suggested bands, wrote reviews, covered independent festivals and shows, and even invited bands to tape live sessions at Trama's studios.

But Trama Virtual was innovative in two other, key ways. First, it forecast some of the current impetus to compensate bands for free streaming or download. It launched a program called *download remunerado*, or paid download, in 2007. Users downloaded tracks for free, while the bands received a proportion of advertising money relative to the amount of downloaded tracks. This scheme was highly successful for a small number of bands, such as Forgotten Boys, Rock Rocket and Dance of Days, who received decent sums of money (around $1300 for the latter band) for the songs that had become hits on the site. This also further helped propel their fame – Trama Virtual displayed the current top downloaded and streaming songs on the home page.

But with limited sponsorship money and a huge number of registered bands, most musicians saw little or no financial benefit. Trama thus launched, in 2008, the "Virtual Album", with the release of Tom Zé's *Danç-Êh-Sá Ao Vivo*. Like most virtual albums to come, Zé's included all the tracks, digital cover art, photos and exclusive videos. Sponsored by particular brands, virtual albums remained on the site for free download for 90 days. Depending on the contract, virtual albums could be later released in other formats. This was the case, for example, with Cansei de Ser Sexy's eponymous debut album before it was picked up by the American label Sub Pop.

Unfortunately, technological snags often plagued the site, and Trama managers didn't quite know to how to continue innovating and adapting to new tools for online music consumption and networking. They slowly relinquished this role, by default, to newer foreign music services ever more eager to grab a piece of the Brazilian market. Trama Virtual is now dead, but let it be known that the world's first real digital music networking site was Brazilian through and through.

Fora do Eixo: Cyberhippies Who Do-It-Together

Fora do Eixo is one of the most interesting examples of Brazilians' attempt to rewire the connections between social media, economy and culture. Meaning "Outside the Axis," it was first established as a network of autonomous cultural-political collectives in Brazil's interior, outside the dominant Rio-São Paulo axis of cultural and financial power. Modifying DIY to DIT (Do-It-Together), Fora do Eixo tries to embrace the possibilities of burgeoning digital networking tools both in ideology and practice. In terms of communication, Fora Do Eixo strategizes its social media use to have maximum viral effect and geographic reach. It also tries to extend the Internet's basic logic – distribution and circulation through collective sharing – to structures for music touring and financing.

In 2005, Fora do Eixo consisted of just four collectives around Brazil. It has since grown to nearly one hundred collectives and affiliates throughout the country and even abroad. Often living in large houses run as communal structures, where everything – including money and clothes – is shared, the collectives work together in a type of musico-laboral exchange, where bands and members of the collectives exchange performances, rehearsal space, recording time, food, lodging and online promotion by Fora do Eixo's vast army of members.

Fora do Eixo even created its own currency, called *card*, to facilitate this exchange, such that a collective could pay a band in *card* instead of *reals*, which the band could then trade for other network services. Aided by this system, Fora do Eixo has produced independent festivals across the country and financed band tours on previously nonexistent routes, thus creating touring circuits where there weren't any and strengthening the indie music scenes outside the "axis" cities of Rio and São Paulo. Fora do Eixo also helped create, and now manages, Toque No Brasil (TNB), or "Play in Brazil", an online database that allows artists and event promoters to find each other, listing the conditions of travel, payment and lodging required by bands or provided by promoters.

Members of Fora do Eixo could be thought of as cyberhippies for their belief in the revolutionary ability of digital technologies to create a non-hierarchical, cooperative society. They've even developed a unique technology-based lingo. For example, they call their greater challenge to Brazil's dominant cultural tropes a *disputa memética* (memetic battle) – a war fought by the meme-like viral spread of their own tropes through social media and by the creation of new spaces and possibilities for independent band performance. During Fora do Eixo discussions, you might hear somebody use the phrase *botar efe cinco* (hit F5), referring to the common browser refresh hotkey, which translates into a shift in tactic for a particular project.

The network's music promotion is part of a larger goal of social transformation. Fora do Eixo has sought to fundamentally remix the connections between culture, economy and politics. Now conceiving of itself as a "social movement of cultures", Fora do Eixo regularly helps document and spread public demonstrations of all sorts. These have included "slut-walk" protests, pressure for cultural policies and politicians, and the June 2013 protests set off by a hike in public transportation fares. Fora do Eixo, in fact, is behind the Mídia NINJA live streaming of these protests and public interventions.

The Mídia NINJA project has recently brought Fora do Eixo into the national spotlight, dredging up a heated controversy that has been part of the Brazilian independent music world for many years. Most musicians, producers, and journalists agree that the availability and quality of performance spaces, press coverage and overall economic health of independent rock and pop music needs to improve. But they take issue with many of Fora do Eixo's means for bringing about these changes, and question the extent of Fora do Eixo's actual impact on Brazilian cultural life. Fora do Eixo has been successful at promoting the bands made up of network members, but struggles to tip this promotion outside of the confines of network affiliates. The network's *card* currency is partially responsible for this. Because members of Fora do Eixo work for *cards* instead of *reals*, outside resources that enter the network stay within it. So *card* helps keep Fora do Eixo running and in fact strengthens it, but does not necessarily support stronger production structures overall. Meanwhile, Fora do Eixo is known to exaggerate the amount of events it produces as well as the impact of its actions, in order to negotiate with financial and political bodies from a better position of power. Combined with the network's increasingly overt political actions, many critics see Fora do Eixo as more interested in growing their own political power than in improving musical aesthetics and economy.

The new national interest in Fora do Eixo owing to the Mídia NINJA project has in fact provoked a wide range of public denunciations of the network's practices. These range from musicians speaking out on contracts being broken, to activists accusing Fora do Eixo of appropriating their image, to former Fora do Eixo members describing cult-like conditions within certain Fora do Eixo houses, where psychological manipulation and sexual coercion are used to keep members working and vying to move up in the strict hierarchy of power. Fora do Eixo, for its part, has launched a fierce media counter attack, calling in favours from top politicians and public figures to denounce the denunciations. Meanwhile, longtime participants in the indie pop/rock world largely roll their eyes; they've heard almost all of it several times before.

Some side with Fora do Eixo's preferred image as tech-savvy cultural revolutionaries. Others favour the counter image of exploitative 21st century labour barons who ride the political current that favours networked cultural production for their own political gain. But all can likely agree that Fora do Eixo's unconventional ways help keep music's relation to technological potentials and economic organization a hot topic of debate.

Queremos! Crowd-Funding Global Cool

Queremos appears to be the world's first crowdfunded concert booking company. It was launched and still primarily operates in Rio de Janeiro, a city that, until Queremos came along, was often left off the touring routes of indie bands from the Anglo world. Such bands are usually brought to the continent via São Paulo, making stops in other major South American cities like Buenos Aires and Santiago, and even passing through smaller Brazilian ones, like Porto Alegre. But Rio was frequently kept out of the loop.

Queremos founders blame this problem on several factors. One is that people in Rio just like to go to the beach, another is the culture of VIP event invites or "getting on the list" thanks to the city's film and television industries. But the biggest element in this tour exclusion owes to the relatively small number of interested listeners. This is generally true for all South American cities when compared to their counterparts in the north. But *carioca* fans appear less willing to make up for smaller audiences by paying exorbitant ticket prices, like *paulistanos* do. Local promoters, meanwhile, are less willing to take on the financial risk in what is a very precarious business environment the world over.

The founders of Queremos have resolved this problem by crowdfunding the booking deposit required to guarantee a band. Once the band is confirmed, regular tickets go on sale, and if enough are sold, the initial investors receive a full or partial refund. This model eliminates much of the risk of buying and selling shows. But its greatest advantage is promotion: since fans have a stake in the show, they mobilize attendance through their social networks, using Facebook, Twitter and other social media tools to spread the word. Curiously, while it would seem that those initial investors would become major promoters of the show in order to get their money back, most appear much less concerned with the monetary return than having a packed, lively show. Attendees as well as the performing musicians often report a heightened atmosphere brought about by this collective effort to make the show happen.

In this way Queremos is an example of some of the best uses of online social networking platforms – creating a sense of connectedness to others through sharing in cultural delights. Queremos has so far been successful in all of its endeavours in Rio, expanding to the production of festivals, to the performances of local musicians, and to shows in other Brazilian cities and beyond. In 2012 it launched in the US as WeDemand!, successfully booking a North American tour of the Canadian experimental jazz group Badbadnotgood.

O Futuro

These examples aren't the only ways Brazilians creatively use digital technologies to distribute and finance music, of course. *Funk*, one of Brazil's most popular music styles, has long relied on a system of amassing huge dance parties through the "social distribution" of new tracks – once hand-to-hand on cassette and CD, now pinged around the Internet via MP3s and YouTube. This is also the model of the increasingly popular *tecnobrega* artists, who download global hits, remix them, give them to street vendors for distribution and finally get paid by performing at giant sound system dance parties on the edge of the Amazon. These and other "copy & share" methods of music distribution produce hundreds more recordings than the big labels and generate multimillion-dollar revenues. And their digital roots show in both their unique musical mixtures and in their global uptake – from M.I.A. (*funk*) to the Strokes (*tecnobrega*) to Diplo (both).

Unsurprisingly, many of these genres that eschew traditional copyright norms and payment structures are made and consumed by social groups that never really got to participate in the cultural industries anyway. But middle class artists and intellectuals have also fiercely advocated for new ways of producing music and defining rights, as with the cases shown earlier. This is partly because digital tools help resolve some of the problems of making culture in a vast country with lopsided transport infrastructures and national media conglomerates controlled by conservative elites. Most artists and intellectuals are committed to the radical potential of the Internet as a democratic tool. In one example, in 2012, they actually successfully lobbied to oust Ana de Hollanda as Minister of Culture for reversing the innovative course set by Gil in the area of copyright reform and digitally-led cultural democracy.

Currently, Brazil's first ever legal framework for Internet use, itself produced collaboratively by over 800 participants, is being debated in the national congress. If passed without major concessions to the telecommunications industry, it will make Brazil the most progressive country in the world when it comes to privacy protection, net neutrality and fair use of art and music online. So far, the lack of a legal framework has likely hurt the ability of Brazilian inventions like Trama Virtual to compete with foreign services like Soundcloud and Bandcamp, which have achieved broad global reach.

But the creativity occurring in Brazil despite the legal uncertainties, along with the rise in home and mobile Internet service, suggests that Brazil's new online tools for music sharing and financing have a shot at taking off globally in the future, whether or not the law passes. So don't be surprised if you soon find your music apps flooded with *funk*, or if the next big innovation in music production is "Feito No Brasil" – Made in Brazil.

SETTING THE SCENE: SALVADOR

by Jody Gillett

Incubator, lab and launch pad, the northeastern state of Bahia is the source of so many pivotal shifts in Brazilian music it's almost inconceivable that one place could generate all those shock waves.

The roots of samba originated in Bahia. It was home to bossa nova dreamer João Gilberto, crazy cool rock 'n' roll legend Raul Seixas and *Tropicália*'s star players (Gilberto Gil, Caetano Veloso, Gal Costa, Tom Zé). In the 80s, Bahian *axé* music began its long domination of the national charts. And today Brazil's top commercial sound, *sertanejo*, has become infiltrated by the sauntering beat and sketchy lyrics of Bahian *arrocha*, the state's favourite romantic melody-machine. So what powers the powerhouse? And what's going on in Salvador right now?

Bass Is The Place

Bahia is the state with the strongest African heritage in Brazil. For three hundred years, until abolition in 1888, Salvador was a major centre of the slave trade to the Americas. As a result, Salvador today is steeped in African culture. It's a de facto cultural capital of the Black Atlantic, a city that has more in common with New Orleans than Brasília. That heritage of cultural collision is played out in Bahia's music at a profound level and today's artists also make the connect with contemporary worldwide currents.

Body-shaking bass beats run through Bahia's DNA. *Candomblé*, the widely practiced Afro-Brazilian religion, has transcendental African percussion at its core. Those rhythms have long been channelled into popular music in Bahia and give a euphoric kick and heady identity to much of its sound.

"When [carnival *blocos*] Olodum and Timbalada hit the streets playing *surdo* drums, the whole neighbourhood vibrates. In Bahia it's bass, bass, bass – it's all about the language of the drum. We want to put that into a dialogue with electronic music," says Rafa Dias, a softly spoken 23-year-old with cosmic tattoos who hails from Paulo Afonso, in the northern *sertão*/desert zone of the state.

His band Os Nelsons is a pioneering young presence emerging on the Salvador scene. They're mixing digital beats, dub delays, dancehall and metal guitar with *pisadinha*, *pagode* and *arrocha* – the ubiquitous pop styles of the day, pumped out of every bar in the region and routinely discounted as neon chart fodder. Os Nelsons fuse all this into a hectic, infectious blast of accelerated romantic melodies, heavy bass beats and rapid-fire vocals.

"We look at the ghettotech movement as a worldwide movement from the global periphery, creating original electronic music made with elements of traditional music from their own cultures. Sometimes people here look at what we're doing like we're extraterrestrials – but *pagode* is totally ghettotech! We call our sound Música Periférica Brasileira," says Dias. Loosely translated as "Brazilian Music from the Margins", it's a new coda for MPB, cranking up the volume for the sounds streaming in from the disenfranchised periphery.

Os Nelsons (photo by Flip Thomaz)

Syncretic Soundsystems, Dub Resistance

In 1950, musical duo Dodô and Osmar famously fixed a speaker to a Ford Model T and changed Salvador's carnival forever with the first amplified party on wheels. Soundsystem had arrived! Ever since then carnival has been all about the *trios elétricos* – mega wattage stacks rolling through town on trucks blasting samba-reggae, *afoxé* and *axé*.

Away from the spectacle, in clubs and bars throughout the year, there's a wave of new artists bridging Bahian and Jamaican soundsystem culture. A key name in this syncretic syncopation is BaianaSystem. They mix the liquid riffs of Bahia's trademark mini electric "guitarra baiana" (essentially an electric mandolin) with dub effects and psychedelic ragga for a new kind of tropical dance floor mayhem.

BaianaSystem's vocalist Russo Passapusso is also a member of Bemba Trio. With Fael 1st and DJ Raiz, their dub flow is rich with Bahian slang and stories, mashing up northeastern *repente* poetry and Miami Bass beats.

"Bass frequencies took hold in Brazil, just like they did in the rest of the world. In Bahia, samba reggae drums always had that vibration, so I think we were already hooked into that current in a tribal, roots way," says Passapusso. "Today, what's interesting is to explore those rhythms and combine it with what's going on globally. Here, we've got the *trio elétrico* and we've got sound engineers who are looking to develop the musical aesthetic in a really natural way, just like in Jamaica or London."

On that deep dub tip, the MiniStereo Público soundsystem who formed in 2003 were forerunners, along with the Dubstereo collective. As much cultural activists as purveyors of trembling bass lines, they started a long-standing weekly club night, Quintas Dancehall, now running in Salvador's hip party quarter, Rio Vermelho. MiniStereo Público also stage neighbourhood cultural happenings in the outer boroughs as Mutirão Metemão, with graffiti artists and community groups. For them dub is a way to mobilise. Calls for black consciousness and social justice come through loud and clear in the work of many artists involved in Salvador's dub scene.

Bahia's affiliation with Jamaican culture stretches back before dub. "Roots reggae has always been very strong here – in Salvador and in Cachoeira," reflects Luciano Matos, editor of Salvador's leading music blog El Cabong. Cachoeira is Bahia's reggae capital and home to one of Brazilian reggae's biggest names, Edson Gomes, whose 1988 watershed album *Reggae Resistência* became the genre's first national hit.

"Dub is a more recent thing", Luciano continues. "Because up until 5-10 years ago Bahian reggae had got stuck in time, nothing new was happening, it was all in that Bob Marley/Peter Tosh/Jimmy Cliff vein. Hip-hop was growing and taking reggae's place as the music of protest. Then the dub scene started gaining momentum – with young artists, with other influences, and its own Bahian characteristics and I think today it is definitely one of the most innovative local music scenes."

Hip-hop, By Any Means Necessary

Brazil's hip-hop hubs are way down in São Paulo and Rio de Janeiro. In Bahia, hip-hop has an utterly different cultural backdrop and very little of the hefty rap infrastructure they have further south. OQuadro, from the coastal town of Ilhéus, are a seven-piece hip-hop crew who got together as teenagers 15 years ago and created their own route forward, by any means necessary. With no resources or access to digital equipment, OQuadro's line-up looks more like a rock band plus three MCs.

OQuadro, *OQuadro* (2012)

"We are hip-hop, our thinking is hip-hop. But we didn't have samplers or decks... so when we started out we transposed the sound of Afrika Bambaataa, Run DMC or Beastie Boys onto bass, guitar, drum kit and percussion", explains one of the MCs, Professor Jef (he's also a philosophy teacher). "We don't have an established hip-hop market in Bahia so when we play live we can end up playing alongside death metal bands, punk or reggae bands... this kind of influences us. I mean we like Bad Brains, Massive Attack, Sepultura, Anti-Pop Consortium, Lee Perry, Geronimo, Black Uhuru... All that falls into the frame we call OQuadro. We allow ourselves not to be defined. What hip-hop gives us is the framework for our music and it's also the way we use to construct our own poetry." With conscious rap courtesy of MCs Jef, Freeza and Rans backed by *candomblé*, dub, *ijexá* and afrobeat, OQuadro found their own hip-hop flavour, Bahian-style.

"Excellent this is why rap around the earth has made the USA mainstream seem a bit backward..." Chuck D's tweet recommending Opanijé's latest video "Se Diz" says it all. On a mission to put Bahia's African heritage centre-stage, Opanijé's sound mixes *candomblé* calls and old-school hip-hop vibes with a full-on cultural manifesto. The band's name is an acronym for Organização Popular Africana Negros Invertendo o Jogo Excludente (Popular Black African Organization Combatting the Exclusion Game). The sound is very, very funky and the lyrics are non-stop sense.

Back in the 70s, the pioneering *blocos afro* (Salvador's Afrocentric carnival troupes) Ilê-Aiyê and Olodum defied fierce municipal resistance to Afro-Brazilian rhythms at carnival by bringing *candomblé* beats to the heart of the parade. Directly influenced by the Black Power movement, at the time this was seen as a controversial, militant stance. Right now, those same rhythms are still proving to be a powerful force for battling the "exclusion game" for Salvador's black majority.

Enter The Portal

Salvador is a unique music hub, rooted in its vast hinterland yet progressive and always reinventing itself. For young reggae singer Soraia Drummond of Dubelétrica: "In Salvador everything is brand new. Everything here is born in an unexpected way." Journalist Luciano Matos agrees. "Bahia has always been innovative, always created new sounds, and I think we are living a very fertile moment," he says. "There is a sense now that you can do anything, everything is allowed and that has produced many new directions."

Any snapshot of new music in Salvador will manifest that the city's sound is always on the move and takes many forms. It's a portal into diversity. Take Letieres Leite's Rumpilezz – a 20 piece big band playing *candomblé*-jazz; composer Hugo Sambone, writing *pagode* arrangements for his classical youth orchestra. Or ethereal singer-songwriter Tiganá with his enigmatic ballads, inspired he says by "life, death and the ocean, the horizon and things we don't see beyond it."

As BaianaSystem's Russo Passapusso notes, "To me, it's like Bahia had a cry caught in its throat. I think now there's a new aesthetic that values what it is that makes us different. And since we have so much raw material to work with, I think this is going to explode."

THE GAME PLAYERS

AN EXPERT OPINION: BRAZILIAN ANTHROPOLOGIST HERMANO VIANNA TELLS THE STORY BEHIND THE SENSATIONAL SUCCESS OF "AI SE EU TE PEGO"

by Hermano Vianna

What I find most interesting about the story of Michel Teló's "Ai Se Eu Te Pego", the Brazilian "Gangnam Style", was not its worldwide success but the epic journey it took, from its composition to subsequent spread, long before first reaching the ears of Michel Teló.

The details of the story may seem exceptional, unbelievable even, but in truth, they betray a familiar pattern found in the cultural industries in the post-Internet age, one that's particularly common in Brazil. It's important to analyse exactly what happened if we hope to understand the odd musical world we've come to inhabit.

It all seems to have begun in an airplane carrying a group of middle-class girls from Paraíba, a state in northeastern Brazil, to Disneyland, in Florida. To pass the time on the trip, they started to make up songs. Without the slightest intention of becoming composers, they came up with the chorus "assim você me mata, ai se eu te pego, ai, ai" ("This way you're gonna kill me, oh if I catch you, oh oh"). They liked the song so much that they started to sing it on all the trips they took thereafter, including one to Porto Seguro.

Porto Seguro, a town in the south of Bahia, is full of tourist attractions. One of them is Axé Moi ("moi" being the French word for "me", in stark contrast to the Yoruba word "axé" meaning "life-force"), whose website describes it as a "leisure complex" and "the biggest beach attraction in Brazil." Personally, I like to imagine that the complex was built on the sands where Pedro Álvares Cabral, the Portuguese explorer, first set foot on Brazilian soil.

It was at a party at Axé Moi that the girls from Paraíba first met Sharon Acioly, who was for many years the high priestess of fun in the complex. Acioly held a variety of roles at Axé Moi, ranging from singer to hype-woman. She wasn't there to create great works of art, rather, her job was simply to keep the crowds entertained at all times. To do this, she would make up games for the guests. One of these games took Brazil by storm a few years ago: the *dança do quadrado* (square dance), which she stole from a group of visiting students from São Paulo and Minas Gerais.

But the show must go on, and it can't sustain itself on last season's hits, so when Acioly heard the girls sing the refrain "ai se eu te pego," she quickly took it and began chanting it over a *funk carioca* beat. It became the soundtrack for the part of the show when female tourists were invited on stage to cavort with the scantily-clad male dancers, experiencing the men's natural gifts up-close by way of some skin-to-skin dancing. This *funk* song can be found in dozens of videos that tourists have posted on YouTube as digital mementos from their holidays.

While passing through Porto Seguro one day, Antônio Dyggs went to check out the entertainment at Axé Moi. Dyggs was an event producer from Feira de Santana, an interior city which lies on the edge of the Bahian *sertão*. "Ai Se Eu Te Pego" stuck in his head and he decided to make a *forró* version of the *funk* song. He proceeded to record it with Os Meninos do Seu Zeh, one of the bands that he worked with. The band categorized themselves as *forró universitário pé de serra*, the "pé de serra" signalling the use of "traditional" instruments such as the accordion.

Despite having a slower tempo than most *forró* tunes, the song was a hit in many Bahian cities, attracting the attention of other *forró* bands who immediately released their own versions. Gradually, it became more and more upbeat. Michel Teló first heard his future global hit when it was already part of the repertoire of the bands Cangaia de Jegue and Garota Safada, just to name the more famous ones, and revving up parties throughout the northeast.

Antonio Dyggs observed all of this in wonder. In July 2011, he wrote on NaCola.com (a music events website): "The feeling of having a single song of yours played by more than 50 bands is fantastic. I get a shiver every time I hear "Ai Se Eu Te Pego" being played as a *forró*, *pagode*, salsa, mambo, *funk*, *arrocha*, etc. And I thank my colleague Sharon

Acioly, also a composer of this hit, and the Meninos de Seu Zeh, the great pioneers of this whole story!" (The girls from Paraíba had long been omitted from the equation and only reappeared later, claiming rights and a share of the profit after the song became a money-making global hit.)

The musical promiscuity Dyggs observed is probably the most significant characteristic of Brazil's music scene today. All the hits are quickly rearranged to fit every Brazilian genre, when they're not mixing all the genres already (Michel Teló's version of "Ai Se Eu Te Pego", for example, contains elements of *sertanejo, forró, arrocha, vaneirão*, among others). This is because the majority of groups playing music in Brazil work as dance bands for parties: you don't animate crowds playing originals, so they play the hits of the moment, regardless of genre. Everything has its purpose, after all, and the musicians are there to get the party going, just like Sharon Acioly at Axé Moi.

In light of this trend, the very concept of composition, which once seemed solid, has quickly melted into air. Another example is the Brazilian summer hit of 2010, "Minha Mulher Não Deixa Não." The origin of the chorus seems to have been a children's song released decades ago by a record label in Pernambuco. This would traditionally be "plagiarism", but it became less of an issue given the avalanche of online videos of people making their own unauthorized versions of the hit, each responding to the other in a very decentralized manner, part of an endless conversation.

I had already come across a similar phenomenon when I visited more than 100 municipalities in the country documenting, on CD and on film, so-called "traditional" or "folkloric" rhythms for the Music of Brazil project. I kept finding the same snippets of melodies, lyrics and choreographies at different parties I went to. One group appropriates the invention of another, in a pattern of continuous transformation. In the end, nobody is the owner.

In this way, everything becomes a *brincadeira*, or "game", the word most commonly used to refer to these traditions. Rather than being called "authors", participants are referred to as *brincantes*, or "game-players". How beautiful the public domain was. Was? Is, and will continue to be: public domain is our destiny and our unshakeable future condition. In certain ways, it seems that digital culture has brought us closer to forms of artistic creation once regarded as archaic.

Some of Michel Teló's versions of "Ai Se Eu Te Pego" that have been released around the world:
Portuguese version; English version; Spanish version; Worldwide Remix featuring Pitbull

GONZAGA & ME

A FORRÓ ODYSSEY

by Rob Curto

When I bought my first accordion, I had already become established in New York City as a keyboard player, working with singer-songwriters, playing in clubs and beginning to travel with some more successful bands. Picking up the accordion, with its roots in Europe and a connection to immigration and colonial expansion, connected me to traditional music throughout the world. I fell into the accordion traditions of countries as diverse as Sweden and Madagascar, or as distant as Egypt and Colombia. I began to feel that I was waiting for one of these traditions to adopt me and my newly adopted instrument as one of their own. It finally happened in full force when I discovered Brazil's own accordion music: *forró*.

The first time I heard a *forró* song, I was immediately drawn to the intricate accordion patterns and lines. From my distant spot in New York City, I had heard the music only by CD, leaving the many techniques of the music a mystery to me. "How could I recreate that sound on my own instrument," I wondered. This fascination ultimately led to a personal quest that would send me to the heart of Brazil's *forró* scene, meeting and playing with some of the country's most accomplished musicians.

Soon after these early discoveries, I became connected with a community of Brazilian musicians living in Astoria, Queens. I first met Ana Fonteles, a brilliant vocalist from Ceará, who was working in relative obscurity. She introduced me to other Brazilian players, and soon we were playing in what I am certain was New York's first band ever to play *forró pé de serra* (traditional-style *forró*, literally "foot of the mountain *forró*"). The style's roots reach back to the pioneer culture of the *sertão* – the dry, tough-to-

61

survive-in, interior region of Brazil's northeast. With this small cadre of musicians, a dark and badly decorated Brazilian sports bar in Astoria became a laboratory for my first, exhilarating attempts at this music, learning the repertoire of great innovators such as Jackson do Pandeiro, Dominguinhos and the legendary Luiz Gonzaga.

I studied voraciously, practicing the various *forró* rhythms such as driving *baião*, sensual *xote* and the frenetic, polka-like *arrasta-pé*. I learned that the way I created sound with my accordion and interacted with the percussion instruments affected how people moved on the dance floor, and I became sure that this was the music for me. My new Brazilian friends were amused by this gringo who took to the music so intensely. I remember sitting around a table in the bar, asking them questions about Brazilian culture and drinking a beer as they encouraged me, "Man, you need to learn Portuguese. Go and visit Brazil!" I took their advice and ran with it, and soon found myself in Recife, in many ways the epicentre of *forró*.

Forró is the dance party music of Brazil's northeast. Couples dance closely glued to one another in a kind of two-step, but with a Brazilian swing, Originally danced in small houses and communal spaces in the *sertão*, the idea of an intimate, rural dance hall or *sala de reboco*, with dust rising and sweat pouring down has become the stuff of *forró* legend. In its traditional form, it's played on small button accordion, or *oito baixos*, and a variety of Brazilian percussion instruments. The music itself is based on the accordion repertoire of 19th century Europe but fused with musical styles and rhythmic syncopations of the Arab world and Africa. *Forró* became a staple at any wedding or party, especially in the month of June, which culminates in the feast of St. John, celebrated in Brazil with bonfires, delicious foods like *pamonha* and *canjica*, and *quadrilha*, a type of French-inspired square dance.

When I arrived in Recife for the first time I had the good fortune to soon find myself in the one place that most resembles one of those old-time parties: the backyard *forró* of Arlindo dos Oito Baixos. A musician friend from New York and I were invited to a rehearsal in Old Recife of the city's municipal *frevo* band, led by Maestro Duda. Chatting with one of the trombone players, I inquired about where to go to hear good *forró*. He immediately gave me the phone number of the great accordionist Mestre Camarão. On the phone, Camarão, in the hospitable manner of people from the region, invited me to come hear him play at Arlindo's backyard that very same night.

I expected to encounter a mere few accordion players sitting around a table, drinking *cachaça* and trading tunes. Upon arriving and descending the narrow stairs to the backyard behind Arlindo's house, I heard an incessant beat made up of the *zabumba* (the low *forró* bass drum), triangle (a big steel one, not your grandmother's little orchestral triangle), *pandeiro*, and an *agogô* bell ringing its high and low clock-beat. And there beside the percussionists was the *sanfoneiro* himself: Mestre Camarão killing it on his Excelsior 120-bass accordion. This was going to be much more exciting than I could have imagined.

I made my way immediately to the front of a small plaster stage, mesmerized as people danced behind me and ate food at small folding tables, enjoying the warm night. Strings of small lights and triangular coloured flags hung above the dance floor, packed with couples moving back and forth to the rhythm. Steady streams of notes flew from Camarão's accordion as his left-hand provided a swinging accompaniment. Already, the mysteries of the *forró* accordion were revealing themselves.

I didn't know it at the time, but in some ways, Arlindo's backyard is the most important spot for *forró* in Brazil today, a true embodiment of the old-school *sala de reboco*. Arlindo has created a meeting point for Brazil's greatest *forró* musicians, receiving regular visits from legends such as Dominguinhos and up-and-comers like Beto Hortiz and Cezzinha. Arlindo, who has been blind for at least 25 years, explained to me how he had been the favourite accordion tuner and technician to the great Luiz Gonzaga. Gonzaga advised Arlindo to put down the piano accordion and concentrate on the original *forró* accordion, the *oito baixos*, feeling that this would set Arlindo apart from many of the other players who were recording at that time. It was fruitful advice, and Arlindo has become a legend in his own right, playing and composing on the difficult button accordion. Several years later I would sit in Arlindo's living room as he tuned my own accordion.

Later that night, around a long table in the back, I found myself drinking *cachaça* and sharing a table with Arlindo and some of his friends. A local delicacy, *buchada*, was brought to the table. *Buchada* is the internal organs of a goat, prepared in the intestines, cooked in blood and often served in the goat's skull. I was told I didn't have to eat it if I didn't want to, but I dove in – I wasn't in the mind-set to say no to anything.

Arlindo was my first direct link to the great Luiz Gonzaga. Gonzaga is a legendary cultural figure in Brazil, and nearly considered a saint by many in the northeast. He was born on December 13, 1912 in a small town called Exu, in the deep interior of Pernambuco. Gonzaga's father, Januário, was an accordionist, and also fixed accordions in a small shop. The young Gonzaga was forbidden from going into his father's workshop on his own, but would sneak in anyway, eventually learning to play the *oito baixos* and animating the dance floor at local gatherings.

As a young man, Gonzaga had some romantic troubles and, upset at his mother, left for Fortaleza to join the army. This fateful move eventually led him to study the cornet, purchase a 120-bass piano accordion and find himself playing in Rio de Janeiro's bars after World War II. There he performed the popular international repertoire of the more cosmopolitan south of Brazil: samba, *choro*, waltz, bolero, tango and foxtrot. Only when urged on by some students from the northeast, who recognized his origin through his distinctly northeastern manner of speaking, did he finally play some of the music that his father had passed on to him.

Gonzaga went on to get a contract to play on the radio, and eventually become an important recording artist. During the 1940s, the northeast of Brazil was looked down upon and misunderstood by the dominant culture of Rio and São Paulo. It was seen as backward and poor. Its people, the *nordestinos*, were discriminated against as migrants flowed into the south in search of work and an escape from the enduring droughts of the *sertão*. When Gonzaga dared to play northeastern music, it struck a deep chord with the *nordestinos* struggling to survive in the urban jungles of Rio and São Paulo.

Likewise, Gonzaga's music and life story struck a deep chord within me. Before long the accordion had become not only integrated into my professional life as a musician, but a passion. To be able to have a life as a performer and recording artist on this instrument became a dream, and as I learned more and more about Gonzaga's life and the moments where he found his own path and calling, the more connected I felt to him and his music. Through his accordion, Gonzaga found a way to help people of the northeast understand their experiences. Along with lyric-writing partners such as Zé Dantas and Humberto Teixeira, he wrote classics such as "Baião", "Xote das Meninas" and "Asa Branca," which would become a *nordestino* anthem. Gonzaga revolutionized the way the accordion was played and codified the *forró* ensemble of *zabumba*, triangle and accordion. His greatest genius however, was the creation of songs that brought a new respect and dignity to the people of the northeast. He gave a voice to an entire culture.

Meeting Arlindo opened up new possibilities for me. Through his contacts, I spent time with other accordion players from Recife, asking questions about techniques I had heard on recordings but was not able to fully understand until I saw them first-hand. Later, the musicians I knew from New York introduced me to Luiz Gonzaga's nephew, Sérgio, as we all went to see a rare New York performance of another great *forró* accordionist, Oswaldinho. Oswaldinho, like Sivuca, Dominguinhos and Camarão, is a member of the next generation after Gonzaga, and meeting him brought me into closer contact with my idol. I remember playing a tune for Oswaldinho in the dressing room as he answered my questions about what timbres he used to play different styles of music: the violin reed for *choro* and the full master reed setting for the more robust *forró*. Later I would go to Recife and get to know Luiz Gonzaga's sister, Chiquinha Gonzaga, also an accordionist and singer. I was shown home movies of the Gonzaga family at their house in Rio de Janeiro. I learned about the immense respect that Gonzaga commanded when he entered a room, about his dislike for the dirty double-entendre *forró* of his brother, Zé Gonzaga, and saw how even among his own family, the late Luiz Gonzaga is remembered and revered with great affection.

In 2001, I finally sublet my apartment in New York and moved to Brazil, renting an apartment in Brasília. Brasília was built to represent the spirit of modernism and progress and, in many ways, the musicians I met there embody those ideals. They were constantly striving to create the best music possible; ceaselessly practicing, writing and performing. This environment mirrored my own desire to learn. I spent hours on end practicing the virtuosic music style *choro* during the day, then playing in a *forró* band in the evenings.

Through friends in Brasília, I would eventually be invited to perform with the legendary

Dominguinhos. Dominguinhos was Luiz Gonzaga's protégé, the guy who took over the role of accordionist in the band, freeing Gonzaga to concentrate on singing. Dominguinhos went on to surpass Gonzaga as an instrumentalist, integrating elements of jazz into his music and becoming a great composer and singer in his own right. After Gonzaga's death in 1989, Dominguinhos ascended to the throne, to become recognized as the king of *forró*. When I was asked to sit in on a performance and play with him I jumped at the chance. I remember trying to decide with him what tunes we would do. I mentioned a few of his own songs, such as "Zé Pequeno Você é Grande," which I had learned from recordings, only to find that Dominguinhos didn't really remember all of his own compositions. I played for him, and once he saw that I knew what I was doing, just said, "Don't worry, we'll figure it out when we get up there." We played his composition "Lamento Sertanejo" and the famous *choro* "Noites Cariocas." Being on that stage trading licks with Dominguinhos was like receiving a blessing from a king for me.

Forró went out of fashion in Brazil in the 60s and 70s, with the ascendance first of bossa nova, and later, the *Tropicália* movement (even though *Tropicália* musicians, such as Gilberto Gil and Milton Nascimento, drew much inspiration from Gonzaga and from *música nordestina* in general). Brazilian culture turned its gaze inward again in the 90s, sparking a revival for iconic Brazilian styles such as samba, *choro* and *forró*. This movement, which continues today, turned what was once considered old-fashioned or provincial music into the favourite styles of Brazil's younger generation.

Eventually, *forró*, reinvented by Luiz Gonzaga and disseminated by mass media throughout Brazil would become internationally recognized, spawning bands and fans in cities as far-flung as New York, London, Paris and Munich. My own role in that movement began when a Brazilian percussionist friend, Mauro Refosco, came over to my apartment in 2005 to play some tunes and rehearse for an informal gig at his birthday party. That night we played our first performance at a small club in New York's East Village called Nublu. Focusing on the repertoire of Gonzaga, Dominguinhos and other great *forrozeiros* such as Jackson do Pandeiro, we created a new focal point for *forró pé de serra* (traditional *forró*).

Since then the *forró* scene in New York City has grown exponentially, thanks to a group of dedicated *forró* dancing enthusiasts and musicians such as singer Liliana Araujo from Ceará, violinist Eliano Braz, percussionist Scott Kettner and others. My own band Matuto, together with guitarist Clay Ross, is bringing the *forró* sound, mixed with other roots music influences, to audiences throughout the world. In tandem with New York and other cities in the US, the *forró* scene in Europe has blossomed. Luiz Gonzaga's dream and vision for the music of the *sertão*, the music of his father and his small town of Exu, has come true in ways that he could never have imagined. The voice of his people is being heard and appreciated all over the globe, through songs like "Asa Branca", which talks about the white-winged dove that is the last to depart during troubled times. Every time these songs of resilience and *alegria* (happiness) are played, the story of the *nordestinos* is told, couples dance, and the spirit of *forró* lives on.

Recife's cultural icons Gilberto Freyre and Chico Science are illustrated above by Pedro Gutierres. These days Recife's music scene is developing without reverence to any one icon.

SETTING THE SCENE: RECIFE

by Diego Albuquerque & Rodrigo Édipo

"There are thousands of small scenes, small manguebits, trying to make a connection amongst themselves." – Siba Veloso

Independent music in Recife is living a unique moment. There are no leaders, no Chico Science to show the way forward. Instead, we're living in the new logic of a networked society, musical niches scattered across the city, pockets of creative power diffused in just a few locations.

Three of these pockets of creativity have emerged from very different projects, the currently-on-hiatus Monodecks, the urban crew Coletivo Êxito D'Rua and one of the city's most popular bands, Mombojó. These projects are what we like to call Recife's "Mother Projects". Additionally, we see two constant threads in Recife's music scene, artists that have emerged from the remnants of *manguebit* and those that show the wealth of good music in Recife's peripheries.

It's All About Beto

Monodecks were an instrumental quintet that formed in 2004 and have been "in limbo" since 2011. It was a project that didn't get enough recognition in its own lifetime, reaching only a small audience. However, the fruits of this project emerged in the shape of many important names in contemporary independent music in Pernambuco, where the tendency to use technology and a homemade lo-fi sound became a common trait for us all. For example, Marditu Soundz, the project of former Monodecks drummer Tiago Barros, is a highly original experimental noise project, free from conventional "obligations"; Sãomer Zwadomit, an audiovisual Dadaist duo formed by Luiz Pessoa and Daaniel Araújo (bassist and guitarist with Monodecks respectively) flirts with psychedelic 70s sources such as Pink Floyd, Frank Zappa and The Beatles, as well as sci-fi movie soundtracks. Then we have the creator of Monodecks, Domingos Sávio's solo career, today recording under the nickname D Mingus. He is currently one of the biggest names in Recife's music scene, releasing three great albums that he made in the "back room" of the apartment where he lives.

This modus operandi, of recording at home, is common among members of the Recife Lo-Fi scene, which is also curiously known as Cena Beto, or Beto's Scene. Beto, short for Roberto, is actually a fictional character that was created by some musicians in Recife to play with the media's need to seek a leader or central character that would centralize the actions of the scene, just like Chico Science had done with *manguebit*.

Other important musicians in this scene include great artists like Graxa (with the album *Molho*), Matheus Mota (with the essential *Desenho*), Ex-Exus and Zeca Viana.

Success Comes From The Street

The second "Mother Project" is Coletivo Êxito D'Rua, a collective formed in 2000 with members that work across all aspects of hip-hop culture: music, graffiti, breakdance and organizing workshops and important social projects across the state of Pernambuco. Many of the group's members are important names in Recife's independent rap scene. For example, DJ Novato has a project of acutely refined beats, an alchemy of rhythms called Batida de Novato. Together with MC Anêmico (member of Coletivo Êxito de Rua and Inquilinus), Novato also created the project Sem Peneira Pra Suco Sujo, with creative (and honest) rhymes and beats. Another prominent name in local rap is the excellent MC Rimocrata, member of Coletivo A Firma, that despite his young age, already possesses a strong sonic, and especially vocal, identity.

The Children of Mombojó

Formed in 2001, Mombojó is one of the most influential and critically-praised bands post-*manguebit*. Mombojó are still active today, but we want to call attention to the projects that sprang from the group. For example, the refined and low-profile Trio Eterno, featuring Felipe S (singer in Mombojó), André Édipo and Missionário José, which has a versatile aesthetic that is slowly moving away from that of Mombojó; and Diatron, a creative duo formed by Chiquinho (Mombojó's keyboardist) and pianist Vitor Araújo has a real attention to sonic details and a great admiration for the French electronic scene. While listening to them it's easy to identify influences such as Air, Daft Punk and *Kid A*-period Radiohead.

Manguebit's Remains

Sharing this scene of innovative artists and new movements are the artists from the

D Mingus, *Fricção* (2003); Alessandra Leão, *Dois Cordões* (2009); Trio Eterno, *Suite Pistache* (2013)

1990s that constantly reinvent themselves and still follow the path of independence. A good example is the singer and poet Siba Veloso, known for being part of one of the most creative groups of *manguebit*, Mestre Ambrósio. He currently plays guitar [as opposed to the *rabeca*, the Brazilian fiddle with which he played for many years] and moves much closer to a global pop music than the regional sound he previously characterized, while still retaining and making good use of the past. Another name is Cinval Coco Grude, a project started in 2002, after the end of the band Querosene Jacaré. In this period of 10 years, Cinval has released more than 20 albums, all handmade at home, creating a huge expanse in the field of free experimentation.

A third interesting project is Areia e Grupo de Música Aberta, headed by bassist Walter Areia, member of the group Mundo Livre S/A. Areia e Grupo de Música Aberta are an instrumental group, working solely with acoustic instruments, following a line of improvisation with strong influences from African and Portuguese music. Last, but not least, Rodrigo Caçapa, who began his contact with music in the times of *manguebit*'s fermentation and today uses the reference of popular songs and guitar instrumentals to perform his work. Together with the voice of Alessandra Leão - who was part of the group Comadre Florzinha - they are developing and subverting the traditionalism of samba, uniting the rhythm with elements of popular music from northeastern Brazil and Africa.

Music From The Periphery

Within this niche are artists who are massively popular in Recife but are constantly targets of prejudice by a more puritan wing of high musical culture. As their creative driving force they all possess a combination of self-taught skills and new democratic means of production, flirting with the aesthetics of black electronic music, such as ragga, *funk carioca*, R&B and hip-hop. One of the central figures of this whole scene is the hedonistic MC Sheldon, whose creative output focuses on controversial lyrics and questionable morals that have already earned him lawsuits. Also present are the equally controversial and nihilistic Alaca, Troz & Dedê with lyrics full of sex, drugs and bingeing. Then there's the half-laidback, half-romantic *tecnobrega* of Vício Louco and Kitara, thus closing this extremely personal, sarcastic, subversive and detached (from judgement) portion of Pernambuco's independent music scene.

A City of Niches

It's clear that there is a growing independent scene in Recife, where demand for music is growing along with the population of the city and surrounding areas. It's a city where there will always be musical niches and, though it may be increasingly difficult to keep an eye on all of them, it will be left to those who hear the music and to the media as to which will be the next scenes to gain attention, whether they rise to the popularity of *manguebit* or smaller current scenes like Recife Lo-Fi or Cena Beto.

CARNAVAL
DO RECIFE

by Beto Figueiroa

MULHER RENDEIRA

FROM THE SERTÃO TO THE WORLD: THE STORY OF A
BRAZILIAN SONG'S JOURNEY TO BECOMING A GLOBAL STAPLE

by Robin Perkins

Sing the simple melody of "Mulher Rendeira" to any Brazilian and though they may not know who wrote it, they will almost certainly recognize it. With its roots in the dry, bandit-plagued *sertão* plains of northeastern Brazil and originally written in the 1920s, the song has come to represent a symbol of the region's traditions and its legends. Covered by countless Brazilian artists including Astrud Gilberto, Raul Seixas, Gerson "King" Combo and Luiz Gonzaga, for over 90 years it has captured Brazil's imagination and become firmly established within the national cultural consciousness. However, there is another, deeper history to this simple melody, one that reaches much further than Brazil's borders, traversing genres, continents, cultures and languages.

I first stumbled across the song in 2008. However, it wasn't the line "Ole mulher rendeira" I heard in the chorus but "Ole mujer hilandera", as sung by Peru's legendary *chicha* band, Juaneco y su Combo from their 1970 recording. A year later as I sat watching Lima Barreto's classic 1953 film *O Cangaceiro* I heard that same, familiar melody once more and it got me thinking. How did that same song make its way between these two contexts, separated by nearly 20 years, a language barrier and thousands of kilometres of dense rainforest?

Intrigued, I began to dig further into the song's history and found over 160 versions of "Mulher Rendeira" spanning 90 years, 19 countries and six languages. There was the swooning cover by German *schlager* singer Heino, a Franco-Brazilian disco hit from the Bandits of Love, the Mexican-tinged version by short-lived US psychedelic-pop band The Eighth Day and even a surprise appearance on Joan Baez's classic album 5. Behind each version there lies a fascinating story.

The origins of "Mulher Rendeira" are shrouded in mystery and myth. The story goes that the song was originally written in the 1920s by the divisive bandit-hero Lampião. According to historians, the "king of the badlands" penned the lyrics on February 22nd, 1922 paying homage to his grandmother, a lace maker or *mulher rendeira*. "Mulher Rendeira" was soon adopted by Lampião's bandits as a war hymn that would be sung during their long marches across the *sertão* plains. The ever-changing lyrics would recount the exploits and bravery of the *cangaceiro* bandits and be accompanied by that simple melody played on a dust-covered accordion. The most well-documented record of the song was during Lampião's attack on the city of Mossoró when some 50 *cangaceiros* attacked the city to the tune of "Mulher Rendeira".

Volta Seca, accordionist and former member of Lampião's troop recorded a version in 1957 that may most resemble the original. This version, released nearly 20 years after Lampião's death, is a slice of the mythical *sertão*, transporting the listener back to the wild, old days when bandits roamed and ancient traditions flourished. This was in stark contrast to the quickly modernizing, urban Brazil of São Paulo and Rio de Janeiro of the

Lampião by Ronald Guimaraes

50s. The release of Volta Seca's *Cantigas do Cangaço* LP was undeniably tied into the resurgence of the *cangaceiro* myth, which was fostered by the release of Lima Baretto's iconic hit film *O Cangaceiro*. In the film, "Mulher Rendeira" lies at the heart of Zé do Norte's celebrated soundtrack, appearing in the opening and closing credits. From that moment on, the song would be forever tied to the myth of the northeast and enshrined in Brazilian cultural consciousness.

Baretto's *O Cangaceiro* is a sanitized and romanticized, Hollywood interpretation of the Lampião myth. Though criticized by many, it went on to become an international box office hit, gaining global distribution and recognition at the 1953 Cannes festival. *O Cangaceiro* reinforced the image within Brazil of the northeast as a land that time forgot where a real "authentic" Brazilian culture could still be found. The *sertão* appears as untouched by the modern world, a place of bandits, guns, romance and mystery. The film not only exported this image to the rest of Brazil but to the rest of the world, and with it, the symbolic sound of the *sertão*, "Mulher Rendeira."

"Mulher Rendeira" was soon incorporated into the booming Latin canon pushed by the leading major record labels. Essentially, they were in the business of exporting Latin American exotica. Versions of "Mulher Rendeira" could be found alongside songs like "Mexican Hat Dance", "Tico Tico" and "Guantanamera" on albums by crooners like Bruce Lowe, James Last, Jean Sablon and even Cliff Richard's The Shadows. These versions often appeared not as "Mulher Rendeira" but as "O Cangaceiro" or "The Bandit", based on Zé do Norte's then standard version and containing mostly translated lyrics. However, these weren't direct translations of Lampião's ballad, but rough adaptations based on the film's exoticized image of old-world Brazil. The lyrics indulge in stereotypes and result in strange cultural or linguistic inaccuracies. Take, for instance, the use of the Spanish "adios" in the Shadows' 1962 version "The Bandit":

"She was sweet and she was tender, there was love light in her eyes,
In my arms she soon surrendered, very much to my surprise.
I refused her father's ransom, and I kept the greater prize,

Now at night we ride together beneath the blue Brazilian sky.
Adios to you, Amigo, Adios to you, my friend.......
Ole, O Cangachero, the Bandit of Brazil."

As the tune reached a new global audience, it began to mean different things to its different international listeners. In the US, audiences instantly identified the heroic bandit figure of Teodoro in "O Cangaceiro" with the country's own bandit myth – that of the cowboy. The image of the "good" outlaw – on-the-run, kidnapping and seducing beautiful maidens across dusty landscapes – resonated with the cowboy films of the same period. "The Bandit of Brazil" recorded by singing cowboy Tex Ritter in 1962 encapsulated exactly this, complete with a horse riding rhythm, a good helping of "yeeehaaaws" and lyrics like:

Os Cangaceiros by Ronald Guimaraes

*"I'm the quickest on the trigger, when I shoot I shoot to kill
I'm a hero down in Rio, where they talk about me still."*

Meanwhile in Peru, some fifty years after Lampião's original homage to his grandmother, the *mulher* took centre-stage once more. "Mulher Rendeira's" transformation into a Peruvian *chicha* classic represents one of the most intriguing twists in the song's history. The *chicha* movement emerged in the 70s as a fusion of Colombian cumbia with psychedelic guitars, surf rock and indigenous symbolism. At the centre of this movement were Juaneco y su Combo who, with their electric guitars slung over traditional Shipibo clothing, would go on to lead the emergence of the so called *cumbia amazónica* strain of *chicha*.

Released in 1970, one of the band's earliest and most popular recordings was "Mujer Hilandera", a Spanish language cover of Zé do Norte's 1953 arrangement. According to José Luis Carvallo, a key figure in the 70s *chicha* scene, the idea of recording "Mujer Hilandera" came from their producer Albert Maravi, who knew the song from having been a DJ in Brazil. Twenty years after the release of *O Cangaceiro*, "Mulher Rendeira" crossed the Amazon and found a new context and a new home.

Much as lace makers are a central part of northeastern culture and identity in Brazil, in Peru the Andean weavers, or *hilanderas*, represented a powerful image of national Peruvian identity. As such, Peruvian listeners identified with "Mujer Hilandera" despite being completely unaware of the song's Brazilian origins. As the song's popularity grew, so "Mujer Hilandera" went on to become enshrined in Peruvian culture, tied to the symbol of the weaver woman.

***

Four years after I first immersed myself in the story of "Mulher Rendeira" I heard that familiar melody in an unfamiliar place once more. This time I was in Italy and Peruvian *chicha*-revival band Bareto's 2008 version was booming out of a beat-up old stereo at a Sunday afternoon meetup for Latin American immigrants in Rome. It was at that moment that I realized just how timeless and spectacularly global "Mulher Rendeira" had become. But the question I kept coming back to was "why?" It doesn't possess the universal sentimentality of "You'll Never Walk Alone," nor the infectious rhythm of "La Bamba" or "Lambada", to name a few other omnipresent songs. Was it the melodic simplicity? The catchy chorus? Or, perhaps, its "outlaw" attitude? There's probably no one answer, so perhaps the key to understanding the song's endurance is recognizing its ability to resonate on different levels in so many different cultural contexts around the world. Chance meetings across the Amazon, seemingly random cover versions, culturally insensitive translations, nostalgic endeavours and surprising cultural assimilation have all shaped "Mulher Rendeira's" trajectory around the world. And surely, its history doesn't stop here. I can't wait to here its next incarnation.

WELCOME TO THE JUNGLE

THE RISE OF THE AMAZONIAN SOUND

by Marlon Bishop

You might have noticed that something was a little off. At shows of the Rio indie rock band Do Amor; on the latest album by *novo-MPB* star Céu; in the all-vinyl DJ sets from São Paulo's hip Veneno Soundsystem. In these places and elsewhere, something about the rhythm pumping out of the speakers hasn't been your typical Brazilian fare. Instead of the manicured bounce of samba or the manic whirl of *forró*, a different groove has been sounding: slow and slithering, the percussion moving like gravity towards the pounding downbeat. A low and dirty guitar repeats the same hypnotizing figure forever. Meanwhile, up above, a battery of razor-sharp horns traces lines in the air. The music swelters.

That beat is *carimbó*, a classic rhythm from the Amazonian state of Pará, in Brazil's far north. Along with other genres from Pará, it's becoming something of a sensation right now. The boom for music from this part of the Amazon was, in part, sparked by tecnobrega queen Gaby Amarantos, whose whirlwind rise has drawn attention to the many musical treasures waiting in the rainforest. In the wake of her star turn, several artists with updated takes on Pará's *música regional* – older genres like *guitarrada*, *lambada* and *carimbó* – have become hot items as well. Local talents Felipe Cordeiro, Dona Onete and Luê Soares have all become in-demand touring artists in Brazil. And beyond Pará, artists ranging from the legendary Marisa Monte to underground electro-jazz outfit Projeto Ccoma have been hungrily absorbing northern sounds into their diet. Bloggers are blogging about it. Crate-diggers are digging for it. Five hundred years after Portuguese explorers first claimed the emerald expanse, Brazil is at last discovering a musical El Dorado in the Amazon.

The Caribbean Connection

Life in Pará is centred around its capital city, Belém. The port city of almost 1.5 million inhabitants is located at the confluence of the massive Amazon and Tocantins rivers and is one of the largest population centres in the entire northern region. As many Brazilians are now discovering, it's also one of the country's most musical cities.

"I'm just amazed by the scene," says Geraldinho Magalhães, a Rio-based artist manager, who has taken various trips to Belém.

Magalhães got interested in the music after attending a concert organized by Terruá Pará, an initiative started by the Pará state government in 2006 to promote the region's music. He was so impressed that he started travelling to Pará and eventually produced a documentary on the topic for TV Globo. "There are so many artists and so many new styles, and they really preserve their musical roots. It's like a big island within Brazil."

A large part of the music's drawing power is that, even in a country as musically diverse as Brazil, it's just so different from everything else. "When I travel, I always realize how unique Belém is. Our lines of music and culture are totally distinct from other places in Brazil," says Pio Lobato, a major figure in the regional music scene in Belém. Lobato says that Belém's uniqueness has a lot to do with the city's isolation from the rest of the country – it's a four day boat journey just to Manaus, the Amazon's other major city. "Belém was for a long time cut-off from Rio and São Paulo, which are the communications centres of the country. So we made our own thing."

The Pará sound is the result of a long history of musical influence from Latin America and the Caribbean. As Brazilian styles like samba and *forró* came in from the south, sounds like merengue, calypso, *kadans* and cumbia flowed in from the north in equal measure, burrowing deep into the region's musical DNA. You can hear it clearly in the Pará artists of today. There's a certain Brazilian vibe present, but it's overshadowed by a potpourri of Caribbean musical elements: the repeating *montuno* licks of Afro-Latin music, the steady ch-chch-ch scrapers culled from Colombian cumbia, and the syncopated guitar strumming common in the West Indies.

The most common origin story about the Caribbean influence in Pará is that in the mid-1900s, residents would use shortwave radios to pick up signals from places like Havana or Martinique. (Scholar Darien Lamen says this is probably a myth, since only the wealthiest *paraenses* would have been able to afford shortwave sets in those days). More likely is that vinyl from the Caribbean and Latin America arrived in the Amazon through the many contraband boats that stopped over in Belém's waterways, carrying goods between Brazil and the neighbouring Guyanas.

Regardless of how they got there, records from the likes of faraway merengue star Angel Viloria and Colombia's Los Corraleros de Majagual became huge on local radio. Those influences filtered into the region's first home-grown pop music movement in the 70s, when artists like Pinduca adapted the rainforest's traditional Afro-indigenous *carimbó* rhythm to a dance band format.

By the mid-70s, Belém was full of horn-driven dance bands imitating Caribbean music with a local accent. Local radio personalities baptized the high-energy music they made with a new name: *lambada*, referring to the snap of a whip. A popular type of *lambada* band was fronted by virtuoso electric guitar players like Mestre Curica and Mestre Vieira, who would make instrumental music full of acrobatic riffing, played out of jury-rigged amplifiers. In the 80s, this style would be rechristened *guitarrada* on a series of releases on the Gravasom label.

If you've heard the term *lambada* before and never connected it to the Amazon that's because it was the brief subject of a global dance craze in the late 80s which somehow managed to ignore the original music almost completely. The style blew up in Brazil in the summer of 1988 through the hit *lambada* "Chorando Se Foi" by Marcía Ferreira (an artist who was not actually from Belém but from Belo Horizonte). The song proceeded to get picked up by a French producer, re-recorded in Paris and made into a watered-down global pop hit. The resulting *lambada* fad had little to do with the hard-driving dance pop happening in Pará, or with any other Brazilian music for that matter.

Rise Up!

The classic dance sounds of Pará faded in the 90s when the schlocky Amazonian radio-pop known as *brega* took over. Their resurrection – the event that single-handedly kicked today's revival into motion – occurred in 2003, with the creation of the *Mestres da Guitarrada* project, which reunited master guitarists of yesteryear to perform and record golden-age *guitarrada*. The project was the brainchild of Pio Lobato, a guitarist for the Belém rock band Cravo Carbono. When he wasn't rocking out, Lobato had been researching *lambada* history for his thesis at a local university. After all, it was the 90s, and regional roots music had suddenly become fashionable for students all over Brazil, mostly thanks to the massive success of Chico Science & Naçao Zumbi's *manguebit*, which made Recife's traditional sounds hip by mixing them with hard rock and hip-hop. Cravo Carbono was adapting the concept to Pará and earning a loyal local following. But with *Mestres da Guitarrada*, Lobato sparked interest in *paraense* music on a truly grand scale. "We never expected so much to come out of it," says Pio Lobato. "It was surprising because here was an album that was 80 percent old instrumental music, and it ended up being this big, pop success."

Mestres da Guitarrada generated excitement about Pará's musical heritage among Belém hipsters and the local government. The former started to create new bands, with plentiful support from the latter. One of the first (and best) musical projects to form was La Pupuña. The band makes "psychedelic *carimbó*", taking advantage of the natural synergy between classic Amazonian pop and surf rock. More recently, La Pupuña grabbed headlines for putting out *Charque Side Of The Moon*, a full-length, Amazonian-flavoured remake of Pink Floyd's *Dark Side Of The Moon* (featuring Gaby Amarantos on "The Great Gig In The Sky" wailing over a *tecnobrega* beat, of course). Bandleader Luiz Félix Robatto ended up being tapped to produce music for Gaby Amarantos' major label debut record.

Felipe Cordeiro is another major artist to emerge from the *música regional* revival. Cordeiro is the son of one of Belém's greatest 80s-era *lambada* producers, and his closeness to the tradition shows. On his 2011 album *Kitsch Pop Cult*, he takes the region's fast-flying electric guitar style and brings it up to date with modern production values and aesthetics. Even though his music is built around *lambada*, he's not shy about mixing in the occasional *tecnobrega* beat.

Not all the Pará artists to break out are young bloods. Dona Onete is a traditional *carimbó* singer (as well as history professor and local secretary of culture) who is just starting her professional touring and recording career at the ripe age of 71. Her band, directed by Pio Lobato, has cut a slick record full of tumbling percussion and tight horn arrangements. Other notables include Luê Soares, a young singer-songwriter with an MPB approach to the region's music, and Lia Sophia, a new singer who was born in French Guiana to Brazilian parents and skilfully mixes pop, *tecnobrega* sounds and Amazonian guitars.

What's interesting is that this whole movement, in a lot of ways, has been made possible by government cultural policies. Revival artists have had the very strong support of the state communication department, known as FUNTELPA. Following the release of the *Mestres da Guitarrada* album, FUNTELPA invested millions of dollars into promoting regional music; allowing artists to record in their studios, pushing them on public TV and radio, and spending big bucks on the splashy Terruá Pará concert series in Belém and in São Paulo.

The results have been impressive. In a few years, there's been a true viral spread of the music throughout the country. Already, Pará is poised to gain a reputation in Brazil as a musical hotspot on the level of long-adored states like Pernambuco and Bahia. In the meantime, Brazil has caught Amazonian music fever. On one hand, it's meant the rise of alternative *tecnobrega* acts like Banda UÓ. But it's also meant artists taking an interest in other regional sounds and pushing them into new directions. For example, Rio indie rockers Do Amor gave *carimbó* the Vampire Weekend treatment on their 2010 track "Isso é Carimbó." In Fortaleza, DJ Guga de Castro expertly remixes the sounds of Pará for the club with his Iracema Hot Sound project. Brasília's Criolina turned Aldo

Aldo Sena / Mestre Curica / Mestre Vieira, *Mestres da Guitarrada* (2004); Gaby Amarantos, *Treme* (2012); Felipe Cordeiro, *Kitsch Pop Cult* (2011)

Sena's classic "Lambada Classe A" into an electro-party anthem on their 2013 *Space Night Love Dance Laser* release. And major recording artists are paying attention as well: Céu, Lucas Santtana, Titãs, Marisa Monte and Orquestra Imperial have all borrowed Pará's sly guitar licks and heavy beats in one way or another. As for the world beyond Brazil, global bass producer Schlachthofbronx released an EP titled *Carimbó* in 2011. Its eponymous lead single pairs a heavy breakbeat with *guitarrada*-inspired synth lines.

Hot, Humid and Undeniably Latin

All of this begs the question: what is making people interested in Pará's music? "The heat, I think," says Marcel Arêde, a Belém native who manages Waldo Squash and to whom I pose this question. "It's music with lots of energy, with strong drum beats. And here people don't make music thinking about the market, they do it because it's fun. So you'll find a lot of music in Pará that's not well-produced, but it's honest."

There's no doubt that Pará's music is hot, but one of the biggest factors in its appeal may be its strong Latin connection. When I asked Céu about the influences on her 2012 album *Caravana Sereia Bloom*, she mentioned *lambada* and *guitarrada*. "I was really interested how up there, music from the rest of Latin America mixes with Brazilian music," she said. Producer Geraldinho Magalhães had a similar sentiment: "Brazil has nothing to do with the rest of Latin America, and it's quite a shame. I never even heard Latin music like salsa until I moved from the northeast to a bigger city like Rio. That's a big part of what amazed me about Pará."

It's true: despite bordering nine other South American countries, Brazil has remained remarkably apart from its Spanish-speaking neighbours, especially when it comes to music. Outside of very small circles, Latin American music just isn't known in Brazil. But there are signs that this is changing. Salsa bands and dedicated salsa club nights are popping up more and more in Rio and São Paulo. Puerto Rican star Don Omar's club hit "Danza Kuduro" was remade into a Brazilian *sertanejo* hit in 2012. This kind of interchange is going the other way too – Michel Teló's Latin crossover success with "Ai Se Eu Te Pego" led to a *sertanejo*-style duet with Colombia's Carlos Vives that was huge around Latin America.

There are many possible factors as to why this is happening. For one, there's the Internet, which has opened Brazil up to all sorts of new influences (see this book's article on Brazilian afrobeat, for instance). There's also the growth of a South American festival circuit, which often brings Latin bands to Brazil and sends Brazilian bands the other way. Plus, Brazil's rising leadership role in the region has deepened its political and economic ties with other Latin American nations. Overall, Brazil seems to be more and more interested in participating in the Latin American cultural conversation, and it makes me think that the growing popularity of Latin-inflected music from Pará right now isn't a coincidence. With the help of jungle beats and some nasty guitar playing, Brazil could finally be settling into the neighbourhood.

TECNOBREGA RISING

WILL WORLDWIDE ATTENTION REPRESENT THE BEGINNING OR THE END FOR A REMARKABLE NEW DANCE MUSIC STRAIGHT OUT OF THE AMAZON?

by Amaya García-Velasco

Tecnobrega's rise has been meteoric. In record time, it went from "soundsystem-only" status to official Patrimônio Cultural (cultural heritage) in its Amazonian home state of Pará, declared in 2011 by then-governor Simão Jatene. What started with cheesy synth lines and MIDI melodies made with cheap software is now a major genre in the global electronic dance music scene. Over time, tecnobrega has gotten harder, faster, more bombastic and more creative, mixing in genres from elsewhere in Latin America like cumbia, merengue and even a little bit of reggaeton.

But it wasn't always that way. As with many genres originating from Latin America's slums, tecnobrega was not particularly well-received at first. Many deemed it too ridiculous, too sexual, too banal, or just plain bad. These same kind of debates have gone on, and continue to go on for Rio's *funk carioca*, as well as *cumbia digital* in Argentina, *changa tuki* in Venezuela, *champeta* in Colombia, and so on. But, things have changed, as Pará's sonic child has gone national, and global, thanks to international beat hunters and the visibility of emissaries like Gaby Amarantos, Gang do Eletro and João Brasil, who have given the genre a fresh start and inspired new regional spin-offs.

A Brief History of Tecnobrega

The term *brega* (meaning "tacky" in Portuguese) didn't come into common use until the 80s, when it became shorthand for popular music of bad taste. According to Brazilian music historian José Teles, brega is "music with simple melodies, romantic lyrics, full of clichés." He sees it as starting life at the end of the 60s when "young people from the lower middle class started playing iê-iê-iê [Brazilian rock 'n' roll, heavily influenced by early The Beatles]." Teles compares those early brega sounds to the old boleros of Mexico, with that same mix of guitars, organs and drums. Daniel Haaksman, founder of Man Recordings, sees a European comparison: "Original brega is like *schlager*, as we say in German. It's what old people listen to. The lyrics are very romantic. They don't sing about guns or sexual positions, they sing about love, being left."

The sound reached its peak in the 80s but ultimately fell out of fashion, its predilection for syrupy ballads and anthemic sing-along choruses giving way to newer styles such as *axé*, *pagode* and *sertanejo*. A more danceable, Caribbean-influenced variant from Pará known as *brega paraense* – the kind made by Banda Calypso, for example – seems to have reached its peak during the 90s and eventually transitioned into what we know as tecnobrega today. In using this term, the originators of the genre are continuing its legacy: not taking themselves too seriously, and focusing on making music "for the people, by the people."

When plain old brega no longer satisfied the youth of Pará, DJs and producers began remaking Top 40 songs using "computers with software downloaded from the Internet and instructions in English we don't read," according to an MTV Iggy interview with breakout tecnobrega star Gaby Amarantos. The resulting music - which had now added the 'tecno' to brega - would play at Belém soundsystem parties alongside plenty of dancing, beer and pyrotechnics. "By putting beats together, we created and developed a new beat which has a bit of Amazonian music in it, a little flavour of indigenous drumming mixed with brega music that speaks of love, betrayal, relationships, happiness, drunkenness and having fun," says Amarantos.

Better words could not describe the topics

BRAZIL'S SONIC MUTANTS

There are few people with a knowledge of underground Brazilian music as vast as that of Wolfram Lange aka SoundGoods. Here, he reveals some of the new fusions which are shaking things up in nightclubs around Brazil.

Brazil is vast, with regional musical styles that reign supreme in certain corners of the country but are barely heard in others. Sometimes though, as people move from state to state, from north to south, Amazon to *sertão*, these styles transform, creating new genres, and nowhere is this more apparent than in electronic music.

While *funk carioca* has stagnated musically in Rio, interesting changes are happening to the *tamborzão* beat [as the classic *funk carioca* beat is known] elsewhere. Not only is there a new *funk* scene in São Paulo, traditionally known for its hip-hop crews, but it's also percolated to states lesser known among tourists and music aficionados. *Eletro funk* mixes *funk carioca* with the more widespread dance beats of electro and house. It's produced everywhere from the southern states of Paraná and Rio Grande do Sul to Midwestern Tocantins and Acre in the far west. The DJs and producers often pick lyrics and samples from original tunes out of Rio and put them together with their own beats or loops from other tracks.

Although the result is more often than not a rudimentary house beat, cheesy female vocals and an MC rapping in *funk carioca*-style, there are some tunes that can definitely compete with the remixes coming from the Western global bass scene. As for the lyrics, sadly they are just as overly macho and sexist as their Rio-based source material. The sound is played in regular clubs, but finds its true home in a venue more easily spotted on boastful Internet videos. Car-crazy Brazilians install huge sound systems in their nouveau riche sport cars, so huge they defy the imagination of how they fit in the trunk. At automotive events or just hanging out on weekends in the town square, eletro funk blasts out of the massive rig, rattling the car, while girls with peroxide blond hair and micro hot pants accompany the beaming owner.

While eletro funk draws on the international club sound that is currently dominating global pop music, there are other hybrids that incorporate Brazilian music styles. Axé funk is the self-descriptive name for a blend of Bahian and carioca music styles. As with eletro funk, it's the lyrics that have made the jump from Rio to Bahia, while the backing track consists of the more charming Bahian style of axé, softer than funk's hard-edged beats.

Aside from the country music twang of sertanejo and the eminently danceable samba offshoot known as pagode, axé is actually the most popular music in Brazil according to the radio and sales charts. Thus, it is not surprising that the tecnobrega and eletro melody producers from Belém have jumped on the bandwagon and created another intra-Brazilian musical mutant. Called axé melody, it brings together the cheesy vocals and weird keyboard riffs of Amazonian electronics with the high-speed beats of axé into a fusion of pure craziness.

by Wolfram Lange

addressed in the tecnobrega lyrics. But what really drew me personally to the music is the lack of restraint tecnobrega artists demonstrate when it comes to mixing genres, sampling diverse sources and just doing whatever they want with the music, no questions asked. Banda Djavu, veterans of the aparelhagems, handily turn Top 40 fare like David Guetta into syrupy tecnobrega goodness. But they do so while mixing in 90s happy hardcore synth lines, reggae beats, calypso sounds and cumbia rhythms, among other genres. Through tecnobrega, these sounds have gained a new life in northern Brazil, not ironically, but as a legitimate way to repurpose the old into something new and original.

Another aspect that defined tecnobrega is its DIY method of production. "If you don't have much musical knowledge, you just play around with what you find," says Haaksman. "That's the same sort of ethos that punk rock had at the beginning. No one in punk rock could play an instrument. The same is happening with [tecnobrega]. Sometimes they use the same samples and it's just the singers that change. But sometimes you find really interesting tracks and music in this context."

DJ Cremoso is one of the prime examples of such innovation. Cremoso, who keeps his identity a secret, turns the music of revered indie icons like Nirvana into tecnobrega jams. As Haaksman touches on, tecnobrega artists are returning to the rich sampling culture that the music industry in the US, for example, has effectively outlawed with copyright legislation. This fear of the "sample and I'll sue you" technique of the big labels isn't really a threat in Pará, but the lack of radio airplay has made it harder for the genre to become known. Even without support from broadcasting, tecnobrega eventually found its way to the wider world.

A New Strain Of Tecnobrega...

In the beginning, it was virtually impossible for people outside of Pará to access tecnobrega. Unless you went to the soundsystem parties yourself or had friends in the scene, you wouldn't have known about it. Even if you did discover tecnobrega, the music's reliance on cheap recording technologies, MIDI files, and the CD-R culture meant you might not have liked what you heard. It was hard to wade through all the muck to find the genre's gems. A lot of the stuff floating around was what Daniel Haaksman (who eventually put together a tecnobrega compilation on Man Recordings) describes as "really cheesy, really badly sounding, and full of jingles where DJs or artists will advertise themselves."

Nonetheless, the music gained profile via artists' television appearances in Brazil, international documentary films like *Good Copy Bad Copy* and *RIP: A Remix Manifesto* which featured the tecnobrega scene, and the curatorial work of electronic dance music producers like Diplo and Haaksman. Attention from abroad made the genre more accessible and gave it credibility within Brazil. In turn, recognition upped the ante for tecnobrega artists, encouraging them to become more creative and recording high quality albums.

"Currently in Belém, good tecnobrega has to have an energetic introduction with lots of jittery synthesizers," explains Gang do Eletro's Waldo Squash. "The creativity of the producer is important here. He has to know if the music will work well during the parties. If he plays the music and the people dance, then it's good."

But aside from making people dance, tecnobrega geared towards the larger market needs to be recorded and mixed in a real studio. With her first record *Treme*, Amarantos set the bar for the new strain of tecnobrega. In terms of quality, *Treme* is a top notch production with a full band, careful arrangements and professional mastering. She says she realized that she needed to invest in tecnobrega if she wanted the world to get to know it. "The scene has already existed for 15 years in Belém but had never left it. When we did *Treme* we managed to bring the quality that we believe that the music deserves to have," she told MTV Iggy.

Gang do Eletro and João Brasil followed suit with high-gloss tecnobrega productions. The new tracks made a difference in bringing the music beyond Belém. "Waldo Squash's high quality productions really surprised me and made me pay attention to the genre," says Omulu, a Rio de Janeiro-based electronic music producer. Eventually, the wider world started to listen too.

From Belém To The World

The current stars of tecnobrega are getting exposure both in and outside of Brazil. Amarantos and Banda UÓ have both had national hits, Gang do Eletro have toured

Europe and João Brasil's profile just keeps getting bigger. The genre has also gained an international following from the likes of British pop group Pet Shop Boys, who commissioned a tecnobrega remix from DJ Waldo Squash for the song "Memory of the Future." Even Madonna has cashed in, borrowing João Brasil's "L.O.V.E. Banana" for her 2012 hit "Give Me All Your Luvin'." And then there's The Strokes, whose "One Way Trigger" includes some undeniable tecnobrega sounds, even though the band hasn't credited the genre. In an interview for Globo, Gaby Amarantos claimed that the song "has those videogame-style solos that we use in tecnobrega. The guitar, the beats, the tempo and the synths are all characteristic [of tecnobrega]." Waldo Squash says the influence goes beyond The Strokes. "From what I've seen, the sounds of the ghettos have influenced much electronic music around the world," he explains. "Tecnobrega fits within this group, and already I've started to hear music with the same beats, identical sounds to those that we're using to create music, and so on."

Even as tecnobrega defines itself, it's already beginning to change. Brazilian producers have begun to rework the style into their own compositions, creating sub-genres like Jaloo's sci-fi brega and Omulu's *bregabass* (which could be seen as a step into the more generic ether of "global bass"). Banda UÓ, on the other hand, have approached the genre from a more rock perspective. Omulu told me that he thought the creation of these updates will eventually cause resistance from more established artists, but when I asked Waldo Squash, he said he sees the new subgenres as a positive thing. "I believe that the emergence of more bands working with this style from other places is going to make the rhythm more stable", he said.

There is no doubt that the future of tecnobrega is bright, but there is no sure-fire way to predict where the genre will head next. Omulu believes that "the style will spread around the world, just like cumbia." Haaksman agrees. "This genre really is starting to circulate globally," he says.

Tecnobrega will inevitably change over time. As the sound grows even further, the need for innovation may force tecnobrega artists, as it has done already, to look for newer rhythms, and use samples that are more in line with international electronic dance music trends. For example, on João Brasil's *Tropical Brittania EP* (2012), you can hear the incorporation of *trap* in "Dadinho". You can also hear more sophisticated house and bass rhythms in the rest of the tracks. Gang do Eletro have already incorporated reggaeton beats to their repertoire. And, Gaby Amarantos has mined cumbia and merengue on *Treme*, drawing on Pará's history of Latin American musical influences while also appealing to fans of electronic cumbia in the global bass community.

Whether future changes strengthen tecnobrega's "genetic code" or sees it conform into a more international-friendly variant remains to be seen. But, whether or not the music fades into the global bass background, there is no denying that the people of Belém have given the world two incredible gifts: a new beat to dance to, and the audacity to let go of the rules and freely experiment with pop culture. That uncompromising belief in creativity will ultimately be the legacy of tecnobrega, no matter where it goes from here.

TECNOBREGA IN BELÉM
BY
HENRIK MOLTKE

Street vendors selling tecnobrega CDs at the comercio central

These photos were taken by Henrik Moltke in October 2006 when shooting footage for *Good Copy Bad Copy*, a documentary about copyright.

The documentary is available from goodcopybadcopy.net

This free Super Pop party was held by local politician/crook Wladimir Costa, on the same day as the then-President Lula was in town, so as to lure people away from Lula's speech. Clever.

Fans... "S" for "Super Pop"!

Super Pop during the magic moment - this was MAD - shooting fire from his instrument, and from the cannons on the sides of the soundsystem!

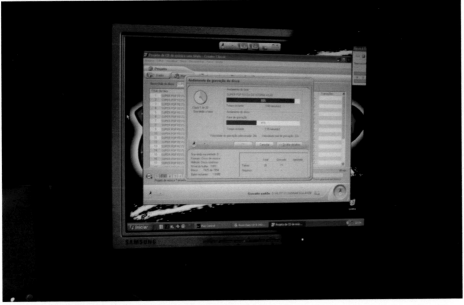

Burning live CDs during the Super Pop show - they will be sold straight to fans or to street vendors who will duplicate them and sell them in the street the following day

This is the oldest of all the brega soundsystems, Brazilandia. Stylish!

Tupinambá soundsystem.

TWENTY INFLUENTIAL BRAZILIAN ALBUMS

Rather than picking what we thought were the twenty best Brazilian albums of all-time, we decided to opt for twenty Brazilian albums which we feel have had – and continue to have – a huge influence on music in Brazil and the rest of the world. So, as well as a few classics , in the following pages you will find some lesser-known, but just as important, gems from Brazilian music's vast well of great albums (if only we could have included all the albums we wanted!)

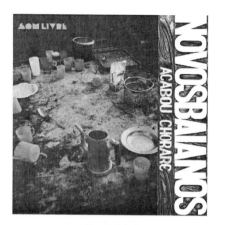

1 OS NOVOS BAIANOS
Acabou Chorare
(1972)

"The gift that they had. Now it sounds closer, smarter, more sure of itself. They discovered silence." – Augusto de Campos (from original liner notes to Acabou Chorare)

While Os Novos Baianos were preparing the material for their second album, following their well-received but slow-selling debut *Ferra Na Boneca*, a surprise encounter caused the band to ditch the electrified "rock" direction their music had been taking and opt for something far more "Brazilian". Nobody other than João Gilberto himself knows quite why he turned up at the Rio apartment where Os Novos Baianos were staying one night in 1971, but that's exactly what he did. Over the course of the night and into the morning the band and Gilberto played songs to each other until sleep finally prevailed. In the process a seed was sown, a need to get in touch with their "Brazilian-ness", that resulted in the group reappraising samba and its role in their music, as well as incorporating native instruments such as the *cavaquinho* and *pandeiro*.

Nowhere was this change more apparent than on "Brasil Pandeiro", the track that opens *Acabou Chorare*. This samba – originally written by Assis Valente for Carmen Miranda – was suggested by Gilberto and works as a perfect showcase for the band, allowing all three singers to shine: Baby do Consuelo's exuberant pop rasp, Moraes Moreira's dry delivery and the versatile range of Paulinho Boca de Cantor; as well as the Hendrix-inspired guitar-work of Pepeu Gomes and the horde of acoustic instruments that give the track its huge carnival-esque exuberance.

The title of the record also comes from Gilberto, who had told Luiz Galvão (the band's main lyricist) about a time when he was looking after his baby daughter Bebel when she had an accident and hurt herself. As Gilberto struggled to deal with the situation, the young Bebel steadied her emotions and told her dad: "acabou chorare", roughly translating as "no more crying". The group thought the name, which could also be seen as referring to a period after bossa nova and the sad nature of that genre, would be perfect for the blissful tone of many of their new songs. And blissful they are. *Acabou Chorare* is like a burst of light; the pace shifts from slower bossa nova numbers to exuberant *baiãos* and sambas but never dips below serene. It's no coincidence that by the time they came to record the album the whole band and their families had relocated to the countryside, where they lived as a hippy commune. Far from the city, they would spend all their time writing and performing music, intermittent with games of football. This communal, idyllic atmosphere spills into every nook and cranny on the album.

Moraes Moreira would later describe their new style as "samba with rock energy." It's an apt description. Tracks like "Preta Pretinha" and "A Menina Dança" helped define MPB and show how great pop music could include both rock and traditional Brazilian influences, something that wasn't common at the time. The fact that *Acabou Chorare* also captures a group of highly talented singers, musicians and songwriters at a perfect moment in their lives only adds to the record's enduring reputation.

by Russell Slater

2 MILTON NASCIMENTO E LÔ BORGES
Clube da Esquina (1972)

"Clube Da Esquina is a great introduction to Brazilian music. Beautiful singing, beautiful songs, lyrics, arrangements..." – Mia Doi Todd

The easiest thing would be to call *Clube da Esquina* a Brazilian *Abbey Road* or *Dark Side Of The Moon*. Or, owing to its status as a double LP, a Brazilian *White Album* or *Electric Ladyland*. And while it has become the universal entry point into the magical world of Milton Nascimento and his friends, the truth is that it's only one chapter in an artistic journey that actually reached its peak in the mid-to-late 70s. But *Clube da Esquina*, credited to Milton and his extremely talented young friend Lô Borges, and elaborated throughout 1971 for release in early 1972, ropes you in immediately from its striking cover and the sense that something wonderful is going to happen when needle hits groove. And so it is.

Nascimento's career in Brazil up to that point wasn't a sure thing commercially. He first came to public attention when his classic song "Travessia" won a song competition in 1967, and word of his special talent spread quickly in US musician circles due to Quincy

Jones' presence at that festival. By the following year Nascimento was signed to A&M Records in the US and releasing an album largely consisting of re-recordings of his Brazilian debut, only this time featuring the likes of Milton superfan Herbie Hancock.

His next two Brazilian-released albums in 1969 and 1970 were brilliant but out of step with the prevailing commercial winds in Brazil. So when Milton, Lô, Toninho Horta, Márcio Borges and the rest of their friends started recording songs they'd largely written at a beach retreat outside Rio, the brass at EMI-Odeon Records understandably got a little nervous. This would be only the third double album of pop music ever released in Brazil (and first of all-new studio material), and it was coming from an artist without a huge commercial profile, albeit with a growing notoriety among American jazz musicians.

The cover, of two anonymous young boys sitting on a roadside, was very evocative but there was no artist name or title on the front. The album itself is a beautiful, moody and reflective mix of folk strains, pop-rock, psychedelia, Beatles influences, a certain classical something and non-clichéd Brazilian cultural elements. It was definitely not what was on the radio at the time in Brazil. The album's classics ("Tudo Que Você Podia Ser", "Cravo e Canela" and "Nada Será Como Antes") were the kind of hits that made their presence felt via covers by other artists in Brazil, and the album slowly found its audience, primarily on college campuses and eventually spreading out from there.

Uniquely for a Brazilian album of its vintage, *Clube da Esquina* has never been out of print in the 41 years since its release, proving that other records may have won the short-term sales battle at the time, but this monster classic won the war. Truly a work of art to be experienced from start to finish, *Clube Da Esquina* will always hold a special place in the Brazilian pop-culture canon, even if it's really just preparation for equally powerful Nascimento masterpieces, *Minas*, *Geraes* and *Clube Da Esquina 2*. You've been warned!

by Greg Caz

3 TOM ZÉ
Estudando o Samba
(1976)

"In 1975 samba had been defamed, the whole world said that it was repetitive, that it was bad. Then one day Rogério Duprat said something that illuminated me. He said: 'Tom Zé, you've seen that the samba is being ridiculed, but you could take the framework of samba... analyse it and find a sophistication that it doesn't have so much these days.' When he said that to me, it left me contented that I had found the idea for Estudando o Samba." – Tom Zé

By 1976 – the year Tom Zé released his fifth studio album, *Estudando o Samba* – the monumental *tropicália* movement was over, and Zé had disappeared from the spotlight. His contemporaries, like Gilberto Gil and Caetano Veloso, were approaching stardom at the time, and the pop sound of their albums reflected that. But celebrity didn't faze Tom Zé, nor did the end of *Tropicalismo*. Zé's work has always been about his own personal interests and pursuits, regardless of who was listening, especially with an album like *Estudando o Samba*.

Zé had immersed himself in samba, and could easily have made an album focused on the style in its purest form. But as a musical savant, having studied under such luminaries as European composer/instrument inventor Walter Smetak, something basic and tra-

ditional was not an option. He took the foundations of recorded samba (acoustic guitar, polyrhythmic percussion and a 2/4 time signature) and infused them with his own distinct sounds. Zé showed his *tropicália* past, mixing in elements of rock and roll, such as the fuzz guitar of opening track "Mã" and the driving bass line of "Doi", but he also added new elements that no one expected, such as the sounds of a typewriter and countless other effects on "Toc." This particular song is perhaps the most unorthodox: though it has a samba rhythm, the rest of the track is a frenzy of sound.

Yet *Estudando O Samba* is not a complete distortion of samba. While there is a flurry of unusual noises, group vocals and bizarre note patterns, the majority of the album is propelled by Zé's voice and his acoustic guitar. There are recognisable sambas such as Antonio Carlos Jobim's "A Felicidade;" collaborations with renowned *sambista* Élton Medeiros on "Tô" and "Mãe (Mãe Solteira)"; and even amidst the madness of "Toc," the *cavaquinho* remains the defining instrument.

Despite all of his ingenuity, the album didn't gain much notice on release. The little attention that it did receive was from critics, who denigrated Tom Zé for his strange use of rhythms, lyrical structure and notation. Little was heard from Zé until 1989, when David Byrne stumbled upon a used copy of *Estudando o Samba*, thinking that it would be an introduction to the musical fundamentals of samba. He was obviously mistaken, yet what he heard exceeded his expectations. Byrne eventually signed Zé to his US-based Luaka Bop label, releasing almost all the tracks from *Estudando o Samba* and a few extras as *Brazil Classics 4: The Best of Tom Zé*.

While the album has gained subsequent popularity, Tom Zé doesn't seem to be affected by it. If anything, he uses the album's success as a springboard to focus on new material, rather than basking in former glory. Tom Zé writes and records what he wants, no matter who likes it. And that's exactly what makes *Estudando o Samba* worth listening to.

by Steven Totten

Tom Zé by Pedro Gutierres

4 TRIBALISTAS
Tribalistas
(2002)

Take three mega-stars from vastly different Brazilian popular music sub-genres, add eclectic songwriting and production with serious hit-making potential, and what do you get?

Tribalistas, a 2002 collaboration between MPB chanteuse Marisa Monte, avant-rock poet Arnaldo Antunes, and *axé/bloco-afro* impresario Carlinhos Brown, was one of the most appealing albums in Brazilian popular music at a point when MPB had become far too serious. By bringing these disparate approaches together in one radio-friendly package, they proved that "sophisticated" and "pop" could exist harmoniously in Brazilian popular music.

Tribalistas produced four singles, one of which, "Já Sei Namorar," was so infectious that it spawned covers in numerous genres, including *frevo* and *forró*. The album continues to be the biggest hit that any of the three musicians involved has had, and it is no coincidence that there is always talk of a reunion. The reasons for Tribalistas' success are numerous, but its influence is best explained through its balance of eclectic personalities and unique arrangements, creating unpretentious songs in topic and craft. The collaboration between Monte, Antunes, and Brown was not unprecedented. They had previously worked together to a varying degree (Monte's *Verde, Anil, Amarelo, Cor-de-Rosa e Carvão*, Brown's *Omelete Man*) and would continue to collaborate afterwards. However, Tribalistas' distinction was that while Marisa Monte was heavily featured, she often sang alongside Antunes and Brown, showcasing the broad gaps in their vocal ranges. For many of the songs, the listener is treated to the sonority of Antunes's gravelly voice one octave below Monte's as the two sing together atop a mix of acoustic instruments and unimposing electronic effects.

The album ranges from pop hits to lullabies, anthems and even a Christmas song. What lends gravity to many of the quieter moments is the balance between Antunes's poetic lyrics and Brown's unique approach to instrumentation and texture. At times you can hear instruments as varied as clay pots and Peruvian *cajón* alongside samplers, which, when coupled with the more traditional acoustic guitar and voice, lend the tracks an unexpected openness. For example, "Velha Infância" features a simple, cyclic chord progression that belies its lyrical complexity. Its lyrics underscore the playful possibilities of love, as with "E a gente canta / E a gente dança / E a gente não se cansa / De ser criança / A gente brinca / Na nossa velha infância" ("And we sing / and we dance / and we don't get tired / of being children / We play in our old infancy"). *Tribalistas* is clearly focused on universality.

A hit like "Já Sei Namorar" represents an alternate approach: an upbeat song that leans more towards slick contemporary electronics than acoustic instruments. It's extremely catchy, with short phrases and singable melodies. And that's exactly the kind of sensibility that informs most of the album. Even listeners who barely understand Portuguese can sing along, investing themselves in their lyrical elegance and basking in the openness of sophisticated pop music that's unafraid of mainstream appeal.

by Kariann Goldschmitt

5 LOS HERMANOS
Bloco do Eu
Sozinho (2001)

"Instead of following the formula that begged for another "anna-something," the ska/hardcore/pop sound of the first disc gave way to broken tempos, intricate melodies and reflective lyrics. [The group] returned to play in small venues and renewed their audience, which would crystallize on their third album and reach messianic proportions on the fourth. The cult began here." – Bruno Natal (Rolling Stone Brasil)

Bloco do Eu Sozinho is the second album from one of the most influential Brazilian indie rock bands of the last 15 years, Los Hermanos. Formed in 1997 by Rodrigo Amarante, Marcelo Camelo, Rodrigo Barba, Bruno Medina and Patrick Laplan (who left before the recording of *Bloco*) the band became a musical reference for almost every Brazilian indie rock band created since then. It is possible to say the amount of influence Los Hermanos had in Brazil was the same as The Strokes had internationally. The influence of Los Hermanos can be heard in artists and bands such as Cícero, Wado and Velhas Virgens. Despite only recording four albums, the band even got its own tribute in 2012; *Re-Trato* featured 30 different artists from Brazil's "new" generation of indie, pop and rock musicians.

The album title *Bloco do Eu Sozinho* (loosely translated as "Street Party for Just One Person") introduces the album as a very unique and audacious work. *Bloco* is a much more mature album than their first self-titled album and less commercial as well. From a musical point of view *Bloco* was a great success, but the record company was not very pleased. Its absence of possible hits like "Anna Júlia" — the song that made the band famous — made the record company ignore it at the time. Despite that, *Bloco* is considered by many critics to be Los Hermanos' best album. Rolling Stone Brasil placed it #42 in their list of the 100 Best Brazilian Music Albums, published in 2007, with their third album *Ventura* also featuring at #68.

Bloco made it clear the path Los Hermanos would follow on their following two albums (*Ventura* and 4), an original signature sound mixing samba and rock. On *Bloco* the group had become better musicians but most impressive of all were the lyrics. *Bloco* was a watershed, typified by the lyrics of "Sentimental" and "Todo Carnaval Tem Seu Fim", showcasing both Amarante and Camelo as remarkable songwriters.

In 2007 Los Hermanos announced they were taking a break, claiming lack of time to develop their private musical projects. Marcelo Camelo now has a solid solo career, releasing two well-received albums (*Sou* and *Toque Dela*); Rodrigo Amarante is part of Little Joy, alongside Fabricio Moretti (The Strokes) and Binki Shapiro, as well as recording with artists like Tom Zé and Marisa Monte; Barba has played drums in a variety of little-known Brazilian bands including one, *Ventura*, that is clearly living off old memories; and Medina is now focusing on journalism after touring with Adriana Calcanhotto for a brief time. The four of them got back together for their 15th birthday, celebrating with a tour in 2012, but a return to the studio together unfortunately still seems a long way off.

by Debora Baldelli

6 MARCOS VALLE
Garra
(1971)

"This is the man who gave us [referring to London's 80s acid jazz/dance scene] the first big tracks from Brazil, 'The Crickets Sing for Anamaria' and then 'Batucada'. . . the back-catalogue is immense!" – Gilles Peterson, after awarding Valle The Worldwide Lifetime Achievement Award at the Worldwide Awards 2013.

Marcos Valle, like his musical brothers from other mothers Stevie Wonder, Paul McCartney and Burt Bacharach, created a new kind of pop music as the 60s became the 70s, fusing regional styles, jazz and even classical elements with the new lingua franca of rock music: big drums, guitar, bass and occasionally horns. His eighth career album could have come off as a cobbled-together set of remakes of tunes he composed for Brazilian soap operas played by anonymous session players. Instead, *Garra* stands as a towering achievement in Brazilian pop. Funky *baiãos* segue into tender bossa novas followed by torchy, bluesy burners and slinky jazz-funk grooves on this musically diverse outing.

"I always had the freedom. Always. Always," Marcos says emphatically. "That's what's absolutely so important, now that I see everything that I have done. They [Odeon Producers] never told me what to do. They let me be free," Marcos says. "You see, at that time, all the record companies had the orchestra in the studio all the time. You could use the orchestra any time. That's why the old records, you can hear a lot of orchestration," Marcos explains. "These are the musicians that would be playing the Municipal Theatre, but they also made money in the recording studio doing sessions."

Marcos' music is only part of what makes this album so interesting. "Because my music is very moving, very merry," Marcos explains – in contrast to the usual counter-culture suspects (Gilberto Gil, Caetano Veloso, Edu Lobo, Chico Buarque and Milton Nascimento) whose songs delivered critical lyrics over experimental, bombastic or foreboding musical backdrops –, "it's easier to hide the intentions so they don't find out." Take this translation of the first stanza of the album's title track, "Garra" (translating alternately as "tenacity" and "talon"): "I run after money, ha ha / 'Til my whole body / Collapses to the ground, ha ha / I'm gonna live downtown, ha ha / I don't even know my city that well, ha ha / But I'm gonna win." The lyrics to this 40+ year-old song by Marcos' older brother and go-to lyricist, Paulo Sérgio Valle, about an arrogant, money-grabbing Brazilian yuppie is just as poignant today, describing a contemporary Wall Street serf or a recently wealthy 21 year-old Silicon Valley programmer.

Whether all of their fans and listeners, unlike the censors, were clever enough to pick up on the nuanced cultural commentary hidden within *Garra*, is irrelevant. Paulo Sérgio's jokes, jabs and humour-laced political commentary are still clever over forty years later, go-going to Marcos' paisley-printed and rose-tinted musical arrangements.

by Allen Thayer

7

QUARTETO NOVO
**Quarteto Novo
(1967)**

"You know who opened up the northeast for instrumental music? We were called Quarteto Novo. Before us there were no records, nothing. Quarteto Novo were influenced by the Beatles, even our own Quinteto Violado. [Before] the musicians in Brazil only listened to jazz... [they] had a lot of prejudice towards the baião." – Hermeto Pascoal

A supergroup formed by Hermeto Pascoal (keyboards, flute), Airto Moreira (percussion), Heraldo do Montes (guitars) and Théo de Barros (double bass), Quarteto Novo started out as Trio Novo in 1967. They were created as a backing band for the singer and composer Geraldo Vandré for a series of shows by French-based fashion label Rhodia. It is said that in the early days there were concerns that the albino Hermeto Pascoal wouldn't be photogenic enough for a fashion event. It was only later, once they finished their contract with Rhodia that he became an integral member of what became Quarteto Novo.

All four came from a background of playing with samba jazz combos. Moreira and Pascoal had played together in the group Sambrasa. Théo de Barros had just won the prize at a major MPB festival alongside Geraldo Vandré, sharing first place for

their song "Disparada" with Chico Buarque's "A Banda". Heraldo do Monte was a highly sought after session musician.

What made Quarteto Novo different, apart from the huge talent of its members, was their conscious decision to move away from the sound of bossa nova and samba jazz. They created music with northeastern-style scales and jazz improvisation, but nothing excessively "cool" or bebop. Théo de Barros was from Rio and Moreira from Santa Catarina so most of the northeastern influences of their sound came from Heraldo do Monte (born in Recife, Pernambuco) and Hermeto Pascoal (born in Lagoa das Canoas, a village in Alagoas).

"O Ovo", a composition by Pascoal that opens the album is a variation on the beat played by *bandas de pifano* (typical flute-led groups of the northeast). Heraldo de Monte brought the twang of the steel guitar of the northeastern improvisers to the music, nothing the likes of which had been recorded in mainstream music besides Luiz Gonzaga's accordion at the tail end of the 40s. In "Fica Mal Com Deus" (by Geraldo Valdré) the *baião* of protest is made without lyrics, enriched by the tones of do Monte's 10-string, by the innovative percussion of Moreira, the improvisations of de Barros on bass and by Pascoal's prowess on the flute.

The group existed from 1967 until 1969, when Airto Moreira left for the US. He played with Miles Davis on *Bitches Brew*, and then with Chick Corea on *Return to Forever*, creating a completely new, hugely-influential style of percussion. Hermeto Pascoal, the man of a thousand instruments, also went to the US where he too played with Miles Davis, among others. Heraldo do Monte went to Europe before later returning to Brazil, where he is still playing. Finally, Théo de Barros also went to the US, but only for a short while. He recorded three solo albums, worked as a producer and arranger, and just like do Monte has maintained a low profile up to the present day.

by José Teles

8 SEPULTURA
Roots
(1996)

The album Sepultura released in 1996 could have been the first of a victorious series. It ended up being the swan song from a band that simply couldn't bear the external pressures and continue at the top of its game.

There is unrestrained anger in *Roots*, an aggressive rancidity, an inevitable sourness, a contagious bad mood. At first listen, it is hard to understand the source of these feelings. It is not a simple equation to solve; Sepultura aim for the bull's-eye and hit where it hurts most. There's anger, hatred, revenge, resentment and feelings of inadequacy. Nobody is happy, and how could they be? "What goes around comes around," Max Cavalera warns on "Straighthate." It's hard to sleep peacefully after hearing that.

In fact, you don't need to go too far to interpret *Roots* as a personal manifesto from Max Cavalera. The fact that this is the last album featuring him as the band's leading singer is no coincidence either. Each song feels like the final words of an argument, a declaration of war on an anonymous enemy that must be fought immediately. Like an army general on alert, Cavalera is someone you would want on your side in any conflict. No one escapes the wild storm coming from this underworld, as uncontrollable as it is impossible to be tamed: politicians, military, corporations, competitors, critics, invaders, enemies of nature and enemies of natives too. *Roots* is hot and urgent, as if the bomb was about to explode and nothing could be done to avoid it. *Roots* was the obvious soundtrack for a third world riot, in which the impure and rejected of the world protest for justice and acceptance.

But not everything is sticks and stones in *Roots*. There are rare moments of pure celebration; the pagan insanity of "Ratamahatta," the smoky tenderness of the instrumental track "Jasco" (Brazilian slang for marijuana), the hypnotizing "Itsari," in partnership with the Xavante tribe ("no overdubs!!!", warns the liner notes). Never has hard rock sounded so Brazilian, whatever this really means. At that time, the expression "tribal" was constantly used by the foreign press to define what Sepultura did, as if to justify the omnipresence of elements of rough "Brazilian-ness" in the square concept of traditional heavy metal, as mathematical as it is predictable. The tribal beat from Sepultura was never off tempo, but the precision had something organic – which did not come at all from the European roots of the band's four members, who by the way, were no "jungle boys". They came from and were raised far away from the tropical rainforest, buried under layers of grey concrete and decorated with the stain of pollution, in the urban, hilly and dry centres of Minas Gerais (in the case of bassist Paulo Xisto, Max and his brother, drummer Igor Cavalera) and São Paulo (guitarist Andreas Kisser). The jungle influence was in the subconscious of the members of Sepultura. Like most Brazilian people, they were born with their feet on cement, but with their spirit connected instinctively to the heart of the unexplored forest.

As an album, *Roots* may not be Sepultura's most cohesive work, much less the most consistent. Its predecessor, *Chaos A.D.* (1993), has more memorable songs that the group's current formation still perform, and the two previous albums, *Arise* (1991) and *Beneath the Remains* (1989), were more faithful to the thrash bias proposed by the band's promotional department. *Roots*, in contrast, seems a collage of sounds, a dirty quilt in bold colours, adorned with percussion, downtuned guitars and Max's brutal voice seaming the fabric. Wildness is offered vastly and in different levels of insanity. There is some polish, but it wasn't idealized by the band, more the result of Ross Robinson's stylized production. "Groove" is also a term that suits the new Sepultura: all songs are invitations to unlimited rioting and partying, even when based on traditional metal rules. In addition to the opening track, "Roots Bloody Roots," the album may be most remembered by the participation of Bahian percussionist Carlinhos Brown on the single "Ratamahatta." Obviously, the native Brazilian inspiration is impossible to be dismissed, floating like a heavy shadow over the album.

This inspiration can be seen on the cover, with its illustration inspired by the native Brazilian on the back of the old 1000 *cruzeiros* note and on "Itsári," recorded live during a ceremony of the Xavante tribe; nearly five minutes of religious trance, with the four Sepultura members sharing acoustic guitars and timbali percussion in synchronicity with the chants of the healing ceremony Datsi Wawere. The beauty of this recording is the fact that it has virtually nothing to do with the rest of the album's context. If on one hand "Itsári" could only exist on an album like *Roots*, the mythic aura *Roots* carries to this day only exists because it includes "Itsári". The experiment with native Brazilians came thanks to the success of "Kaiowas," from the previous album, where the band traded electric for acoustic guitars and drums in a session recorded in an European castle – the track became one of the band's greatest moments live between 1993 and 1996. There was no time for "Itsári" to gain this status: Sepultura crumbled apart before that.

Roots was released in February 1996. I remember I got the CD from a friend, as a gift for my 18th birthday. I also remember feeling much differently

than I had when *Chaos A.D.* was released, three years earlier. You could not help compare them: on *Chaos A.D.* there was real weight as part of the band's sound; a clear evolution from *Arise* and *Beneath the Remains*. The latent Brazilian-ness was also present – the introduction of "Refuse/Resist" caused a mixture of laughter and excitement, with drums inspired by the percussion group Olodum alternating with guitars heavier than the E-flat tuning could offer. Then, the primal war scream "Territory" continued a pulsing, newly-acquired groove, with the most exuberant drum introduction ever written by Igor Cavalera. We started wondering what Sepultura would be capable of doing next, but also didn't want to think about it. Where to go after *Chaos A.D.?* It seemed better not to have any expectations. The top of the world was the limit.

And then came *Roots*, taking boldness to an unexpected extreme. It is worth remembering that this was a moment of transition in public acceptance of metal. Years before, Metallica went from being a thrash phenomenon to reaching the Olympus of mainstream with their multiplatinum same-name album known as the *Black Album*. The period on the top of the world didn't make Metallica get heavy again – in fact, the following album, *Load* (released months after *Roots*), proved the more accessible direction the band would take for the following years.

So, it could be said, with some degree of injustice, that *Roots* was Sepultura's *Black Album* – the album with which the band was finally accepted by the system. Not coincidentally, it was far from receiving unanimous approval from the fans. There was little thrash with progressive flair and precise millimetric structures, or an insistent pulsing groove tied to all the tracks. The guitar tunings were even lower – in D, sometimes D-flat, one and a half tone lower than usual. The ill-fated Brazilian percussions were also featured at every opportunity. Even the solos from Kisser were off standard, putting the layers of voluminous, high-speed notes aside and concentrating on the generation of synthetic noises with wah-wah pedal. The unmistakable touch of nu-metal with traces of industrial rock was also perceptible. Producer Ross Robinson had his share of responsibility in the elaboration of the new sound: he was the one who polished Korn's first two albums. History says that Korn was highly influenced by *Chaos A.D.* – which, in a way, means that a band inspired by Sepultura inspired Sepultura. The fact of the matter is: without the old Sepultura, the new Sepultura would not exist.

Maybe it wasn't a secret that *Roots* was the album Sepultura created so that the rest of the world paid attention to them. There are elements clearly positioned to please foreign listeners, such as the lively percussion throughout the album, using instruments whose names any non-Portuguese speaker would struggle to pronounce. Brazil, in a way, is there and everywhere. The thank-you section shows the longing generated by life on the road and pays tribute to a long list of famous Brazilians; the football team that won the 1994 World Cup, Ayrton Senna, Coffin Joe, the Gracie family and the Xavante tribe. On "Dictatorship", Cavalera sends the message in Portuguese: "Tortura nunca mais!" (No more torture!). On the hook of "Ratamahatta," he is more direct and less poetic: "Vamo' detoná essa porra, é, porra!" (Let's burn this shit down!).

This is the dirty, crazy and percussive Brazil that perseveres throughout *Roots* – on the noisy celebration of "Endangered Species" (an angry ode about Amazon exploitation), on the nervous *baião* "Ambush," the crazy samba of "Born Stubborn," the *berimbau* riff of "Attitude," and on the Pelourinho percussion of "Cut-Throat" and "Breed Apart." The odd one out is "Lookaway," which sounds like a mix between Faith No More and Korn simply because this is what it is – the track features the lead singers from both bands, Mike Patton and Jonathan Davis, and is too weird to fit the context of the album. Summed up and disregarding excesses, this may be the least Sepultura album ever released, and ended up being the one that still defines the band, for good or bad.

Roots must be the Brazilian rock album most heard worldwide, notably ranking #27 on American's Billboard charts on its first week. But there was no time for *Roots* to make a bigger difference because Sepultura ended prematurely. It is, in a way, emblematic that none of the members have since achieved success like *Roots* offered in such short time. After a breakup as sudden as it was inevitable, Max followed his own path and continued in the same musical direction with Soulfly. Isolated in the USA, only recently has he started visiting Brazil regularly, when he reconciled with his brother Igor and, together, they began creating music again. Kisser and Xisto are still active, still carrying the heavy and valuable cross that is Sepultura. Some people still dream of a reunion with the classic lineup, but it seems increasingly unlikely due to the circumstances (and the constant public spats between the former band mates).

The Sepultura that went their separate ways in December 1996 has never said a proper goodbye to the Brazilian audience. The concerts that year were probably the most significant since the acclamation of *Arise*. The last concert in Brazil was in São Paulo, on November 7th, at the Olympia, which then had the tradition of hosting the best concerts in the city. The following week, Sepultura would take the *Tribalism Across the World Tour* to South America and then Europe. I close my eyes and still see flashes of that evening: black and red stains – the uneven mass that comprised the nearly all-male audience – hit by yellow light beams coming from the top of the stage, and also the smell of sweaty bodies mingling with an invisible wall of low-end. Of the songs, my most vivid memory takes me back to the peak of the instrumental "Kaiowas" – the band positioned front stage, carrying drumsticks, pounding drums, calling for war. After the last dry thump, Max raised his arm, exultant as a tribe chief, and threw a drumstick to the crowd. It flew freely until landing right on the side of my head. I ignored the pain and quickly hid it under my shirt. I still have it.

by Pablo Miyazawa

9 ARTHUR VEROCAI
Arthur Verocai
(1972)

"This album, a commercial failure but a tremendous personal accomplishment for its then 26-year-old composer, is a complex fusion rivalled only by the likes of David Axelrod's Capitol trilogy. It took thirty years for this record to see a worthy resurgence in interest and, forty years since its creation, it's still as ponderous and sublime as it was when it was first issued and lost in the musical deluge of 1970s Brazil."
— Eothen "Egon" Alapatt (Now & Again Records)

Arthur Verocai's mysterious solo album, demonstrates more than any other album on this list just how deep Brazil's recorded music tradition goes. I read somewhere once that Brazil is the only other country besides the US that consumes more domestic music than imported music. Just like in the US, Brazil's musical "golden era" of the 60s and 70s delivered both quality and quantity, resulting in countless commercially-challenged releases, like those of David Axelrod and Arthur Verocai, getting lost in the noise.

As with Axelrod, whose output as composer/arranger/producer overshadowed his solo work,

Verocai was best remembered (if remembered at all) as a "Waldo" [or Wally, if you're British] of MPB album credits – look hard enough and you might find his name. After scoring some commercial work arranging records for Ivan Lins (his first album *Agora*) and a couple of albums for jazz/bossa singer Célia, the record label offered Verocai a solo record as a reward. Without time or money to worry about, Verocai took it as a challenge – a one-time opportunity to make his musical personal statement. This musically curious *carioca* with roots in Minas Gerais and adventurous tastes in international pop music synthesized countless musical elements into a masterful album with a variety of Brazilian rhythms, often augmented by alternately jazzy or soulful drums, orchestral flourishes (20 strings alone on some tracks), searing horns, and diverse and mysterious vocals from Célia, Carlos Dafé, Luiz Carlos (ex-Abolição, future-Banda Black Rio) and Verocai himself on the haunting opening track, "Caboclo".

After the album tanked, Verocai didn't disappear like Sixto Rodriguez, he just kept on working – arranging and writing records for most of the 70s and then advertising/jingles in the 80s and 90s. He even recorded another solo album in 2002, before his rediscovery.

Just like Dr. Dre and DJ Shadow (re)introduced David Axelrod to the world, DJs and tastemakers from Gilles Peterson to Brazilian DJ Nuts and Mochilla's B+ all sung Verocai's praises, sampling his music, reissuing his work and giving him the opportunity to make new music (Verocai's 2011 album *Encore* on Far Out Records) and an unforgettable performance in Los Angeles of the original album in its entirety for the first time ever by over 40 musicians in 2010 as part of Mochilla' Timeless Series. Since the Timeless concert he's been "discovered" by his countrymen, performing the record in São Paulo, Recife and Amsterdam so far . . .

by Allen Thayer

10 LUIZ GONZAGA
Juazeiro/Baião
78rpm (1949)

Released in 1949, by Luiz Gonzaga and writing partner Humberto Teixeira, as two sides of a 78rpm single, "Juazeiro" and "Baião" are two of the most covered songs in the history of Brazilian music. The B-side "Baião" wasn't anything new, having been recorded in 1946 by Quatro Ases e Um Coringa, a vocal group from Ceará. The importance of Luiz Gonzaga's version is his interpretation of the instrumental arrangement. Quatro Ases e Um Coringa had not learnt the nuances of the *baião* rhythm, which they sang as if it were a samba.

Baião can trace its melodic heritage back to the guitar interludes of the northeastern *repentistas*. These poets/musicians would challenge each other to create lyrics ad lib, plucking at 10-string guitars between verses. They come from a tradition that harks backs to the provincial troubadours, brought to Brazil by the Portuguese, that remains one of the foremost cultural expressions of the region.

At parties in northeast Brazil the instrumental melodies of the *repentistas*, the *baião*, served as a rhythm to be danced. The opening lines of "Baião" are an open invitation to this format: "Eu vou contar pra vocês / como se dança o baião / e quem quiser aprender / é só prestar atenção" ("I'm going to tell you how / to dance the *baião* / and anyone that wants to learn / just needs to pay attention"). And pay attention they did. *Baião* would remain the most popular music in Brazil for a decade, and Luiz Gonzaga its highest selling artist. At its peak, *baião* music was recorded by practically every big name in Brazilian music.

Luiz Gonzaga (1912-1989) and Humberto Teixeira (1915-1979) were both born in northeastern Brazil's vast interior; Gonzaga in Exu, Pernambuco, and Teixeira in Igatu, Ceará. They met in Rio de Janeiro. Interestingly, the first seeds of their partnership were sown in a building in Avenida Calógeras, a busy street in the centre of the country's then capital, between the four walls of an import/export company, where Humberto Teixeira was working as a lawyer. A large number of their early compositions were stylised versions of songs that already existed in the public domain ("Juazeiro" has its roots in a song called "Catingueira").

The impact that the rhythm of *baião* had on Brazil was more or less the equivalent to what rock 'n' roll would have in the US. Luiz Gonzaga created a formidable musical line-up: an accordion played by himself in the middle, a bass drum to one side and a triangle to the other [creating what is now the classic *forró* line-up]. The melody of the *baião* came from the *repentistas'* guitar, but the beat found its inspiration in the *maracatu* of Pernambuco, in the drumbeats of the state's African roots, the *samba-de-matuto*. It was irresistible.

The *baião* took over the country and even influenced the writers of Tin Pan Alley, who were drawn to the success of "El Negro Zumbon" (a *baião* from the 1951 film *Anna*). Leiber & Stoller's use of the *baião*-style bass drum created a subgenre of R&B called "Jewish Latin" (cited by Ken Emerson in the book *Always Magic in the Air*). It can be heard in The Ronettes' "Be My Baby", and also Dionne Warwick's Burt Bacharach and Hal David-written "Do You Know The Way to San Jose"; Bacharach discovered *baião* when he accompanied Marlene Dietrich on a trip to Brazil. *Baião* also found its way to Japan, where Japanese versions of "Paraíba" and "Juazeiro" were produced.

Baião fell out of favour with the emergence of bossa nova. However, whilst the A-side of the first bossa nova single was "Chega de Saudade" by Tom Jobim and Vinicius de Morais, its B-side was "Bim Bom", with its creator João Gilberto singing: "This is it, my baião / There's nothing else to it."

by José Teles

11 JOÃO GILBERTO Chega de Saudade/ Bim Bom 78rpm (1958)

"I saw in 'Chega de Saudade' the manifesto and the masterpiece of a movement: the mother ship. A samba with some traces of choro, immensely rich in melodic motifs, with a flavour so Brazilian it could be a recording by Silvio Caldas from the 30s. 'Chega de Saudade' managed to be a modern song while having enough harmonic and rhythmic daring to attract any bop or cool-jazz musician." – Caetano Veloso (Tropical Truth)

Nelson Rodrigues, a great Brazilian writer from Recife, Pernambuco, used to say that it was difficult to see the obvious. This is especially true for bossa nova. The obvious being that if it were not for João Gilberto, then bossa nova would not exist. The style is built around João Gilberto's guitar playing and his vibrato-less singing, seemingly simple but, in fact, extremely complex.

"Chega de Saudade", the emblematic song of bossa nova, confirms the assertion. Tom Jobim and Vinicius de Moraes's samba-choro has a harmonic structure that could be played by a regional group of guitars, ukulele, flute and tambourine. Before João Gilberto recorded it, in 1958, there had been other recordings of the song. It had been the B-side of a 78rpm by the vocal group Os Cariocas (the A-side was "Always And Forever". It was also the B-side of a rare single by Osvaldo Borba ("Lover" was the A-side).

In 1958, the year in which João Gilberto recorded it, the song had already been recorded by Marisa Gata Mansa, Agostinho dos Santos, Nelson Trombone, Sol Stein, and last but not least, Elizeth Cardoso, whose *Canção do Amor* LP was dedicated to the music of Tom and Vinicius. What made this last record historical was the fact that João Gilberto played his guitar "differently" on two tracks: "Chega de Saudade" and "Outra Vez" (written by Tom Jobim); a taste of what was to come.

None of these versions of "Chega de Saudade" were considered extraordinary releases at the time, nor were they called bossa nova. It was the way that João Gilberto interpreted the song and played guitar on his own version that created the revolution [the combination of voice and guitar or *voz e violão* in Portuguese]. The first listen of João Gilberto's "Chega de Saudade" can be compared to hearing "I Want To Hold Your Hand" for the first time, a real "do you remember where you were?" moment.

The *carioca* Edu Lobo, of the second bossa nova generation – one of the most brilliant Brazilian music composers – told me the story of when he first heard the song, while on holiday with his parents at 18: "I was walking down the street, when I heard 'Chega de Saudade' coming from a radio in someone's home. I remember I stopped and listened. I couldn't speak". [Four years later Lobo would win a festival of MPB with "Arrastão", a collaboration with Vinicius de Moraes.]

Caetano Veloso was similarly blown away in his hometown of Santo Amaro da Purificação, Bahia, as was Geraldo Azevedo in Petrolina, Pernambuco, and a *carioca* teenager living in São Paulo, Chico Buarque (whose sister, Miúcha, in a few years would marry João Gilberto). A new generation of Brazilian musicians had been inspired. After João Gilberto's "Chega de Saudade", Brazilian music would never be the same again.

by José Teles

12 BADEN E VINICIUS Os Afro-Sambas (1966)

"These antennas that Baden had linked to Bahia, and ultimately to Africa, enabled us to create a new form: to carioquizar [i.e. to create a "Rio" version of] Afro-Brazilian candomblé within the spirit of modern samba and at the same time give it a more universal dimension. It's [...] the latest response from Brazil to the overwhelming musical mediocrity that bogs down the world." – Vinicius de Morais

Os Afro-Sambas starts with "Abertura" and the sound of Baden Powell's guitar playing a searching classical melody that dips and swoons before finding a rhythm, the samba rhythm, and bursting into life. It doesn't last though, the rhythm stutters, Powell flies into a series of acrobatic *choro*-esque runs before finally switching to a menacing, manic riff which plays out the song. It's an incredible introduction to Powell's guitar playing and his distinctive style, mixing the classical and traditional, but most of all, it's an audacious track to open the album with, for after that Powell's guitar is just one of the elements that comprises the sound of *Os Afro Sambas*. On the rest of the album, Powell is joined by Vinicius de Moraes' plaintive singing, the youthful female

voices of Quarteto Em Cy, lots of percussion and the use of Afro-Brazilian instruments such as the *berimbau* and *agogô*; as well as what Vinicius called the "choir of friendship", a group of friends and lovers who sing on many of the songs. As Vinicius' quote makes clear, the album was an attempt to bring to the surface the Afro-Brazilian spirit of modern samba, and continue a journey that they had started years before.

At the start of the 60s, Vinicius – who was already well-known, having written lyrics for the likes of "A Garota da Ipanema" and "Chega de Saudade" – was given a copy of *Sambas de Roda e Candomblés da Bahia*, an album that allowed him to discover an African-influenced facet of Brazilian music that he previously knew little of. Conversely, Baden Powell had already been educated, getting his chance to learn about Afro-Brazilian traditions when he visited Bahia in 1962 to play some shows with Silvia Teles and ended up befriending the capoeira master Canjiquinha who showed him the chants (*cânticos*) and sounds of candomblé. Powell had been studying Gregorian chants at the time (under the tutelage of Moacyr Santos) and saw a similarity with the Afro songs he heard in Bahia. Back in Rio, and with Vinicius eager to write songs influenced by *candomblé* and the Afro-Brazilian gods the duo began recording *Os Afro-Sambas* with the group of singers, musicians and friends they'd assembled.

When it was released in 1966, *Os Afro-Sambas* became the first album in Brazilian musical history to mix typical instruments from *candomblé*, *atabaques* and *afoxé* with instruments like the flute, violin, drums and double bass. More than that though, it was the musical formula they'd concocted that got people's attention, the mix of the samba beat with the melodic beauty of Baden Powell's guitar playing and the voices that had the same otherworldly quality as Gregorian chants. It was a formula so original that few have been able to copy it, though its ability to mix the African and European and the traditional and modern lives on.

by Russell Slater

13 SPEED
Expresso
(2001)

"When I was in a band, it was almost like a business. Always there was a guy in charge. Now I do 100% what I want." – Speed, discussing the release of Expresso

Speed is one of the most talented MCs and producers in Brazilian hip-hop history. His musicianship was deep-rooted and evident not only in his flow and beats but his singing and bass playing. Murdered in his hometown of Niterói, by circumstances still unknown, he took his stage-name too seriously and left us too soon, on 26th March, 2010.

Some UK heads may remember him for "Follow Me Follow Me (Quem Que Caguetou?)", a track with partner-in-rhyme Black Alien and producer Tejo that made some noise as the theme song for a Nissan ad in 2003. In a pre-M.I.A. scene, that tune caught the dance floor's attention for its infamous *baile* beat, and it was no surprise that Fatboy Slim remixed it or that it featured on the *Fast & Furious 5* soundtrack.

Even though he recorded a lotta stuff during his short lifetime; as a solo artist, in a duo with Black Alien or in partnership with pop names such as Fernanda Abreu, Lúcio Maia (from the almighty

Nação Zumbi), Marcelo D2 and Herbert Vianna (from Os Paralamas Do Sucesso), his masterpiece is without a doubt his 2001 solo debut *Expresso*.

Released independently and currently out of print, that album was the pioneering full-length in what is commonly defined as Alternative Rap in tropical lands. One of those shiny examples of how art can defy technical limitations, *Expresso* was produced entirely by Speed, mostly using an old dirty PC full of cracked programs, with some help on recording and mixing by Alexandre Basa (who later produced Mamelo Sound System's *Urbália* and Black Alien's *Babylon By Gus, Vol. 1: O Ano Do Macaco*).

Beside its heavy beats and timeless "espresso" (i.e. fast, strong and real-time) concept, it remains fresh for new listeners today for its original flows and out-of-the-box lyrics that have been Speed's trademark since day one. If you need a comparison, I'd say the dude was the Brazilian answer to Kool Keith: genius, dope, surreal, odd, intense, a sucker for bass, multifaceted, and ultra-magnetic for sure!

Another highlight on *Expresso* is the cameo list, a who's who of "green & yellow" microphone check: from BNegão (Planet Hemp, Turbo Trio, Seletores de Frequência) to the undeniable soulmate Black Alien, samba-rap O.G. Rappin' Hood, DJ Nuts, freestyle master Max B.O., DJ Zegon (from NASA), and yours truly, to name a few. It was the first time I got invited to guest on someone else's record. I remember being excited and anxious. Once he was a reference for me and a bunch of other cats. When I reminisce about those sessions, it makes me feel proud to be able to say "I was there", y'know what I mean?

Even though Speed didn't get all the props he deserves and remains one of our Best Kept Secrets, his art stands the test of time and speaks for itself. This is the best album you won't find on most Top 10 Classic Rap Albums From Brazil lists. So if you didn't know, now you do!

by Rodrigo Brandão

14 JORGE BEN
Africa Brasil
(1976)

"I love Jorge Ben, especially 60s/70s when he still played acoustic guitar. I think he is a revolutionary of Brazilian music, because he took the roots of samba and mixed it with funk, but in a way that doesn't sound like samba or funk, it just sounds like Jorge Ben. He has a way of playing the acoustic guitar which is just ridiculous, and also the lyrics, he was in a very spiritual place. It's psychedelic but also Brazilian." – Céu

Trying to pick the most influential Jorge Ben album of all time is not an easy task. *Samba Esquema Novo* brought new levels of energy and invention to bossa nova (as well as the monster hit "Mas Que Nada") in 1963; *O Bidu - Silêncio no Brooklyn* tuned in delightfully with the *tropicália* movement in 1967, with great arrangements by Rogério Duprat; *Força Bruta* was the best album he made with Trio Mocotó, a majestic early slice of samba soul in 1970; the mystical spirit and hypnotic grooves of 1974's *A Tábua de Esmeralda* has made it a critic's favourite; while the public might even vote for the sheer power and non-stop hits on 2002's live *Acústico MTV*.

My choice though is *África Brasil*, the 1976 album

which saw Ben augment his band with horns and numerous percussionists for a record that explored African rhythms, US funk and an all-embracing sense of mythology. In Brazil, folklore doesn't exist as it does in the rest of the world, namely because it is still being lived and Ben beautifully displays that in *África Brasil*. He takes inspiration from football culture on "Ponta de Lança Africano (Umbabarauma)" and "Camisa 10 da Gávea"; searches for the meaning of the Emerald Tablet in "Hermes Trismegisto Escreveu" and alludes to the story of Zumbi, the leader of Brazil's last runaway slave kingdom Quilombo dos Palmares, in final track "África Brasil (Zumbi)".

Ben's knowledge of Greek mythology, the history of his beloved football team Flamengo and the oral history of slavery are only matched by his wordplay (so many of his lyrics delight in using ambiguity and double meaning), his passionate delivery and his distinctive style of playing guitar (just attempt to play along to one of his songs and you'll understand how complex and individual Ben's riffs are). Musically, this was the album where he showed the most muscle, the perfect fusion of his earlier samba soul material and his later cleaner disco sound with a strong influence from US soul and R&B, heard in the funky guitars of "Hermes Trimegisto Escreveu" or the driving bass line and energetic horns of "A História de Jorge", recalling Maceo & The Macks or The J.B.'s.

When ex-Talking Heads frontman David Byrne released his compilation *Brazil Classics Vol.1: Beleza Tropical* he made "Ponta De Lanca Africano (Umbabarauma)" the opening track. It's easy to see why he loved it. In 1980 Talking Heads were the talk of the music world for their masterpiece *Remain In Light*, the critics raving about its polyrhythms, describing it as music with which you can "dance and think, think and dance, dance and think, ad infinitum." Three years earlier, Jorge Ben had already completed the exact same feat with *Africa Brasil*, a stand-out classic in a career full of them.

by Russell Slater

15 CARTOLA
Cartola
(1974)

"You do everything wrong, but it comes out right! Don't ever study [music]." — Heitor Villa-Lobos, to Cartola, 1940

From its first mournful bassoon notes to its stuttering *cavaquinhos*, no record has the power to transport you to a smoky corner *boteco* in 1940s Rio de Janeiro quite like *Cartola*, the self-titled debut from the legendary samba composer of the same name. I was surprised, then, to find out that it was actually recorded not during Cartola's heyday but in 1974, when the founder of the Mangueira samba school was already a ripe 66 years old. I was also surprised to learn that when producer João Carlos Bozelli shopped around the idea of recording a Cartola album, he was soundly rejected by Brazil's record labels, save for Marcus Pereira Records, the self-funded venture of a socialist ad-man with the mission of recording regional Brazilian folk traditions before modernity swallowed them whole.

But those familiar with samba history shouldn't be shocked at all. From the music's early days in the 30s, the great sambas were written by Afro-Brazilian composers from the hillside slums, and recorded by light-skinned singers like Francisco Alves (a great interpreter of Cartola's songs) from the formal city below. The Brazilian state under President Getúlio Vargas paid lip service to samba as the foremost symbol of Brazil's mixed-race identity, but black *sambistas* rarely got a chance to put their own works on wax, and almost never reaped their due rewards.

And so it was that Cartola was found washed-up and washing cars in Ipanema by the journalist Sérgio Porto in 1957, an encounter that set into motion the composer's gradual return to samba as a marquee performer and recording artist.

The 1974 record, which became a sleeper hit that same year in Brazil, captured golden-era samba and *samba-canção* in a way it really never had before. The grooves are slow and loose, with the down-home feel of a backyard jam session. At the same time, there's a stateliness to the recordings; a certain old-world poise to them. The presence of trombones and flutes classes things up, and guitarist Dino 7-Cordas' frenetic bass runs animate the tunes throughout, which are all imbued with a sense of *saudade* (roughly, "bittersweetness") so thick you could cut it with a steak knife.

The true source of the album's magic, however, is in Cartola's intuitive songwriting – the swooping melodic turns, unorthodox harmonies and sudden modulations.

"If Brazil had been different, he could have been our Gershwin," the Brazilian pianist Lilian Baretto once lamented, noting his raw compositional talent. Had Brazil been different, we'd also have scores of hard grooving, early 20th-century samba records by Cartola and his *favelado* contemporaries. All I can say is, at least we have 1974's *Cartola*; samba history is better for it.

by Marlon Bishop

16 TRIO ELETRICO DODÔ & OSMAR Jubileu De Prata (1975)

When Caetano Veloso was imprisoned in Salvador, and awaiting authorization for his exile from Brazil, he, along with Gilberto Gil, recorded the seminal record *Álbum Branco*. Its hit track was "Atrás do Trio Elétrico", a *frevo*, but here, this traditional rhythm from Pernambuco was played by a band, featuring the distorted electric guitar solos of Lanny Gordin.

Frevo is carnival music played by an orchestra, as well as electric guitar, bass and drums; Caetano Veloso would never commit musical blasphemy. He was introducing Brazil to the previously unknown carnival of Salvador, as defined by Dodo & Osmar's *trio elétrico*, who shot to local fame during the carnival of 1951. (A *trio elétrico* is a band which parades through the streets during carnival on top of a moving truck). Although they had been around for a while, Dodo and Osmar only incorporated *frevo* into their repertoire after hearing the rhythm when Vassourinhas, a band from Recife, played in Salvador.

Dodo played guitar, Osmar played bass and Temistocles, the *triolim*, a sort of electric mandolin. At first they played from atop an old Ford 1929 (known as a

fubica in Brazil). The following year, they upgraded to a bigger car, and were soon sponsored by the fizzy drinks company Fratelli Vita. Overshadowed by the carnivals of Recife and Rio, the *trio elétrico* only started to gain renown thanks to the *frevo* on Caetano's album. In fact, Dodo and Osmar's *trio elétrico* only recorded this, their first CD, in 1975, after they had been around for 25 years, with Osmar's son, the virtuoso Armandinho Macedo, leading the band. On *Jubileu de Prata*, the repertoire is almost completely *frevo*, which, as they say in Pernambuco, doesn't draw you in, it completely washes you away. It was a landmark album as it introduced *trio elétrico* music to the whole of Brazil, narrating the story in the very first song: "25 years ago in Salvador / *frevo* and the famous trio / arose on a *fubica*." It was the first time a *frevo* from the group had had lyrics, sung by Moraes Moreira (who had recently left Os Novos Baianos).

Jubileu de Prata was not immediately successful. This happened 5 years later, when Moraes Moreira wrote lyrics for the Bahian carnival classic "Double Morse" and renamed it "Pombo Correio" ("Homing Pigeon"), scoring an instant hit throughout Brazil. This debut album by the Dodo and Osmar trio is the closest to the music played on the old *fubica*; the band's music would become more pop-orientated in the 80s. The trios would only be upstaged at the end of the decade with the explosion of *axé* music. The *axé* bands, whose music included everything from pop ballads to Caribbean rhythms, continued the tradition started by the trios, parading through the streets on large trucks converted into mobile stages, but the success of *axé* artists like Luis Caldas, Ricardo Chaves and Daniela Mercury practically finished the *trio elétricos*. Dodo and Osmar's band still exists, but is now almost a sacred relic of the old carnival, a time when you didn't have to pay to dance within a cordoned off area patrolled by security guards. Or as they themselves sing in "Jubileu de Prata": "This place belongs to everyone / who dances rich or poor / it's enough just to exist / and to see Dodo and Osmar's trio passing by."

by José Teles

TIM MAIA RACIONAL
VOL. 1

17 TIM MAIA
Racional Vol. 1
(1975)

"Tim was the Big Bang who completely changed the scene when he arrived at the turn of the 70s. He took the black American thing and mixed it with Brazilian forms like samba, baião and xaxado, inaugurating a new direction in Brazilian pop that remains popular even today: that of urban black music." – Nelson Motta

Nothing in the history of Brazilian music quite compares to the legend that surrounds Tim Maia's *Racional*. Ignored by both critics and the music-buying public upon its release in 1975, the album has gone on to attain almost mythical status among lovers of Brazilian music, thanks as much to its remarkable backstory as its impeccable samba-soul sound.

The story goes like this: by the early 1970s, Maia was one of Brazil's biggest stars; known for his rock 'n' roll lifestyle and his unpredictability, frequently falling out with band members and failing to show up for gigs. But whilst preparing his fifth album, he picked up a book that would lead him to turn his life around. The book, *Universe in Disenchantment*, explained the teachings of an obscure religious sect called Rational Culture, and Maia became fascinated by the teachings of its leader, Manoel, who believed that humans came from a "super world" of "rational

energy" and were merely visitors to earth.

Maia renounced drink, drugs and sex, and threw out all his worldly possessions. He convinced his entire band to convert along with him, dressing all in white and painting their instruments white too. They scrapped the lyrics to the songs they had been working on and re-recorded them as hymns to Rational Culture. His record label wanted nothing to do with this bizarre new direction, so Maia founded his own label to distribute *Racional*. The Brazilian public turned out to be equally uninterested and so when, by the end of 1975, a disillusioned Maia renounced Rational Culture and set out to destroy every copy he could find, it garnered little attention.

But in a way it was this final act that really assured the album's mythical status. Years later, when artists like Gal Costa began covering tracks from the album and the track "No Caminho do Bem" was included on the *City of God* soundtrack, interest was renewed in the album, though copies of the LP were almost impossible to come by. To this day, the record changes hands for upwards of £200.

Of course, all of this would simply be an obscure footnote to a tumultuous and prolific career were it not for the fact that the music itself is simply sublime. Thanks perhaps to the drug-free lifestyle, or the devotional fervour of his efforts to spread the Rational message, Maia's voice – already a force of nature – is more powerful here than ever before. His band, which at that time included both the legendary guitarist Paulinho and sax man Oberdan Magalhães (who later went on to form Banda Black Rio), pull off a remarkable blend of gospel, soul and funk that often recalls Isaac Hayes at the height of his powers.

Thanks to a re-release on the Trama label in 2006, the album and its follow-up, *Racional Vol. 2*, are easy enough to come by now, enabling a wider audience to finally discover what is now considered to be some of his finest work. The Racional legend lives on.

by Tom Crookston

18 MESTRE AMBRÓSIO
Mestre Ambrósio
(1996)

"For the music... to be possible, we've been through a long process of self-cleansing. Cleaning ourselves of rock, of jazz, of art music. Cleaning not in the sense that these things are good or bad, but in the sense that as we grow up with these other styles, living with them on a daily basis, we completely lose our meaning, our specific references, as musicians, as persons, and even as northeasterners and Brazilians." – Siba *(Brazilian Popular Music & Globalization)*

Released in 1996 amid the fervour of *manguebit*, the first album from Mestre Ambrósio was a revelation: its sound was raw, strong, visceral and unusual, borne from an intense and radical relationship with northeastern Brazil's traditional street music that even cultivated a healthy, yet subtle space for elements of rock and African music.

To understand the impact the band had, you have to realize that although bands like Chico Science and Mundo Livre S/A, the most revolutionary groups of the time, found an original way of using little-celebrated genres of Brazilian music to create their own original musical language, their music was also heavily influenced by hip-hop, punk rock and psychedelia.

Mestre Ambrósio, on the other hand, ventured creatively into genres that were undervalued or even unknown by young people in large urban centres — *cavalo-marinho, maracatu de baque solto, coco de roda, cantoria de viola* — and paved the way for using instruments that were once very popular in the northeast but had become largely forgotten — like the *rabeca*, the *viola dinâmica*, the *fole de 8 baixos*, the *ilú* and the *zabumba*. They became one of the bands most responsible for the revival of *forró pé-de-serra* (traditional-style *forró*). They also helped draw attention to the masters of traditional music from Pernambuco, such as Luiz Paixão and Biu Roque.

The beautiful compositions of Siba, one of the most creative musicians of his generation, are one of the highlights of the album. His songs demonstrate a rare mastery of musical languages and traditional poetry of the northeast, and achieve the even tougher feat of creating a personal style that is immediately recognizable. The strength of these compositions, combined with the mastery of the four percussionists, the expressiveness of Siba's *rabeca* and the band's cohesiveness as a whole, keeps the album fresh to this day. Several of its tracks have since become classics of northeastern music.

There is no denying Mestre Ambrósio's influence on a large number of young musicians, beginning in the late 90s. Some examples of their direct influence can be seen in the work of Chão e Chinelo (of which I was a member, playing *viola* and *zabumba*, alongside *rabequeiro* Maciel Salu and Nilton Jr., current bandleader of Pandeiro do Mestre); of Comadre Fulozinha (whose members included Karina Buhr, Alessandra Leão and Isaar); singer Renata Rosa; Cláudio Rabeca e do Quarteto Olinda; Paraíba's Cabruêra; and Ceará's Fulô da Aurora; along with various groups of *forró* in southeastern Brazil, and even in Europe and North America.

by Caçapa

19 GAL COSTA Fa-Tal - Gal a Todo Vapor (1971)

"There is currently nothing better in 'superexalting' Brazilian popular music. Nothing better than Gal."
– Torquato Neto, reviewing the Fa-Tal show in his Jornal Última Hora newspaper column, October 1971

There are live albums, and there are albums that strangle you and ask you if you want to live. Gal Costa's 1971 two-record aural bitchslap, *Fa-tal: Gal a Todo Vapor* delivers on its promise to be "fatal".

Gal's unstoppable, razor sharp voice explodes in a live performance that knocks the wind out of anyone listening – especially among the crowd present on the day of recording at Rio's Teatro Tereza Raquel.

You know that feeling when you're in a room full of people holding their breath? Listening to this album is that kind of collective experience, the kind that feels historical and important. After all, 1971 was a time in Brazil when young people were participating in (and, like fellow *baianos* Gilberto Gil and Caetano Veloso, being exiled by) demonstrations of political will. The people in the audience were the same people who were trying

by all means possible to change the country they lived in. And they weren't getting far.

The occasional blown-out vocals and errant acoustic guitar strums contribute to how vivid and raw *Fa-tal* is. In Portuguese, one would say that her emotions are "à flor da pele" – they bloom on her skin. As she croons solo through songs like "Sua Estupidez," her mournful delivery is just as powerful as her gnashing cries of "saia, desapareça" ("get out, disappear") in "Luz do Sol." She lets her voice go growly and rough, performing the life out of each note. You want to listen as hard as she is singing.

The crowd is right there with her – you can almost hear the joints being passed. When the flaring electric guitars and smashing cymbals explode in "Chuva, Suor e Cerveja," it's as if Gal summoned the whole week of *Carnaval* to descend on these people and give them a party.

Gal's voice is both transfixing and versatile. She lashes her audience with her varsity-level upper register in songs like "Vapor Barato" and sashays gently and nakedly through the acoustic tenderness of Caetano Veloso's "Coração Vagabundo." Gal has an instrument under her shrubbery of black hair that is as fierce as it is vulnerable.

The wide contours of Gal's performance carries with it the complexities of a place with staggering divisions between poor and wealthy, black and white, north and south, male and female. The album is a hippie bacchanal underscored by a live current of anger and distrust for an unjust government.

And ultimately, whoever came up with the album's title was entirely right: it's killer.

by Julia Furlan

20 OS MUTANTES
Os Mutantes
(1968)

"Hearing Os Mutantes for the first time was one of those revelatory moments you live for as a musician, when you find something that you have been wanting to hear for years but never thought existed. I made records like Odelay because there was a certain sound and sensibility that I wanted to achieve, and it was eerie to find that they had already done it 30 years ago, in a totally shocking but beautiful and satisfying way." – Beck

What made all the best early rock 'n' roll great was love; stupid, naïve, youthful love, from Elvis Presley to The Beatles, the combination of a great melody and a guttural plea to a sweetheart takes some beating. In 1968 Arnaldo Baptista was just 19 years old. He was completely in love with Rita Lee, his first girlfriend. The two of them, along with Baptista's younger brother Sérgio Dias, would release their first album as Os Mutantes that year, establishing themselves as the raw primal force that meant *tropicália* would become shorthand for musical adventure for years to come.

It all begins with "Panis et Circenses", a simple march which builds and builds through "Penny Lane"-esque horns, home-made special effects and Lee singing the surreal vocal refrain of "But all the people having dinner inside / Are very busy with their food / 'Til they die." The pace increases, the rhythm becomes frantic, until we hear the sound of a glass breaking. Then we hear the sound of Jorge Ben's rhythm guitar [he's making a guest appearance] and "A Minha Menina" begins, a silly love song ("Ela é minha menina e eu sou o menino dela" / "She is my girl and I'm her boy") that also happens to be one of the most explosive doses of sunshine ever put to tape. From there we go to the elegiac "O Relógio", a slow French chanteuse-esque creation with a psych garage bridge. In just those first three songs Brazilian pop and rock music has been reinvented into new shapes and configurations that still sound utterly original now; it's hard to imagine how they were interpreted in 1968. This continues through the album; "Baby" is a swooning pop ballad; "Bat Macumba" a lyrical deconstruction backed by tribal drums and deafening guitars, and these genre-defying descriptions could continue for every song.

Baptista would leave Os Mutantes in 1973 after four more albums and go solo. Listen to his later solo recordings now and you hear a man depressed. Rita Lee had left him, the acid had created a barrier between him and his fellow musicians (one of the reasons they're solo recordings), but his ability to play with words and rhythms shone through. Skip back to 1968 and you can hear the love hanging onto Baptista's sleeves. With arranger Rogério Duprat (*tropicália*'s designated George Martin), songs donated by Gilberto Gil and Caetano Veloso to augment their own, and older brother Claudio's inventions – including the fuzz pedal which gives "Bat Macumba" and "A Minha Menina" their unforgettable guitar sound – Os Mutantes created a rock 'n' roll masterpiece. It's an album that easily sits alongside *Sgt Pepper's* and *Pet Sounds* as an historical and musical wonder, the likes of which will never be repeated. As long as new audiences keep listening to Os Mutantes the flame of *tropicália* will never die out.

by Russell Slater

This illustration by Felipe Muanis is called *Dadinho na Terra do Sol* and is a fusion of the character Dadinho from *Cidade de Deus* with the classic poster for the film *Deus e o Diabo na Terra do Sol*, designed by Rogério Duarte, with Dadinho assuming the position of the character Corisco from the classic Cinema Novo film. The illustration was made for Foco Brasil, an exhibition of posters influenced by Brazilian cinema that was organized by the Brazilian consulate in Shanghai, China. After its first exhibition in Shanghai (2007), it has featured in Mostra Foco Brasil in Recife, Brazil (2008) as well as exhibitions in Hanoi, Vietnam (2009); Ilustra Brasil! 5, Rio de Janeiro e São Paulo (2009); Beijing, China (2011) and Abu Dhabi, UAE (2012). The illustration will also be the cover for a book called *Audiovisual e Mundialização: Televisão e Cinema*, written by Felipe Muanis that will be released in 2014 and focus on the relationship between television and cinema in Brazil.

BRAZILIAN CINEMA

AN INTRODUCTION

by Demetrios Matheou

It's 15 years since a little road movie called *Central do Brasil (Central Station)* came, seemingly out of nowhere, to win the prestigious Golden Bear at the Berlin Film Festival. Up to that point international audiences had come to forget that Brazilian cinema even existed; but the success of Walter Salles' potent film – at once a state-of-the-nation statement and an enormously moving, universal story – heralded its return.

For too long Brazil's film industry had been buffeted by the country's misfortunes, 21 years of dictatorship, followed by a democracy that was marred by corruption and economic disarray. The biggest blow was struck in 1991, ironically, by Brazil's first democratically-elected president since the dictators, who withdrew all state support for culture. There was not a single Brazilian film made that year, leading the director Hector Babenco to declare: "Brazilian cinema is dead".

But a new government's introduction in 1995 of far-reaching new film laws prompted what became known as the *Retomada da Produção*, the rebirth of the country's cinema; Salles's breakthrough in 1998, and Kátia Lund and Fernando Meirelles' phenomenal *Cidade de Deus (City of God)* four years later - both of which were Oscar-nominated – sealed the deal.

Since then various factors have been at play to keep the ball rolling; direct state funding, along with tax breaks for private companies and foreign distributors who invest in local film production; the involvement of the media behemoth Globo, which recognized a cinema audience for its TV soaps and comedies; and last but not least, a small number of canny film-makers, Salles and Meirelles among them, who set up independent film houses to nurture a new generation of highly motivated film-makers who have drawn on their country's difficult, but colourful recent history for their stories.

It somehow seemed fitting that as the "everyman" president Lula turned Brazil into a global player, so the country's cinema itself should move out of the doldrums. Lula is now gone, but with the Olympics and World Cup intensifying the international focus on the country, along with a surprising degree of recent social unrest, it's interesting to reflect how Brazilian cinema has progressed since *Central do Brasil*. What one finds is a quite dazzling diversity that isn't always acknowledged, involving trends that reflect both regional influences and those contrasting means of funding and production.

With its vibrant account of the drug war in Rio's favelas, *Cidade de Deus* was a massive hit in Brazil and abroad. Lund and Meirelles followed a tradition of films looking at the country's social problems – notably those of the Cinema Novo directors in the 60s – but also reflected the new phenomenon of drugs and heavily-armed gang warfare in the favelas. As such it was the trailblazer for a new kind of crime movie. In its wake came Hector Babenco's prison drama *Carandiru* (2003) and José Padilha's *Tropa de Elite* (*Elite Squad*, 2007) which dealt with the thorny issue of police corruption. These were hits both domestically and internationally, with Padilha's sequel, *Tropa de Elite 2 – O Inimigo Agora É Outro* (*Elite Squad: The Enemy Within*, 2010) being the highest grossing film in Brazil's history.

Abroad, these crime films create something of a problem, in that they are still the ones most associated with Brazilian cinema by narrow-minded distributors, despite comprising a minority of the 100-odd movies made each year; it's a stereotype that arguably still needs to be countered. In Brazil itself, the genre is matched as a major crowd-pleaser by comedies. Globo's influence, often exporting its TV stars into its formulaic films, isn't creative or artistic, though if it encourages Brazilians to see Brazilian movies, and so break Hollywood's customary stranglehold, perhaps one shouldn't get too sniffy about it. And Variety recently reported that Brazilian cinema has the highest share of its domestic box office than of any local industry in Latin America, a predicted 18% in 2013, with producers targeting up to 30% by 2015.

And Globo aside, there has been much to admire since the late 90s. Amongst a huge variety of genre-defying films, stand-outs include Cao Hamburger's *O Ano em Que Meus Pais Saíram de Férias* (*The Year My Parents Went on Vacation*, 2006), an extremely engaging film that combines dictatorship, football and a young boy's coming of age; Andrucha Waddington's *Casa da Areia* (*The House of Sand*, 2005), an historical and romantic drama set in the Brazilian desert, with a sweep and aesthetic that brings to mind *The English Patient*; Sérgio Machado's *Cidade Baixa* (*Lower City*, 2005), a visceral and vibrant portrait of street hustlers and prostitutes in Salvador, featuring three of Brazil's biggest stars – Wagner Moura (who later went A-list with *Tropa de Elite*), Lázaro Ramos and Alice Braga; Paulo Caldas's unsettling *Deserto Feliz* (*Happy Desert*, 2007), which concerns a young woman's yearning to escape her dreary life for Europe; Karim Aïnouz's *O Céu de Suely* (*Love for Sale/Suely in the Sky*, 2006), which follows a young mother's attempt to control her own destiny in the country's dusty, deprived northeast; Marcelo Gomes's *Era Uma Vez Eu, Verônica* (*Once Upon A Time Was I, Veronica*, 2012), a sexy and poetic portrait of a young woman struggling to deal with her detachment (starring *Suely*'s outstanding Hermila Guedes).

Proving that the favela film isn't the sole domain of men were two refreshing perspectives by women: Tata Amaral's *Antônia* (2006), about a group of friends who try to escape a São Paulo slum by forming a girl band, and Lúcia Murat's *Maré, Nossa História de Amor* (*Another Love Story*, 2007), which sets Romeo and Juliet in a Rio favela.

These encapsulate some of the characteristics of the best Brazilian cinema: an engagement with the country's history, regions and landscape, the poverty of the north and disillusion of the young. The country also has some of the best documentary makers in the world, not least José Padilha, who balances his high-octane *Tropa de Elite* movies with documentaries, such as *Ônibus 174* (*Bus 174*, 2002), which recreated a tragic showdown between police and a bus hijacker on Rio's streets, and Walter Salles's brother João Moreira Salles, whose documentary (with Kátia Lund) *Notícias de Uma Guerra Particular* (*News From A Private War*, 1999) paved the way for *Cidade de Deus*, and *Santiago* (2007), about the Salles's butler, which was a resonant reflection on family, history and memory.

Some of the directors mentioned reflect the abundance of creativity outside the major centres of Rio and São Paulo, particularly in the northeast of the country – which was, incidentally, the richly metaphorical hinterland of Cinema Novo. Aïnouz is from Forteleza, Machado from Salvador, Caldas and Gomes from Recife. A newer director on the block, Kleber Mendonça Filho, is also from Recife, and his *O Som Ao Redor* (*Neighbouring Sounds*, 2012) is one of the very best Brazilian films of recent years. Indeed, if some of the heat generated by Brazilian cinema at the turn of the century had slightly dissipated – with critics' attention being captured by directors in Argentina and Chile – the temperature has just been turned back up.

Continuing a tradition of Latin films that concern class, Mendonça Filho sets his film within a middle-class neighbourhood of Recife, which accepts round-the-clock protection from a security firm whose boss might pose the biggest threat of all, prompting a drama whose every frame is loaded with ambiguity and menace.

O Som Ao Redor won prizes at a number of film festivals, not just in Rio and São Paulo, but also Rotterdam, Copenhagen and Oslo. Also succeeding on the festival circuit recently were *Era Uma Vez Eu, Verônica*, Eduardo Nunes's slow-burning, mysterious fable *Sudoeste* (*Southwest*), Júlia Murat's beautifully crafted, magical realist fable *Histórias Que Só Existem Quando Lembradas* (*Found Memories*) and Luiz Bolognesi's adult-oriented animation *Uma História de Amor e Fúria* (*Rio 2096: A Story of Love and Fury*), which won the top award at Annecy's respected animation festival.

While such films demonstrate renewed critical receptiveness to Brazilian cinema, the growing enthusiasm for international co-productions points the way to a greater international audience. And with production outstripping that of many European countries, the patient once deemed out for the count by Babenco seems to be in surprisingly rude health.

NEIGHBOURING FILMS

HOW RECIFE BECAME THE CAPITAL OF BRAZILIAN INDEPENDENT CINEMA

by Bruno Guaraná

Recife, the capital of Pernambuco state in northeastern Brazil, has become a national and international centre of attention for its film output since the dawning of the new decade, hitting something of an apex with the critically-acclaimed 2012 release of Kleber Mendonça Filho's *O Som Ao Redor* (*Neighbouring Sounds*).

Although some reports have positioned *O Som Ao Redor* as an igniting factor in Recife's scene, the film is in fact part of a large lineage of productions shot in the region in the past two decades, which include other highly regarded features such as Paulo Caldas and Lírio Ferreira's *Baile Perfumado* (*Perfumed Ball*, 1997), Cláudio Assis's *Amarelo Manga* (*Mango Yellow*, 2002), and Marcelo Gomes's *Cinema, Aspirinas e Urubus* (*Cinema, Aspirins and Vultures*, 2005). Mendonça Filho's film, with its success and unmistakable depiction of Recife's present environment, has helped make Recife a permanent feature of Brazil's film production map.

It hasn't always been like this, however. The city only makes brief appearances in Brazilian cinematic history in the so-called regional cycles of the 1920s. These then folded with the advent of sound and the consequential increase in production costs which led to a re-centralization of film production back to Rio de Janeiro and São Paulo. In 1995, new tax exemption laws provided a long-awaited incentive for the national production, enabling the rebirth of Brazilian cinema and the rediscovery of the wider production map.

2012 marked another breakthrough in the history of recent Brazilian cinema, and neatly indicates the growing decentralization of cultural production that began timidly in 1995. In addition to having a special screening of *O Som Ao Redor*, the Festival de Cinema de Brasília put Recife under its spotlight by featuring four recent films from the region in its competition's line-up. Marcelo Lordello's *Eles Voltam (They'll Come Back)* and *Era Uma Vez Eu, Marcelo Gomes's Verônica (Once Upon a Time Was I, Veronica)* shared the prize for best fiction feature; Daniel Aragão was awarded best director for *Boa Sorte, Meu Amor (Good Luck, Sweetheart)*; Gabriel Mascaro's documentary *Doméstica (Housemaids)*, whose project consisted of lending production equipment to middle-class teenagers to document their respective maids, received a special prize, given to its characters and film-makers.

If, for the first years after the reemergence of Brazilian cinema, the production in Recife was rather scattered and limited, the city now contains a large web of film production companies, and a number of active film-makers whose approaches oscillate between a professional mode of production and a guerrilla, near-amateurish, style of filming. Within the Recife production, much like most Brazilian independent films, friends of friends commonly offer their time as extras, and lend furniture and vehicles for the shoot. Shoots, in turn, often run overtime, productions extrapolate their planned schedules, and producers need to deal with an overwhelming load of bureaucratic paperwork.

Yet, with all its impediments, the regional film production culture seems to have been established with a consistent practice, aided by a growing interest in exhibition, research, and critical reviews. The end results vary accordingly, and, as the Brasília film festival demonstrated, Recife has seen the production of feature film accompany its already-mature culture of making short films.

From Marcelo Pedroso's quiet documentary *Balsa (Raft)* to the sensible docu-drama *A Onda Traz, O Vento Leva (Ebb and Flow)* by Gabriel Mascaro; from the handmade animation in

THE SOUNDS OF THE STREET

Brazilian singer/songwriter Lucas Santtana tells us why the message of Neighbouring Sounds extends beyond the screen, spilling onto the streets in Brazil's recent protests.

The films produced in Brazil at the start of the 21st century seem to have been cast in just a few moulds. The most recurrent were the shallow comedies made by Globo Films, which were more like straight-to-TV movies or of a religious theme. The films made during this period which attracted the most attention, both within Brazil and abroad, were *Cidade de Deus* and the two *Tropa de Elite* films, all focused on the life of poor people in the favelas.

I remember a friend asking me why people don't make films about the lives of millionaires in Brazil. The banks here have an annual turnover of over 10 billion *reals*. Surely, it would be really interesting to know how these people live.

Last year, contrary to all expectations, director Kleber Mendonça Filho released such a film, entitled *O Som Ao Redor (Neighbouring Sounds)*, surprising the cinema world in the process. Mendonça Filho chose to film a few select characters in a district of Recife to talk about Brazil's middle class.

And just in case you didn't know: to talk about the middle class in Brazil is to talk about all of the social classes and the differences between them; of slavery, of racism, of the growing use of new technology, of real estate speculation, of television, radio and pop culture, of floating hornyness and how all these things fit together in a promiscuous, surprising and not-so-Cartesian manner in our tropics.

The film brings all these nuances together in an explosively poetic way. There are so many scenes full of metaphors and lyricism that you forget about the narrative until the final scene, when everything suddenly gains new meaning.

To cite just a few such scenes: the moment when Bia sings with her vacuum cleaner while smoking a joint, or when she masturbates with the washing machine. Or when Clodoaldo, the private guard employed by the street, shows men on his mobile phone being assassinated as if it were a night watch video game.

What seduces Brazilians who see *Neighbouring Sounds* is the fact that it tells the story exactly as it is without resorting to stereotypes about the rich or the poor.

As protesters flood the streets, new kinds of conversations about social class are happening in Brazil these days. On June 17th, 2013, alongside more than 300,000 people, I took part in demonstrations on the streets of Brazil against corruption, lack of investment in education and health, the exorbitant amount of money spent by the government on the World Cup and rapidly rising cost of living in Brazil.

Those small yet significant, everyday moments that make *Neighbouring Sounds* such a great film were happening all around us, and suddenly, we were all documenting them ourselves. Almost everyone at the protest was filming the demonstrations on their phones, these were their "neighbouring sounds".

by Lucas Santtana

Nara Normande's *Dia Estrelado* (*Starry Day*) to the confrontational "quickies" made by the Vurto collective; from the comedic stop-motion horror of Mendonça Filho's *Vinil Verde* (*Green Vinyl*) to the award-winning experimentalism of Tião's *Muro* (*Wall*); from the critique of beauty standards in Juliano Dornelles's *Mens Sana In Corpore Sano* to the collectively-filmed critique of urbanism and gentrification in *[projetotorresgêmeas]*, the variety of themes and approaches in short films made in Pernambuco in the past five years make up the melting pot of the Recife scene.

Three factors directly relate to the burgeoning film production scene in Recife: funding structures promoted by the municipal and state governments geared towards local film production and the decrease of costs with the advent of digital film-making; the proliferation of undergraduate-level film schools in Recife; and an increased interest in film viewing (with cinéclubs and special programs), film criticism (with digital magazines and blogs), and film-making itself. Mendonça Filho appears as a key figure in this scenario. A film critic himself, and one of the few consistently active film-makers of the earlier generation, Mendonça Filho has helped reconfigure the city's exhibition market by programming the most important local art film house at Fundação Joaquim Nabuco, in addition to founding the Janela Internacional de Cinema do Recife.

The cinema made in Pernambuco, because of its current weight, breaks the traditional privileges of film production development in Rio de Janeiro and São Paulo. What we witness in Recife is an apparent disregard for ample exhibition markets, as those aimed at by Globo Filmes, and a regionalism that makes its films immediately recognisable as northeastern. These films demonstrate an effort to mark the local geography and culture, engendering what I like to call a "universal parochialism" that, while easily assimilated across cultures, is effectively soaked in locally flavoured waters. While translating well across cultural borders, Recife films tend to remain intrinsically attached to the contemporary cultural, social and political atmosphere in which their production is inserted.

The political and economic climates in Recife could not be more favourable to the establishment of such a film culture. The growing economy of the region since the Lula government is a reality felt in the urban centres, with an increasingly intense traffic, a wild real estate market, and a continuous process of construction (especially of residential high rises).

The sounds neighbouring Recife's households don't come only from the stacking of residents on top of one another, but mostly from the unavoidable noises of modernization and verticalization of the city. It is from within this agitated atmosphere that Recife's effervescent film scene emerges. The city's social, economic and political conjuncture has enabled an increase in the local film production, while also motivating the medium to challenge what Recife really needs and wants for its future.

Written by Bruno Guaraná for Cinema Tropical's TropicalFRONT

Neighbouring Soun

A HERO WITHOUT CHARACTER

THE DISCOVERY OF BRAZIL THROUGH MACUNAÍMA

by Bruna Gala
translated by Emily Brown

After some notable successes in the early 2000s, Brazilian cinema became known abroad for its stories about social inequality played out in a style which excited the critics and public alike; but, much before this, at the beginning of the 1960s, an artistic movement was already well underway in trying to authentically portray the Brazilian condition. Cinema Novo, under the command of Glauber Rocha, was a quest for Brazilian identity which continued a strand within fine arts and literature going back to the 1920s by means of modernism and a group of artists who called themselves "cannibalists".

Straddling this vibrant scene came Mário de Andrade's 1928 book *Macunaíma – Um Herói Sem Caráter* (*Macunaíma – A Hero Without Character*) and its film version, simply titled *Macunaíma*, which appeared 41 years later in 1969. For some, they constitute prerequisites for learning more about Brazil and its culture. Joaquim Pedro de Andrade's film is based on the modernist novel, even if many plot points differ, but it's still a comedy full of social critique and folklorisms, that, as they play out, bring together diverse characters from Brazil's history, such as the black African, taken to Brazil during the time of slavery; the white European, who arrived during the beginning of the 20th century; and the Indian, who lived in Brazil even before it was called Brazil.

Joaquim Pedro made a wise decision to choose an iconic book of the cannibalist movement as the theme of his Cinema Novo film, but this quest for Brazilian identity had begun earlier, during Modern Art Week in 1922. Brazilian modernism discoursed intensely with what occurred in Europe during this period; and the cannibalist manifesto of Oswald de Andrade, of whom *Macunaíma*'s author was a disciple, sparked an autonomous development of the culture and character of Brazilians. With the story of the "hero without character" on billboards, the masses finally went to the cinema to watch this tragedy dressed as comedy, something that Cinema Novo had not yet managed to achieve.

To capture the importance of Joaquim Pedro's film, it is necessary to look back and understand what the cannibalist movement was. This "*antropofagia*" of Oswald and Mário de Andrade defended a culture of appropriation, but only of that which was good. The idea was to digest the good and vomit out the bad, so as to search for an accurate portrayal of Brazilian culture and not only to accept what came from the old world. It was necessary to digest the other and only after this cannibalism of ideas would it be possible to define and develop the true Brazilian culture as something new. The endeavour was to decolonise the cultural production of the country. This is the crucial point, since it comes extremely close to the modernism of Cinema Novo, in the way that it sought a national language, but at the same time was opposed to the bucolic idea of Romanticism and a submissive stance in relation to what came from abroad.

In this way, Cinema Novo and *antropofagia* presented themselves as a perfect combination: after all, what could be better than "cannibalism" to understand the intentions of Cinema Novo? The movement of the modernists was a more natural response, already having used and abused this dichotomy between good and bad in its process of selective digestion. Cinema Novo, like Oswald de Andrade and his crew, also searched for an original and innovative Brazilian language, whilst also absorbing what came for abroad, seeking inspiration in the French New Wave and Italian neorealism.

As Cinema Novo invaded the cinema screens, and *tropicalismo*, which also fed from the

Macunaíma

cannibalist manifesto, dominated the alternative music scene, *Macunaíma* presented on the big screen a pessimistic self-portrait of the Tupiniquim people. In making use of a kitsch aesthetic and through juxtaposing archaic and modern elements, Joaquim Pedro introduced to a broad audience a hero somewhat askew, but certainly Brazilian. Joaquim Pedro finally achieved the first truly popular film of Cinema Novo. To attract the masses to the cinema, he chose the well-known actor Grande Otelo, the format of a slapstick comedy and references from popular Brazilian entertainment from the 30s though to the 60s, strongly marked by ties with American cinematographic culture.

In the almost surrealist script of *Macunaíma*, our anti-hero is born black and, once older, turns white inexplicably, this time played by the actor Paulo José, and begins to derive pleasures until then only enjoyed by the while Brazilian elite, besides arousing female interest on a more frequent basis.

Racism in the country is one of the crucial questions of the film, even if approached from a humorous angle. With the change of skin colour, *Macunaíma* incorporates and interplays different types of Brazilians – the white middle class, the guerrilla, the black, the Indian and even a member of a Portuguese royal family – in one great journey through Brazilian history. The characterless portrait remains, and the white skinned person only deceives those who believe that skin colour is synonymous with honesty.

The protagonist sleeps with the wives of his brother innumerable times during the film, does not work, survives through favours, only thinks of money, robs. Essentially the film's protagonist personifies the figure of the scoundrel in Brazilian society, but *Macunaíma* also signifies a man struggling with fate, driving him to try and recover the Muiraquitã, which, according to legend, would bring him luck and protection. The films script unwinds in a wandering saga of the main character in search of this indigenous amulet.

Even though it can seem shocking on first viewing, the writer himself Mário de Andrade defined the Brazilians as a people without an identity in the 20s. You could say that this uncomfortable criticism is still relevant. Even today, Brazilian society is bombarded with mainly North American culture and it is very difficult to define an identity for a population in a country of continental dimensions. The character portrayed by the writer is clearly linked with morality, but not solely; it possesses more profound roots, since, being in a new country, the Brazilian lacks historical references which could unify a certain vision of this world, or even enable a common sharing of social values.

Almost 100 years ago, men who cried out for cultural cannibalization spoke of a process of selective digestion. During the 60s, Cinema Novo came to change the status quo, entombing the slapstick comedy. *Tropicalismo*, in turn, mixed concretism with pop art and Braziliality to form an enduring period of music. This banquet of cultures was delayed in being digested, but, in the globalized world of today, Brazil still appears much like *Macunaíma*: its cinema surprising all with its authenticity, irreverence and, above all, identity. So much so that one could even call it "Brazilian".

LITERATURE, ART & POLITICS

THE FILMS OF GLAUBER ROCHA

by Leo Nikolaidis

If the accolade "polymath" applies to someone who excels at a multitude of humanities and arts subjects, rather than just the sciences, then Glauber Rocha certainly was one. During his comparatively short but intensely influential career he tried his hand at everything from journalism and radical left politics to law, before finally settling on film-making after the critical recognition gained by his first short, *Pátio*. He also continued to write and, alongside his cinematic works, he has left us with a wealth of poems, essays and aphorisms which describe his unique take on aesthetics and politics.

His films are often talked about by cinematic academics due to their alternative take on Italian neorealism and the French New Wave, but they are also held up as popular cultural icons by the Brazilians themselves, who voted *Deus e o Diabo na Terra do Sol* (*Black God, White Devil*) as the best Brazilian film of all time [in a poll conducted by the Brazilian film magazine Contracampo (#27)]. Rocha's films tend to be the embodiment of various strands of his own interests – the literary, the artistic and the political – all drawn together to form rich tapestries buzzing with complex ideas and rich visual imagery.

Those who would be put off by Rocha's overt intellectualism should remember his popularist streak, as they are not intended to alienate the casual viewer. In fact they attempt to push Marxist ideology and give a voice to the voiceless. Much of the Cinema Novo movement which Rocha was instrumental in setting up was based around an "Aesthetic of Hunger" which he expounded in an essay of the same name.

Behind the abstract montages and numerous political references and symbols are actually simple stories or moral parables which are nowhere near as pretentious as they might first sound. The films of this trilogy take the form of folk tales and as such, the plots are fairly easily palatable, even if some of the references to specific political situations might go quite deep and cause confusion. However, this doesn't hamper the possible enjoyment of the films, as challenging scenes are usually side-by-side with simple views of northern Brazil's expansive countryside, or of lengthy shots of whole villages singing and dancing, leaving the soundtrack, usually a mixture of traditional Brazilian folk music and Villa-Lobos, to do the work.

The following reviewed films are part of an unnamed trilogy of some of Rocha's most celebrated works, comprised of two instalments of harsh life in northern Brazil with a recurring hitman/bandit character, Antonio, sandwiching a political allegory set in a fictional country. Rocha was very vocal about the purposes of his films, and so I include some of his own views on each.

Deus E O Diabo Na Terra Do Sol (Black God, White Devil, 1964)

Deus E O Diabo Na Terra Do Sol

"I started from the poetic text. The origin of Deus E O Diabo Na Terra Do Sol is a metaphorical language, the literatura de cordel. In the northeast of Brazil, the blind men in the circus, in the fairs, in the popular theatres start a story by singing: 'I am going to tell you a story which is truth and imagination, or in other words, which is true imagination'. All my upbringing took place in this context. The idea for the film came spontaneously."

Literatura de cordel are popular and cheap printed booklets containing folk novels, poems and songs, sold by street vendors in the northeast of Brazil which the film imitates by tackling maniacal religious themes, warrior saints and violent cults through the epic personalities which you'd find in myths.

Deus E O Diabo Na Terra Do Sol is Rocha's most well known work, and takes the form of a worker's parable, with the story propelled along with Brazilian folk music. The poor and lowly cowherd, Manuel, is pushed slightly too far by his callous and unfeeling boss. Manuel then spontaneously murders him and flees to join a cult in the wilderness which is led by a saint who preaches a doctrine of violence against the rich landowners.

Though certain scenes carry a strong feel of a Western, the film also strongly resembles soviet cinema, and Dovzhenko in particular. The morals of many of those films, where the heroes would bravely stand up against their rich and cruel oppressors, is mirrored here with the rich landowners in *Deus E O Diabo Na Terra Do Sol* being the kulaks in Russia. It would certainly be surprising if a Marxist like Rocha hadn't intended some kind of comparison.

Terra Em Transe (Entranced Earth, 1967)

"Convulsion, shock between different parties, different political tendencies and economic interests, and violent power struggles. These are what take place in Eldorado, tropical country or island. I placed the film there because what interested me was the general problem of the Latin American trance, not the Brazilian one alone. I wanted to open the theme of 'trance', that is, the instability of the consciousness."

Of the trilogy, this is the most avant-garde, complex and ambitious (which is really saying something for Rocha) and the only one not set in Brazil. It has layers and layers of thick allegory and symbolism which give you a choice of enjoying all the imagery in its confusing wonder, or of taking notes, studying hard and trying to grasp the plot in full with all its implications.

It concerns corrupt Latin American politicians, doing as they do, while a poet, journalist and former friend of both of them tries to do his best to oppose them in the next election. The result is a swirling tragic dream sequence which involves black flags, the unruly masses, the Catholic Church and some very ornate staircases.

The forces at work between popularism and conservatism, between the elite and the masses, and between the aesthetic and the pragmatic makes this epic a must for anyone interested in Latin American politics who can stomach high art cinema without feeling too queasy.

O Dragão Da Maldade Contra O Santo Guerreiro (Antonio Das Mortes, 1969)

"Initially, the dragon is Antonio das Mortes and Saint George is the cangaceiro. Later, the true dragon is the landholder whereas the warrior saint proceeds to be the teacher when he holds the cangaceiro's and Antonio das Mortes' guns. Briefly, I wanted to say that such social roles are not eternal or static, and that such components of social groups that are solidly conservative or reactionary or accomplices of the powerful can change and contribute to changes. They only have to understand where the true dragon is."

A cangaceiro was a type of social bandit, a Robin Hood type figure who, in the face of peasant hardships, decided to revolt against the landowners for the good of the population at large. This film focuses on the shifting allegiances of Antonio, the hitman from the first film, who was thought to have exterminated the last of these bandits. It also abounds with myths about the protagonists that are chanted, in the style of traditional song, throughout the film as if we were hearing the reprise in an opera or theatre production.

Some of the grandest imagery is of the bandits, festooned with coloured ribbons blowing in the breeze and impossibly long narrow knives known as peixeiras. They complicate matters for Antonio, who cannot seem to escape the cycle of hardship, death and meaninglessness.

Just like the translations of his writing, Rocha's films are difficult and clunky in places. But that shouldn't put you off what is clearly a brilliant, passionate and exciting mind at the height of its creativity and drive. The aesthetic and conceptual richness of his films merit a thousand viewings, unlike most Westerns or political propaganda pieces and should be properly celebrated and enjoyed as visual and mental overloads, led along by the repeated incantations of the music.

Rocha on Cinema Novo:

This quote, by Glauber Rocha, is taken from his Aesthetic of Hunger essay and summarises his views on, and therefore his relationship with, Cinema Novo:

"From Amanda to Vidas Secas, Cinema Novo narrated, described, poeticized, discoursed, analysed. It aroused the themes of hunger: characters eating dirt, characters eating roots, characters stealing to eat, characters killing to eat, characters fleeing to eat; dirty, ugly and starving characters living in dirty ugly dark houses. It was this gallery of the hungry that identified Cinema Novo with the miserabilism so condemned by the government, by criticism at the service of anti-national interests, by producers and by the audience, who cannot bear images of its own wretchedness."

CINEMA NOVO

LOOKING PAST ROCHA – FIVE BRAZILIAN CLASSICS

by Leo Nikolaidis

To consider all Cinema Novo as imitations of or homages to Rocha is to deeply misunderstand the movement. As Diegues once said: "Because Cinema Novo is not a school, it has no established style. In Cinema Novo, expressive forms are necessarily personal and original without formal dogmas." Of course the movement owes much credit to Rocha for articulating so many of its themes and ideas, but his talents threaten to eclipse a wealth of other directors and further obscure works which are really quite difficult to get hold of.

The films which follow are representative of the broad themes and styles which Cinema Novo had a go at tackling while also highlighting the overlaps which merit them being compared together as a movement at all.

Os Cafajestes (The Unscrupulous Ones, 1962) - Ruy Guerra

This is so perfectly representative of the influence of French New Wave and Italian neorealism on Cinema Novo that, language aside, it is virtually indistinguishable from a Godard or Fellini. The smooth saxophone of the soundtrack, the endless smoking and trendy sunglasses could all be seen as a mere imitation of European art cinema's clichés but just as Rocha showed with *O Dragão Da Maldade Contra O Santo Guerreiro* that the Western could be appropriated into a more Brazilian form, Guerra showed that Brazil also has its share of young nihilistic protagonists who can wax about existential angst while combing their

Os Cafajestes

Brylcreemed hair.

The film contains Brazil's first example of full frontal nudity in a daring and deeply uncomfortable 10-minute scene which highlights how the "unscrupulous ones" of the title are closer to sexist bullies than cheeky chappies looking for love. This ambition backfired as conservative Catholic and governmental forces censored much of the film, explaining why so few people have seen it, even now.

Bandido da Luz Vermelha (Red Light Bandit, 1968) - Rogério Sganzerla

Bandido da Luz Vermelha

"What poverty? A country without poverty is a country without folklore and a country without folklore is a country without tourists."

This semi-comedic folktale, based on a real criminal, could have been another simple Euro-homage but it's firmly kept on its own continent by the oft-repeated phrase: "Those who wear shoes won't survive" and through its treatment of uniquely Brazilian problems, helped by having the whole film narrated as if the bandit's exploits were being discussed on a chirpy breakfast radio show.

Our bandit has come up from the favelas to live a luxurious lifestyle surrounded by consumer goods from the proceeds of his crimes, but the film paints him as more of a lovable rogue than the *cafajestes*. This is perhaps surprising considering the sexual violence he deals out, but we must bear in mind that the aesthetic of these underground films tended towards aggressive immorality and trashing the optimism of the more popular ones. This glamorizing of saintly criminals on society's margins is also done in Rocha's films, and here the population call the bandit Luz or 'light'. Maybe it's his idiosyncrasies which endear him to us: while mid-burglary, he demands a spicy omelette. The woman of the house dutifully complies. On serving, he casts aside the knife and fork in favour of using a spoon which he has brought with him. This could be class symbolism, a long-lost reference or just a red herring. Ironically enough for this instance, Cinema Novo doesn't patronise the viewer by spoon-feeding them the answers.

Macunaíma (1969) - Joaquim Pedro de Andrade

Despite being one of the most recognisable and watched films of the Cinema Novo era, *Macunaíma* represents the movement's values the least. From the outset the film has high production values and revels in bright colours and gratuitous nudity almost as if it were a forgotten Carry On film. Rather than try to make the human form a subject for awkward viewing, or treat it as a natural fact of life (like those featuring native peoples) *Macunaíma* cycles through his love interests at the speed of a Woody Allen character. However, what might look like simple attempts at popularism don't render the film devoid of message, it just doesn't feel the need to tackle its themes subtly. This means that its talking points are inescapable and brazen and what ends up as a clattery, noisy, melting pot is actually an emphasis on the characteristics of Cinema Novo themselves.

One central example of this is the

exploration of the creation story of the Brazilian people. The theory of "Racial Democracy" holds that Brazilians are a perfect mix of American Indian, black slave and white colonist to produce a distinct meta-race. The blunt instrument with which the film hammers its point is shown by *Macunaíma* and his brothers inexplicably being of one race each. This is later confounded by Macunaíma's magical change of race (and gender) to allow him to experience different cross sections of Brazil's society.

The film delights in a love of the absurd with a cartoony aesthetic, culminating in Macunaíma paddling back to his jungle home in a canoe full of electrical kitchen appliances.

Como Era Gostoso O Meu Frances (How Tasty Was My Little Frenchman, 1971) – Nelson Pereira dos Santos

The title is so affectionate that it may be hard to believe that it is not supposed to be taken figuratively. Maybe cannibalism has been given a bad name over the years, most recently with *The Road* treating it as an horrific feature of a relentlessly bleak and dying world. Here we are almost persuaded that it's not such a barbaric thing after all and that human-eating-human can be a beautiful feature of a tropical paradise.

By covering ground which other storytellers and documentary makers fear to tread, this film is close to a Herzog-esque anthropological study, although Pereira dos Santos chooses to do so with significantly more black humour.

The setting is 1594 Brazil where European powers battle for regional control alongside their native allies. The problem for our protagonist is that these allies find it difficult to distinguish between

Como Era Gostoso O Meu Frances

the white people who are on their side and those they are supposed to attack: the French and Portuguese look and sound indistinguishable to them. He is therefore mistaken for a Portuguese (the enemy of the *Tupinambás*) and sentenced to be eaten, after a year of captivity within the tribe. This punishment surprisingly has numerous upsides; he is allocated a wife, enjoys taking part in local customs and helps them to use captured artillery for their protection.

The film is taken to be a high point of the "cannibal-tropicalist" element of Cinema Novo, where European themes are digested and reformed into something which is uniquely of the New World, but just as easily it could be thought of as a light-hearted *Aguirre, Wrath of God*, giving out a few unusual laughs and social commentary by flipping colonialism on its head.

Quilombo (1984) – Carlos Diegues

The film forms a compete history of Palmares, one of Brazil's most notable *quilombos*, the name given to settlements of runaway slaves.

Over the course of around 50 years, beginning in 1650, Diegues revisits themes he tackled in the earliest parts of the movement (notably his *Ganga Zumba*) to tell the tale of the slaves of African descent who defied their captors to go and live in the mountains. Even though, as second or third generation, they are divorced from their origins, their native languages replaced by Portuguese, the scenes of tribal life show happy dancing crowds perfectly in tune with nature, fully appreciating their freedom.

The music is an eclectic fare, going along with Cinema Novo's ability to bring together a variety of clattering styles into one piece. Tribal drums and twanging *berimbau* give way to synths and a light 80s pop-reggae complete with folkloric lyrics.

Although the *quilombos* are also refuges for non-black sufferers of colonialism, such as native peoples and ostracized Europeans, there is an ongoing tension, verging into war with the majority of the colonial Portuguese. The film gives fascinating insights into a so-called "primitive" society as it prepares for attack by cannon. Imagine if a companion film for *Zulu* was made from the opposing point of view. Far from being terrified by the technology, the warriors discuss their tactical strengths and advantages but must also spiritually prepare themselves for their community's possible annihilation.

But is there a future?

It has been pointed out that Cinema Novo contained a deeply problematic paradox: while a primary purpose of the movement was to educate and inform on the widest scale possible to the poorest (or hungriest) classes, the attempts to do so were not always immediately understood by or palatable to your ordinary Joe Bloggs on the street. Also, except perhaps for the works set in colonial times, the average cinemagoer would be actively prohibited from any escapism from the film as so many are anchored by real or imminent problems. Compelling and interesting as the films undoubtedly are, they require an understanding and active enjoyment that is far more suited to ardent intellectuals, political junkies and cinema enthusiasts than for those looking to transport themselves out of this world for 90 minutes.

By filming on low budgets they were able to tackle subjects which may not have had clear market value, even if getting them into cinemas would prove problematic. Maybe it's only now that the movement can live up to its full potential as the Internet opens up simple and far-reaching distribution systems to cater for the discerning cult viewer.

Cinema Novo's influence on modern Brazilian cinema can be detected in the most famous cinematic exports, such as *Cidade de Deus* or *Tropa de Elite*, which, as with the earliest Novo films were set in the favelas, used a mixture of professional and non-professional actors to achieve realism, and strove to portray genuine situations and so bring their issues to a wider audience.

Though the population explosion in the cities since the time of Cinema Novo has caused a greater emphasis on urban stories rather than the mythical and tribal settings seen in Cinema Novo, there is still evidence in films such as *Baile Perfumado* (1997), which essentially deified Lampião, and *Birdwatchers* (2008), a spiritual story of a native tribe fighting a landowner, that this legacy continues. Is it just possible that with Brazil trying to make sense of its new global power and find its identity once more, as well as ensure that it becomes a positive steward of the Amazon and its many indigenous tribes, that the country's film-makers will switch to these expansive natural and mythical narratives once more?

MIRROR, MIRROR

WALTER SALLES' FOREIGN LAND AND HOW BRAZIL'S IDENTITY CRISIS INFLUENCED A NEW WAVE OF CINEMA

by Sofia Serbin de Skalon

In an early scene in *Terra Estrangeira* (*Foreign Land*, 1996), Alex (Fernanda Torres), a young Brazilian woman in Lisbon, determined to escape from her boyfriend's drug addiction, and a dead-end job as a waitress, tries to raise some much-needed cash by selling her passport. Instead of the $3,000 she had hoped for, the unscrupulous Spanish buyer offers her $300. "Brazilian passports are worth nothing," he tells her, making her standing as a foreigner in Europe very clear.

Terra Estrangeira, Walter Salles's first feature (co-directed with Brazilian theatre director Daniela Thomas) is a stylish yet poignant portrayal of a group of twenty-something Brazilians who find themselves in Portugal, searching for a better life. It is often overshadowed by Salles' more attention-grabbing films, such as the universally acclaimed *Central do Brasil* (*Central Station*, 1998), which came immediately after, and which would rocket Brazilian cinema into the international spotlight with a score of accolades including an Oscar nomination for Best Foreign Film as well as a BAFTA and a Golden Globe.

But *Terra Estrangeira* is a crucial piece of Brazilian film-making. The film is set in 1990, shortly after Fernando Collor de Mello, Brazil's first democratically-elected President, came to power following more than 20 years of military dictatorship. It centres on Paco (Fernando Alves Pinto), a university student who lives with his ageing mother in a small apartment in São Paulo. Paco's secret hope is to become an actor; while his mother dreams of returning with him to her native San Sebastian, using the little money she has saved over the years. When the government announces an extreme economic plan, which in effect confiscates all Brazilian savings accounts overnight, Paco's mother suddenly dies, leaving Paco no choice but to rethink his future. This event, which actually took place in March 1990, threw the country into chaos. As a result, nearly a million Brazilians were forced to leave the country in search of new opportunities. Paco's story is one such example: his escape route leads him to become an unwitting smuggler of uncut diamonds and he lands in Lisbon, where his path crosses with Alex, another young Brazilian exile.

Salles' background in documentary film-making (he had produced a string of documentaries before he came to shoot *Terra Estrangeira*) certainly helps to give the story its conviction: not only does he capture São Paulo and Lisbon in raw yet beautiful black and white images (shot with a hand-held camera by the talented cinematographer Walter Carvalho) but the use of Brazilian, Portuguese and Creole argot gives the dialogue authenticity. The influence of Italian neorealism, which also influenced Brazil's Cinema Novo in the 60s, is also clear, but here the emphasis is not just on the day to day struggles of working people, but more specifically, on the experience of those living in exile: Paco, newly arrived in Lisbon and waiting for his contact Daniel to collect and pay for the diamond filled violin he's been asked to bring over;

Terra Estrangeira

Alex, Daniel's girlfriend who is increasingly caught up in the criminal underworld thanks to her boyfriend's illicit dealings; the Angolans in Paco's hotel who keep themselves to themselves and try to avoid mixing with "white folk"; even Pedro the seemingly innocent Brazilian bookseller. They are all brought together in the margins of a society in which a shared language and history should have brought some affinity with the country, but which in the grind of their daily existence, pushes them into further estrangement. What's more, the Portugal they come in contact with is far removed from the past glories of empire; instead it is standing on the periphery, close to, but outside Europe.

When after various days of waiting, Paco sets out to look for Daniel, he soon learns that he has been murdered. Alex, when he eventually tracks her down, offers the only clue as to what to do with the violin, but her actions lead them into further complications and danger. They have no choice but to flee, and the memory of Paco's mother's dream makes him choose Spain in the hope of reaching San Sebastian. Their tense flight north has all the characteristics of a road-movie, a form with which Salles would continue to develop in his later films, and which would become his trademark. Just as in *Central do Brasil* there is the journey taken by the cynical middle-aged woman and the innocent boy to find the boy's father, in *Motorcycle Diaries* (2004) Salles explored how Che Guevara's travels through Latin America changed his view of the continent, and directly influenced the man he was to become. More recently, Salles adapted Kerouac's quintessential road-trip narrative, *On The Road* (2012). In an interview with Film Journal in 2012 he explained what draws him to this narrative device time and time again:

"Cinema, at least for my generation, was what informed you about the world... And road movies quintessentially do that. I personally love to watch road movies in which the crisis the characters are undergoing somehow mirrors a larger crisis of a society or culture as a whole. Those for me are the most potent and powerful road movies, because they allow you not only to comment on the characters from an emotional standpoint, but also allow for you to have an x-ray of that culture in that given moment in time."

Clearly, *Terra Estrangeira* does this, not only by examining the situation of those forced to leave Brazil, but, given the period when it is set, also the uncertainty and crisis in identity which Brazilian film-making itself was undergoing due, naturally, to the social, economic and political upheavals within Brazil at that time. So in the same moment that the government froze a percentage of bank accounts, it also closed Embrafilme (Empresa Brasileira de Filmes) and Concice (Conselho Nacional de Cinema), the main organizations governing national film production and distribution. With nothing to replace them, the Brazilian film industry virtually collapsed overnight, going from an all time high of 102 Brazilian features released in 1980 to 9 in 1991, and just 6 in 1992. It was only in 1993 that a new Ministry of Culture began to once again stimulate film production, with the allocation in 1993 of $25 million support for the industry. As in Argentina, where a new cinema law (*Ley de Cine*) was introduced in 1994 which once again made subsidies available for film-makers – helping to support a new generation of film-making talent, the so called "new Argentine cinema" – so this subsidy encouraged a new cinema to flourish in Brazil. *Terra Estrangeira* is a direct product of this new incentive, and the film not only deals with a specific moment in Brazilian film production, but in the isolation of its characters and the film's mixture of themes and genres it also tries to redefine the notion of Brazilian cinema itself. As Salles explained in a Guardian interview at the BFI in 2004:

"Unlike Europe, we are societies in which the question of identity has not yet crystallised. It is perhaps for this reason that we have such a need for cinema, so that we can see ourselves in the many conflicting mirrors that reflect us."

BUS 174 & THE INVISIBLES

THE PERSONAL STORY OF A BRITISH NOVELIST WHO FOUND HIS LATEST BOOK'S MESSAGE IN THE SOCIAL COMMENTARY OF A BRAZILIAN DOCUMENTARY

by Ed Siegle

The camera speeds in low over a blue sea then floats up and over the shoulder of a mountain before diving, spinning towards the vast sprawl of Rocinha, Rio's largest favela. The voice of a girl kicks in, recounting how she has lived on the streets since she was six. As more kids tell their tragic tales the camera moves on to the mansions and swimming pools of those living the Brazilian dream, finally tilting upwards to show a postcard view of Rio de Janeiro, with Sugarloaf rising pertly beside Guanabara bay.

When I first saw this opening sequence of José Padilha's documentary *Ônibus 174* (*Bus 174*, 2002), in a little screening room in Soho, I had conceived most of the pieces of a new novel but was still searching for something to glue them all together. I knew I wanted to write about someone longing to return to the *Cidade Maravilhoso* (Marvellous City), because I longed to go back there myself. Two years before I'd been lucky enough to have a view of Sugarloaf from my office, but the company I'd been working for had gone bust and I was living back in Brighton. I'd devised a plot about a man scouring Rio for his long-dead (or not so dead) father, planning to put all the *saudade* I felt for Brazil into his quest; I had storylines to bring in the Brazilian music I loved, set against the backdrop of the dictatorship; I knew too that I wanted to touch on the social contrasts of Brazil, although I was under no illusion that I would be able (or had much right) to explain them. But something was lacking. And I still didn't have a title.

Bus 174 is a documentary brimming with scenes from an action movie, a legacy of the TV footage beamed live to 30 million Brazilians. The hijacker, Sandro, paces wildly, waving his gun out of the window, grabbing hostages, ranting at the police. Not far into the narrative, a girl at gun-point scrawls in red lipstick on the windscreen of the bus, "At six o' clock he's going to kill everyone." Throughout the film we are counting down the minutes until the moment of death.

But whilst the tragic drama of that afternoon drives the narrative, equally compelling is the story of the hijacker's life. Notably, as Sandro shouts through the window, he was also present at another infamous Rio tragedy; the murder of 8 sleeping street children at Candelária church in 1993. When I interviewed José Padilha about the film, he cited this connection as a key spark for its genesis. Whilst there is day-to-day violence around the world, some events take on a symbolic significance, he argued. The question was: how did Sandro come to be involved – as victim and perpetrator – in two such notorious events? The question was no less important because after Candelária the authorities had pledged to look after the 62 kids who escaped; 39 of them had since been murdered, we are told.

The power of the way Sandro's story is told comes from the variety of compelling voices which trace his life; from the trauma of seeing his mother stabbed to death before his eyes, through the streets and penitentiaries of Rio, to that final afternoon on the bus. Policemen from the scene, his social worker, street-kid friends, hostages, journalists, his aunt, a hooded cop-killer, all of them give their perspective on his life and actions, lifting him out of the headlines and giving him life.

Padilha made it clear that he wasn't seeking to condone Sandro's actions or hide the central tragedy of that day, the death of Geisa, one of the hostages. Rather he sought to explore how society conspires to turn children like Sandro into monsters. The point is brought powerfully home by the voices of the street kids recounting how they are beaten and abused, but most strikingly by a glimpse inside one of Rio's jails where

Bus 174

inmates crammed like cattle into overcrowded cells rant through the bars about their beatings and their rage.

When I saw the film I was interested in the contrasts and connections to *City of God*, a film which had created an impression of favela life and the underbelly of Brazilian society that was fresh in the mind of many. When I asked him about the differences between the films, Padilha emphasized that the drug dealers have a life with a semblance of structure; they have money and a place to live and operate within a system. To a certain extent, within favela society, they have a choice; of tens of thousands living in a favela, with limited options, some will take that path. Street kids, on the other hand, do not have a choice; they are on the street because they have no one to look after them and nowhere to go, and so they beg and scavenge and commit petty crimes to survive. They exist outside of society: ignored, shunned, invisible.

As a psychologist in the film explains, street kids are rendered doubly invisible by our attitude towards them: firstly because we shun them and deny them any voice and secondly because we impose upon them a preconceived caricature of their nature, as criminal scum, and thus deny each the right to an individual identity. In holding up a bus in front of 30 million viewers, Sandro rejects this conceit, making himself supremely visible, if only for an afternoon.

Of course rendering the undesirable invisible is not a purely Brazilian problem; a tendency towards outrageous blindness is part of the human condition. But it looms large in a city like Rio, where you can stand, like I used to, on the roof of your apartment block in Ipanema admiring the beauty of Dois Irmãos, the twin mountain at the end of the beach, as it twinkles in the night with a garland of favela lights.

I don't know if I came out of that screening room knowing that I would call my novel *Invisibles*, but it certainly didn't take long. It seemed to tie together the social themes I'd wanted to include, as well as underpinning the internal preoccupations of the characters. It became a frame of reference for multiple perspectives of my novel, making it feel for the first time like a whole creation, rather than a combination of so many different parts. It enabled me to write about the Brazil I'd known and loved, whilst acknowledging its complexity and showing a slice of its darker side.

Invisibility is there in my novel in the story of Nelson, a down and out musician and his sister Mariana, forced to live on the streets. It is there in Joel's quest for the truth about his violent father and the fate he may have met at the hands of the military regime. And it is there, most obviously, in the story of Sandro, threaded through the narrative in the days which follow the hijack, as characters watch the news, and read the papers and argue about the truth. I hope in this way that the invisibles of my story, like Sandro on the bus, help to illuminate the shadows of Brazil; aspects less evident than the beach-samba-football culture we enjoy, but no less a part of the Brazil we love.

Ed Siegle's The Invisibles is published by Myriad Editions

DIRETAS JÁ

HOW A NEW FILM DRAWS PARALLELS BETWEEN
THE BRAZILIAN PROTESTS OF 1984 AND 2013

by Nick MacWilliam

On April 10th, 1984, Rio de Janeiro bore witness to an event the scale of which had never before been seen in Brazil. As the singer Fafá de Belém emerged onto the stage in front of the city's Candelária church, a huge roar went up from the multitudes in attendance. More than a million people had crammed into the Pio de Praça, one of Rio's main squares, to hear the voice that had become symbolic of their cause. This was the culmination of a series of public protests in Brazil, commonly known as the *Diretas Já*, or Elections Now, movement, which had been steadily growing for over a year as Brazilians took to the streets to demand free elections and a return to democracy following twenty years of military dictatorship. When Fafá sang "Menestrel de Alagoas", the song which had come to represent the Diretas Já movement, it was as the voice of a nation, a public cry for liberty that shook the government to the core.

The hegemony of military rule had been constant in Brazil since the armed coup d'état of March 31st, 1964 that deposed the left-wing democratic government of João Goulart. Elections and opposition parties were banned while state repression and torture became characteristics of the regime. Diretas Já was the result of a seething public sense of injustice and frustration that united sectors from across the Brazilian social spectrum and which began amid the harsh economic situation of 1983 as inflation soared to 239%, leaving swathes of the population in poverty. As support for the movement swelled, it drew people together from distinct social backgrounds, as well as sections of the highly influential Catholic Church, and even the lower rungs of the military who were as affected by the economic crisis as civilian sectors of society.

A new film set amid the 1983-84 pro-democracy movement addresses the heaving momentum of the time. *Depois Da Chuva (After The Rain)* is the story of a teenage boy, Caio, in the city of Salvador whose social consciousness is aroused by the growing public sentiment for change. Caio becomes heavily involved in the student mobilization against the establishment, a time that coincides with his first love. *Depois Da Chuva*'s semi-autobiographical tone is based on the experiences of Claudio Marques, who co-directed the film with Marilia Hughes. "I was a teenager in 1984 and lived my political and loving awakening while the country was experiencing a rare sense of freedom", says São Paulo-born Marques. "It was a special moment, a period when people breathed the same air. We had a feeling that anything was possible".

Memories of Diretas Já have been stirred by recent protests in Brazil as once again millions expressed anger over gaping levels of inequality and governmental failures to address widespread social problems, even as Brazil's booming economy has sent its international status soaring. This was emphasized by the awarding of both the 2014 World Cup and the 2016 Olympic Games to South America's largest country. Yet while Brazil's elite has been busily backslapping itself for this boost to the global profile, the 2013 protests, which were largely staged during the Confederations Cup (a warm-up for 2014's main football showcase) have blown the lid on public disillusionment at the mammoth investment afforded these events at the same time as more urgent needs are neglected. National funds used to develop the necessary infrastructure to stage the World Cup and the Olympics could otherwise be invested in education, housing and health, and while it is the Brazilian public purse making these investments, it is the World Cup governing body, FIFA, and the Olympic Games Committee who stand to reap the vast financial rewards. And, just to put the icing on the cake, ticket prices for these events are likely to be so high that the majority of Brazilians will get nowhere near the inside of a stadium.

Wasn't democracy supposed to have fixed all this? Didn't Diretas Já arise from the masses being denied a voice in the running of their country and the channelling of wealth into the hands of the elite minority? Although the 1984 Diretas Já amendment calling for reform was defeated by the sizable pro-dictatorship faction within the Brazilian congress, the movement set the wheels in motion for a return to civil governance the following year, with Brazil's first free and democratic elections in almost three decades taking place in 1989.

According to Marques, however, the concept of democracy was one engineered and controlled by the ruling elite. "The professional politicians had understood the moment [in 1984] better than anyone, and they conducted the process. In the end, the first

Protests in front of the National Congress in Brasília, 1984 (photo courtesy of Arquivo da Agência Brasil)

president was a politician who had helped the dictatorship. It was frustrating, terrible."
The president in question was Fernando Collor de Mello, whose first term was cut short
just two years later when he resigned after being impeached on corruption charges.

Nowadays in Brazil the system continues to be geared towards serving a few at the
expense of many, a lack of true popular representation which is strongly felt. "Today
the country lives in a limited democracy. The population is called to vote every four
years and that's it. We need to create better democratic structures," says Marques.
The 2013 protests provide clear evidence of this, as the real desires of Brazilians
are overlooked in favour of grandiose short-termism. "Brazil is experiencing a good
economic moment. We have money and jobs, but life in the big cities is terrible. We
have no good public transport, for example. Politicians are corrupt and key decisions
are taken without public consultation."

Even after more than a decade of left-leaning government, the first since the Goulart
administration which was overthrown in 1964, Brazil still faces grave social problems,
from lack of housing and increased living costs to the curses of drugs and gang violence.
The new age of Brazilian prosperity may have proved highly beneficial to some, but
many more are yet to experience the fabled trickle-down effect that economic growth
supposedly brings.

In spite of *Depois Da Chuva* being set some thirty years ago, its tone and content resonate
with the current climate. As the country once again witnesses public disenchantment
towards the status quo, the film could not be released at a more pertinent moment.
Scheduled for a 2014 release, *Depois Da Chuva* has already been attracting attention,
particularly as it offers a chance to examine the parallels that can be drawn between
the 1980s and modern times. The situation shows little sign of being resolved by next
summer, and The Greatest Show(s) on earth face the potentially awkward prospect of
being played out against a backdrop of mass social unrest. Riot police and burning cars
do not send out the positive image that World Cup organizers seek to project in order
to keep their multibillion-dollar sponsors satisfied.

As global sporting extravaganzas grow more detached from the public realm, subject
to ever greater commercial criteria, there are lessons to be learned from Diretas Já.
The sheer scale of the movement meant that it became impossible for the authorities
to ignore public demands, even if ultimately the return to democracy has not fully
resulted in the inclusiveness that was hoped for at the time. Far fewer in number yet
far greater in political influence, the elite continue to hold disproportionate clout in
public policy, in spite of an increase in governmental initiatives designed to improve
social conditions. However, the fostering of togetherness and the political strength
that can be engineered by popular movements continues to allow people to make their
voices heard, and, as has been seen in other global regions, can be a genuine force for
change. The World Cup stopped being the world's cup a long time ago, the illusory
mask of participation having slipped to reveal the corporate behemoth beneath, yet
in mass unity there will always exist the belief that things don't have to be this way.

BRASÍLIA, 20TH JUNE 2013

**A PHOTO ESSAY OF BRAZIL'S
PROTESTS OF JUNE 2013, AS SEEN FROM
THE NATION'S CAPITAL**

words and photos by Cícero Fraga

Thousands of people shut down the streets and march to the Central Bus Station

The MPL (Movimento Passe Livre / Free Fare Movement) protests in São Paulo, and the antagonistic action of the police during those initial demonstrations in June, were the spark that set off a winter of discontent in Brazil, with people flocking to the streets across the country to continue the protests. As well as the MPL, several other groups and political parties saw the opportunity to bring their agenda to the fore; posters and flags were raised, many were torn down, uncertainty grew about what everyone wanted. The MPL was one of the few movements that from the beginning could clarify what it wanted and went on to win a number of victories, even if they weren't ideal. In the capital Brasília, which has one of the most corrupt, expensive and out-of-date public transport systems in Brazil, the MPL went to the streets to ask for investments and to propose solutions, such as Zero Fare [which asked for free public transport, seeing it as a basic right].

The following photos are a portrait of the people that want transport options other than the car.

"Estado laico, porra!" (Secular state, dammit!), with an evangelical contingency that keeps on growing, the Brazilian congress shows an increasingly homophobic and moralistic stance on issues like abortion and same sex marriage.

A cyclist vents his feelings about the insecurity many bike users feel when using the roads.

Above: The MPL flag is raised after arriving at the bus station.

Right: "Tentei chegar cedo, mas o bau quebrou... de novo" ("I tried to get there early, but the bus broke down... again"). Every day a local radio station counts the number of broken down buses throughout the region.

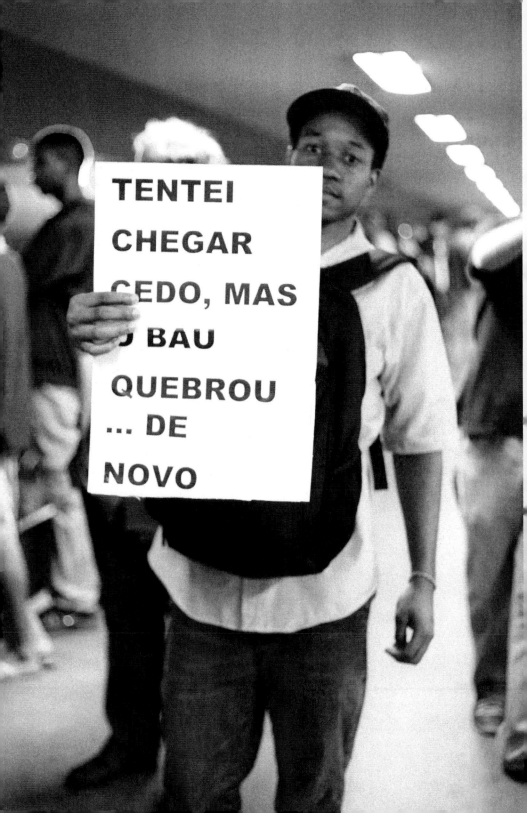

A protester jumps overs the subway turnstile.

After jumping over the subway turnstile, some of the protesters spoke in favour of Zero Fare (Tarifa Zero).

BRAZILIAN ART: AN INTRODUCTION

by Alicia Bastos

There was a time when people used to think about Brazil as being the country of the future. Now here we are, spotlight on the rising economy, iconic events planned and ready to happen. The country is radically changing, and so are the arts within it.

Of all of Brazil's natural resources, there is one precious commodity that will never become extinct: creativity. The openness of Brazilians and their ability to contextualize have caught the eye of the globe and found space to interact within it. Brazil has opened a dialogue with the rest of the world, resulting in many collaborations and projects flying across the seas, as well as significant commercial growth. This cultural exchange sees Brazil exporting artists and importing galleries, projects, festivals and more.

Internally, a number of cultural policies have been supporting artistic production on a grand scale and the money can be said to be "flowing". These policies, along with a rise in collectors and large corporate sponsorships are financing one of the most exciting periods in Brazilian art for some time.

Contemporary Art

The contemporary arts scene in Brazil has, in the last decade, grown significantly in importance in the art world. In 2010, Brazilian art accounted for around 37% of the total sales of Latin American art, while another $2.3 million worth was sold at auction the same year.

The São Paulo Biennial, which began in 1951, has been responsible for creating a dialogue between the art world and the public. Today, the event is one of the most influential biennials and together with SP-Arte, and more recently ArtRio, is motivating higher-earning Brazilians to become collectors.

Contemporary art galleries are opening in Brazilian cities like Recife, Fortaleza, Salvador, Belém and Belo Horizonte, in addition to the Brazilian art capitals Rio and São Paulo, showcasing not only the Brazilian modernist masters but also the younger generations.

The newly-created Inhotim, Latin America's largest "open air" arts centre, in Minas Gerais hosts contemporary art in two dozen specially-designed "art" pavilions dotted among handcrafted gardens. It was founded by Bernando Paz, who was nominated by ArtReview in 2012 as one of the 100 most influential people in the art world.

The more established Brazilian galleries have been taking part in major art fairs around the globe including Art Basel in Switzerland, Miami and Hong Kong, and Frieze and PINTA in New York and London, all supported by Latitude, a programme setup in 2007 to promote Brazil's contemporary art internationally.

Brazilian art first came to worldwide attention towards the end of the 60s with the modernist and constructivist artists Hélio Oiticica, Lygia Clark, Mira Schendel and Lygia Pape. Oiticia's first international show took place in the Whitechapel gallery in London in 1969. These artists are now inspiring a new generation, born after 1985, which is responsible for a quarter of the Tate's Latin American art collection.

Two major art organizations, the Pompidou Centre in France and the Tate in the UK, how now set up a Latin American acquisitions committee. Brazilian curators are becoming more active abroad, introducing younger talents to the world, like Adriano Pedrosa who co-curated the Istanbul Biennial in 2011 and currently works with the White Cube and Serpentine galleries.

Established artists such as Ernesto Neto, Beatriz Milhazes, Vik Muniz and Adriana Varejão head the Brazilian art auctions sales in the world. Adriana's work *Wall With*

AN ART HAVEN FOR POST-CONTEMPORARY SOCIETY

Inhotim is a centre for contemporary art set in a 5,000 acre botanical garden in Minas Gerais conceived by legendary Brazilian landscape designer Roberto Burle Marx. Within the garden are 24 art pavilions housing work by Hélio Oiticica, Anish Kapoor, Matthew Barney, Dominique Gonzalez-Foerster, Cildo Meireles and Vik Muniz, among many others. The garden and art works are owned by Bernardo Paz, a Brazilian mining magnate who has poured his millions into collecting and commissioning contemporary art. While the project started as a personal collection Paz soon realized that he should make Inhotim available to all and the garden opened to the public in 2006. Since then many new installations have been added to the collection and plenty of visitors have been and

gone. In 2012, Inhotim had over 300,000 visitors. A figure that looks set to rise year-on-year in this Eden for "post-contemporary society", as Paz has taken to calling it.

by Russell Slater

Incisions a la Fontana II broke the auction record for a contemporary Brazilian artist, selling for $1,527,980 in February 2011 in London. Artists from the same generation as the modernists art still being discovered, and newer artists, such as Luiz Zerbini, are revisiting those inspirational times and artists to create their own works,

One global trend in contemporary art is for works based on political, social and environmental issues. This has been embraced by some Brazilian artists. Paulo Nazareth's work, for instance, brings attention to social and racial classes. In 2011 Paulo spent five months travelling on foot and by bus from his Minas Gerais home to Miami for the Art Basel Miami Art Fair. The journey, which was undertaken barefoot with Paulo never once washing his feet, became a piece of art entitled *News from the Americas*. Speaking to the curator Janaina Melo on the journey, Paulo said "I have transformed myself, by being the same", in reference to how his racial identity changed significance in the different countries he travelled. Paulo's work is well respected by curators such as Hans Ulrich-Obrist, who invited the artist to be a part of the *The Insides Are On The Outside* exhibition at Casa de Vidro (Glass House) in São Paulo, and Gunnar Kvaran who invited him to be a part of the 2013 Lyon Biennial. Other artists making a big impression on the contemporary art world include Shima, who uses video and technology to make critiques of a systematic lifestyle, and Maira Vaz Valente whose

Paulo Nazareth's *Art Market / Banana Market*, Art Basel, Miami Beach, 2011 (courtesy of Mendes Wood DM, São Paulo)

works feature physical interaction with the audience.

In some cases performance is being used to compose visual work. Another award-winning artist to attract the international eye is Cinthia Marcelle, who hails from Belo Horizonte and creates video pieces from collages, city-wide interventions or land transformations. Her 2010 work *Crossing* was a looped 5 minute video of groups of people in striking colours methodically walking around a road crossing. The contrast between the colours of the people and the rich red of the earth is a great example of how her work evokes the same concern with primary colours that Lygia Pape, Lygia Clark and Hélio Oiticica displayed in the 60s and 70s.

The vibrant trend for collective working in Brazil has grown rapidly over the past decade. These collaborations are happening across a variety of media, including urban interventions and site-specific works. The themes of the works vary in focus, but there are many groups such as Urucum from Macapá who work on tensions connected to life in the Amazon and EthnoHaus, who work on local issues in Rio. There are also many artist collectives and theatre companies which incorporate street performance into their projects, with a strong influence from the circus. The result is a mélange of fun characters that often use this medium to poke fun at Brazilian customs and personalities.

The Lamina Collective run a studio in the centre of São Paulo. The studio and events space acts as a hub for artists, who are increasingly developing street projects that celebrate music, film and performance. Gambiologia are another collective, their name meaning the science of *gambiarra*, a Brazilian practice of DIY, whereby smart and quirky improvisations are used to repair objects or tools, sometimes giving the object a different purpose in the process. Gambiologia represent this ethos, creating objects, structures and installations from recycled materials and electronics.

Theatre

Although the line between theatre and performance has become increasingly blurred there are still many characteristics, such as the use of narrative, which have allowed the two scenes to grow separately.

While performance has moved from the streets into museums and galleries, Brazilian theatre has had a more prominent path, starting with its role during dictatorial times as a way of addressing political and social matters, especially the case at Arena Theatre (1957) and Oficina Theatre (1958). Grand names of Brazilian theatre emerged during this period, including Gianfrancesco Guarnieri, Nelson Rodrigues, Vianinha, José Renato, Miriam Mehler, Chico Buarque, José Celso Martinez Correa and Antunes Filho amongst others.

Augusto Boal, who worked at Arena Theatre and Theatre of the Oppressed, has gained international recognition for his innovative methods of encouraging social liberation through audience interaction. His work continues to influence Brazilian contemporary theatre productions and theatre communities around the world which have studied and furthered his methods.

More recently Gerald Thomas has provoked post-modernism in Brazilian theatre. This is despite criticism from experts that his strong work comes from an "outsider" perspective due to his training in America and Europe, and the personal influences he brings to his work. Nevertheless, his approach to theatre is both shocking and abstract and has been an inspiration for many.

Today we can clearly see two different paths that Brazilian theatre has taken; the commercial path with directors working on profit-making productions, which rely on major sponsorships through the government; then there's the more alternative route, filled with independent groups, especially cooperatives and communities, that are engaged with local projects. These groups, whose limited funding means they often stage pop-up productions in bars, community spaces or public areas, focus on social and political issues and are rooted in the counter-culture tradition.

The Nós do Morro collective has been working since 1986 in Rio's Vidigal slum. The theatre has over 350 participants, mainly actors and technicians taken from the local area, and has produced over 30 plays, winning awards for transforming stereotypes in the process. Nucleo Bartolomeu de Depoimentos – Hip-Hop Theatre is an art collective

THE TWINS ADDING COLOUR TO THE GREY CITY

Any talk of street art in Brazil has to make mention of Os Gêmeos. These identical twins, Otávio and Gustavo Pandolfo, have become synonymous with São Paulo's street art scene and ambassadors for the form worldwide. Emerging from São Paulo's hip-hop scene of the late 80s (see p.28 for more on this) the twins spent years locked up in their bedroom perfecting the elements that would comprise their signature style: a melange of cartoonish yellow characters backed with colourfully surreal scenery. It was the late 90s when they achieved international recognition after artist Barry McGee saw their work and recommended it to a US magazine, followed by an offer to go to Munich thanks to the artist Loomit. After that their profile flourished, leading to high-profile commissions including painting the facade of Tate Modern in London, Johnny Depp's mansion in

Los Angeles and the inflatable pig for a Roger Waters tour. Often, their work has caused controversy, such as the above mural (photo by Chase Elliott Clark) which dominates Dewey Square in Boston, whose hooded character has been criticized by some conservative onlookers.

by Russell Slater

that has existed since 200 in São Paulo and which creates performances that fuse the epic theatre of Bertold Brecht with hip-hop culture. They have produced over nine plays, as well as urban interventions and audiovisual projects using a blend of dialogue, music and poetry. Cia Antropofágica (Company) was formed in April 2002 with the proposal to use *"antropofagia"* (cannibalism) as the guiding principle of their creative and social process. Productions have included *Macunaíma* and *The Tragedy of John and Mary*, an adult version of the Grimm's fairy tale. Their creations and workshops are based in an independent space called *Pyndorama*.

Grupo Galpão is one of the most established theatre groups in the country with 25 years of activity. Their individual style mixes theatre with a touch of comedy. They have performed all over the globe, and are the only Brazilian company to have performed Romeo & Juliet at the Globe Shakespeare Theatre in London in 2012.

Street Art

"Brazilian graffiti art is considered among the most significant strand[s] of a global urban art movement, and its diversity defies the increasing homogeneity of world graffiti." – Design Week

Graffiti in Brazil has its place in history and is considered by many to be paradise for street art. Traditionally, Brazilian graffiti artists used it as a form of expression against economic unbalance and social exclusion. Even if *pixacão* (tagging) could be seen as compromising the acceptance of graffiti, its potential to communicate opinions rather than vandalize is definitely growing. The work of artists like Os Gêmeos are now sold in major art galleries for prices as high as important modernists. Controversially, one of their iconic pieces in São Paulo was removed by the local government, reaffirming that this is still not a universally appreciated art form.

Some of the best Brazilian graffiti can be seen in the streets of Vila Madelena in São Paulo, at the Graffiti Fine Art Biennial and in Rio's Jardim Botânico or Santa Teresa neighbourhood. Over the last ten years, with the help of pro-graffiti (and anti-tagging) initiatives street art has flourished in cities like Recife, Belo Horizonte and Brasília. Key to the recent upturn was the decision to decriminalize street art in 2009, making it legal to paint walls where consent has been given. This has resulted in many social projects in communities with youngsters encouraged to realize their artistic potential.

Some of the most established artists have created seminal projects such as Binho's painting of the sewage system in São Paulo and his curatorship of the 1st Graffiti Fine Art Bienial, or MC Grafiteiro's use of music and graffiti while working with kids in Rio's Favela do Alemão. There are also many street art collectives, of which Acidum, from northeast Brazil, is one of the most influential and active.

If you want to find out more *Graffiti Brasil* by Tristan Manco & Caleb Neelon and the recent *Estética Marginal Volume II* by Allan Szacher do a great job of highlighting the amazing street art and artists currently working in Brazil.

PORTRAIT OF POPULISM

HOW CANDIDO PORTINARI'S
PORTRAITS OF BRAZILIAN LIFE HELPED
THE COUNTRY DISCOVER ITSELF

by Jessica Sequeira

In 1947, at the Centro de Estudiantes de Bellas Artes in Buenos Aires, the Brazilian artist Candido Portinari gave a talk entitled *The Social Meaning of Art*. Addressing the young crowd, Portinari said that "the development of any human activity is linked with historical, political and economic events"; expanding on this to discuss art, he said that "social painting is that which intentionally directs itself to the masses, and painters must possess both artistic and collective sensibility." The applause was resounding.

At the time of the talk Portinari was already an established artist. Throughout the 1940s, his paintings were shown in galleries and exhibitions in the United States and France, the most famous being his *War and Peace* panels in the United Nations building in New York and his mural in the Library of Congress in Washington D.C.. Using a palette dominated by earthy reds, browns and yellows, Portinari's giant canvasses depicted black workers on the coffee plantations and poor farmers in the dry northeast of Brazil. His figures, instantly recognisable by their huge round heads, short bodies and massively over-sized hands and feet, were depicted hard at work in monotonous activity. Western critics praised Portinari's "realism"; in his paintings, they noted approvingly, the "negro" and genuine Brazilian life were openly illustrated for the first time.

Portinari's paintings are also deeply Brazilian in their political context. Portinari perceived himself as something of an intellectual of the people. He was a communist, yet his version of the left co-existed with the "leftist" dictatorship of Getúlio Vargas. His desire to both shape Brazilian art and transform the way people thought about society was riddled with ambiguities. It is precisely because of these tensions in his life and work, bound inextricably with Brazilian politics and the trajectory of his nation, that Portinari remains such a fascinating figure

The Rediscovery of Brazil

The son of Italian immigrants, Portinari was born on December 29th, 1903 in a coffee fazenda near the village of Brodowski, in São Paulo province; an environment that would define him. In one of the poems Portinari wrote late in life, he said that he "came from red earth and the coffee plantation", and he spent his life painting those themes.

As a child, his inclination towards art was so marked that he did not even attend primary school, instead passing the time helping his father and making sketches. He later won a place at the National School of Fine Arts in Rio de Janeiro and subsequently got a job enlarging photos as paintings, forging an early reputation as a portrait artist. When he wasn't working on close-ups of rich clients, however, Portinari preferred precisely the opposite: creating vast landscapes heavy in browns and reds, with the people within them so tiny the pictures assumed an almost surreal quality. His circumstances were humble; he would give people paintings in exchange for art supplies, and sleep on the floor of friends' studios or apartments

The years of hard work paid off. In 1928 Portinari won the Prix de Voyage, a scholarship enabling him to travel to France, Italy, England and Spain. It was a time of quiet transformation for him, taking place under the surface with little artistic yield (although his time was productive in another way: while in Paris, he met a Uruguayan named Maria, who he later married).

It was during this time that he realized what he wanted to paint, and how he wanted to paint it. As Portinari put in a letter from Europe dated July 12th, 1930: "From here I see my land better, I see Brodowski as it is. Here I have no desire to do anything. I am going to paint the people [of Brodowski], with their clothing and their colour." As such, though he saw a lot in Europe – he was particularly impressed by the elegance of Italian renaissance paintings, the thin blank faces of Modigliani, and the horror of Picasso's Guernica – his output was small. Once back in Brazil, however, Portinari set up a studio and attacked his canvasses with a new sense of purpose.

Portinari's realization that his own country could be the subject of art mirrored a wider artistic movement. The 1922 Modern Art Week in São Paulo set the tone for a reinvigoration of art true to the nation's essence. In a comic wink to the nation's indigenous, intellectuals asked: "Tupi or not tupi?" The poet Mario de Andrade promoted the idea of a "descubrimento de Brasil", embarking on ethnographic trips in 1927, 1928 and 1929. The next two decades saw this push towards the "rediscovery" of Brazil deepen in scope and widen into other media. A new literary movement led by Jorge Amado, Graciliano Ramos, José Lins do Rego and Erico Veríssimo emphasised the common people. Blackness became a theme in the work of artists like Jorge de Lima, Hector Villa-Lobos, Oscar Fernandes and Gilberto Freyre. Traditional musical forms like samba were recuperated and given a prominent role in the national identity.

This "rediscovery" was accompanied by the idea of social improvement. In a famous Rio de Janeiro conference in 1942, Mario de Andrade said that the first goal of culture was "the political and social improvement of man". Cultural renovation could not avoid the economic: the financial crash had been felt in Brazil, a "nation of planters and industrialists", just as in the rest of the world. Life in the *sertão*, the vast dry hinterlands of the northeast, had always been difficult; now it was near impossible, and droves of immigrants flooded south to wealthier and more temperate cities like São Paulo. Many new artists produced work which conveyed this dryness: Brazil, stereotypically a land of rich tropical abundance, could also be dusty, hard, and fruitless, as described in Graciliano Ramos' *Vidas Secas*.

Portinari's work can be seen in light of these trends. From the 1930s onward, his figures increased in size to take up almost the entire canvas. His people were now subjects, their natural environment receding in importance. This period also saw the beginning of his distorting effects – the exaggeration of head, feet and legs in his paintings. In Brazil this has been attributed to many causes, ranging from a childhood limp playing football (art as compensation for reality's deficiencies) to the deformed feet of workers seen on the coffee *fazendas* (art as exaggeration of reality's pain). Whatever the case, Portinari's connection to the sensuality and tangibility of these humble feet is clear; in his 1958 autobiography *Retalhos da Minha Infancia* he writes: "Feet that could tell a story impressed me... feet similar to maps: with hills and valleys, and furrows like rivers..."

Portinari wanted to tell the story of humble people. Yet his work was not at first accepted. Where previously he had been criticized for "demoralizing Brazil" with his bleak landscapes, now people did not understand his work on a purely aesthetic level. "They said it was only 'big foot' painting," he said. "They said I was alright at painting portraits, just a head. But with my other pictures, people would come and say: Nice work, the head isn't bad, but why the big feet?"

In 1935 their perception changed when Portinari's *Café* (pictured below), which depicts

the back-breaking conditions of life on a coffee plantation, received an honorary mention at the International Exhibition of Modern Art at the Carnegie Institute in New York. The foreign acclaim made Brazilian critics take another look at "their" painter; this time, they found more to like in Portinari's national vision, big feet and all.

Painting and the Brazilian Left

The intuition that there was a nation to be "discovered", was not purely artistic. The coup d'état in 1930 installed Getúlio Vargas as president, a man marked by populist discourse. Though he had risen to power through association with landed plantation owners, Vargas made it clear that his government would depart from their "*café com leite*" politics. Brazil was bigger than this, and needed a new infrastructure which favoured the growth of private industry and corporations. Promoting industrial development through heavy state intervention was, according to Vargas, the best way to help the nation.

Portinari became the official artist of the regime, chosen for the role thanks to the honours he had received abroad for *Café* and other paintings. Under Vargas he would produce one of his most impressive and enduring works: the 1939 Panel of the Economic Cycle murals for the Palace of Culture (now the Ministry of Education and Culture). Portinari however was not interested in creating bold, polemical art focused on revolution. Using softer colours and organizing space more systematically, Portinari focused not on his country's history of violence but rather on its peaceful economic development.

Meanwhile, political storm clouds were gathering. In 1937, facing the prospect of having to leave power because of provisions in the Constitution legislated by his own government four years earlier, Vargas implemented his infamous *Estado Novo*, dissolving Congress, calling off elections, declaring a state of emergency, and constructing a censorship-driven police state. This highly ambiguous entity, with heavy trade links to Germany and political links to Italy during the war, ultimately sided with the Allies, particularly the US. Despite his repressive tendencies, Vargas improved labour legislation and reinvigorated the national economy. Post-war, however, calls for a return to democracy grew louder, particularly among the middle-class, and in 1945 the *Estado Novo* came to an end.

During the Vargas years, the Brazilian Communist Party had been made illegal. Following "redemocratization" in 1946, Portinari was able to enter the party, in which he'd always had an interest. He attempted to get involved politically, running twice as a candidate for the Legislature, first as federal deputy and then as senator for São Paulo, but was both times unsuccessful. The Communist Party was a minority, with only about nine percent of the vote. But it was popular with the country's avant-garde, and intellectuals and artists within it enjoyed their self-imposed role as directors of popular sentiment. Portinari was no exception. In his talk *Sentido Social de Arte*, he emphasized that a painter had to be technically good – if not, he might as well shout his social ideas in the plaza rather than create art. At the same time, however, the artist also had to connect to common reality through suffering, serving as a representation and interpretation of larger societal struggle.

From the 1940s onward, Portinari grew more daring in his art, applying paint with a thick brush and palette knife. This art was often more appealing to the critic than the "common man." Painting, his medium of choice, itself held a strange status opposed to other graphic arts; collective traditions in wood and printmaking had long existed in Brazil, cultivated particularly by those in the northeast who used woodcuts to illustrate stories they were unable to write. Yet though Portinari preferred painting, and "modern" painting at that, it is clear he thought of the "people" as his audience, and his themes remained social ones.

The question always hovered over his work: should art be inspired by the popular or shape it? Perhaps both, contradictory as this might seem. Artistic "communism" was common currency on the Brazilian left, in which the goal of elites, as de Andrade put it, was "to promote the emergence of those segments of society in shadow, putting them in a condition to receive more light." The lack of knowledge of the "common people" was

Preparatory drawing for "Discovery of the Land" mural, Hispanic Division, US Library of Congress, 1941

something to be rectified, but so was the public consciousness, which could be shaped through, among other things, social art.

During this period Portinari travelled widely, and just as he had learned from his European tour, he also learned from other countries in the New World. Apart from his North American tour, he visited neighbouring countries like Argentina, where he was treated with great respect. At a literary gathering in his honour, the poet Nicolás Guillén wrote "Un Son Para Portinari", which would later gain popularity throughout the continent when sung by Mercedes Sosa.

Yet despite the praise he received, and the project to which he was committed, there are occasional signs that as he grew older Portinari himself began to question the "social" role of painting. "Painting, which was previously the greatest vehicle for the propaganda of ideas, today itself requires an enormous propaganda to survive," he wrote. "Previously it served religion or the state; today it does not serve anybody. Other more direct and efficient media have substituted for it, such as cinema, television, radio and newspaper."

The Ambiguity of "Realism"

The new path that Portinari, and his country, were trying to trace was a shaky one. Portinari's patron Vargas returned to power in 1951, once again pushing a nationalist policy free of foreign influence, and founding companies like the Brazilian oil giant Petrobras. Threatened with a coup attempt on the palace, he preempted fate and calmly shot himself in the chest with a Colt, leaving behind the lines: "Serenely, I take my first step on the road to eternity and I leave life to enter history." But the nationalism he represented was embraced fiercely for years after, a nationalism which would take on its full and terrifying consequences with armed forces' take-over of the country from 1964-1985.

Portinari's use of realism reflected the ambiguities of Brazil. Though paintings of workers' struggles and the poor could have been deemed "communist", such subject matter was always in danger of devolving into popular kitsch if it based itself on traditional bourgeois representational methods of realism. The solution was that if realism was truly to be attuned to the social it had to use avant-garde techniques. The discovery of the "popular" thus entailed the use of elite methods. In the end, Portinari's nationalism served the purposes of the elite world in which he operated more than any "people" this elite imagined.

Portinari lived in a period of Brazilian history during which the cause of the "people" was co-opted with striking ease, with nationalism used as a keyword by everyone from communists to the military. The ambiguity of his work, and the Brazil in which he lived, lies with the enduring question of whether his constant search to represent the social realities of the nation was in fact just a stepping stone to the more vested interests of art and politics, a platform he undoubtedly reached.

ANARKIA BOLADONA

THE BRAZILIAN STREET ARTIST WHO WENT FROM ILLEGAL TAGGING TO MEETING HILARY CLINTON

words by Damian Platt
photos by Damian Platt/Anarkia

"My name is Panmela Castro, better known as Anarkia. I do graffiti. I started on the street in 2005 but before that I was a *pixadora*. In reality I flirted with graffiti for 5 years before I started painting. *Pixação* is more or less what people outside Brazil call tags, which means writing your name with spray paint on a wall, although it grew differently here, as a self contained culture. Here there is the thing about writing names as high as possible on buildings and to make sequences, so *pixação* took on its own characteristics. I started through a friend who studied at the time, who started to *pixar* to get in with the boys at school, and it worked for her.

A *pixador* is a normal person – they could be firemen, policemen or teachers. They are normal people but

instead of going out to a dance or to play football they go out to *pixar*, it's their leisure... just that it's illegal. The adrenaline that someone might get from motocross might be the same that someone gets from doing something illegal that happens to be writing their name on a wall.

I stopped *pixação* in 2002. My career wasn't very long, but I always lived among it, because it generates a circle of friends that you can't get away from afterwards. I think this is one of the motives for *pixação*: to be someone somewhere, to be a member of a group. I stopped because I got married and became a housewife when I was 21, and I only started doing graffiti after I got separated. I wasn't going to go back to *pixação*, I was working and studying, I had set up a house, and there was no way I was going to start running from the police again or getting shot at. At the time of being a *pixadora* it was difficult because there weren't any girls and they always thought that we wouldn't be able to keep up, so I had to work to earn my space. With graffiti, even though the boys were more open, it was still the same thing, I had to earn my space. Nowadays any girl can join in because we already conquered the terrain for them.

I've always been ANARKIA since I began with my first *pixação*. The first thing I ever wrote was the punk A in a circle, the A for anarchy, and then I began to stylize it and it became my logo [see photo on opposing page; and with other *pixação* below]. I know how to do a lot of throw ups, when I started writing graffiti I started doing pieces and throw-ups in the street, then I began to write letters – Anarkia, a big filled in A, then I wrote Anark, and now I write Kia.

I still paint in the street, I have my spots, and now and then I go there and renew. In the Leopoldina area there are loads of walls that are mine. I already argued with almost everyone in graffiti, but we're all friends now. I once fought with a girl from *pixação* and there was a boy in graffiti who I wanted to fight in the past, but when I tried people never let me do it. Now we're friends. I've learnt to respect other people's differences over the years.

Through graffiti I can say what I think and express myself to everyone irrespective of race, gender or social class, it's there for everyone to see. I'm a painting graduate and I've been studying drawing since I was nine. I began to incorporate the theme of women into paintings when I began to turn into a feminist.

Being a feminist means being a politicized woman, conscious of her rights and who fights for recognition of her rights and cultural equality because even though we're equal in our constitution, we haven't managed to conquest this equality culturally speaking and in our lives. But we're on our way there, and the process is going well. However there's still a

lot about the woman being a housewife; we can work, but we still have total responsibility for children, there isn't much division of responsibility with the father, and then there's the triple day of work, study, home/kids. We still earn less than men and I think this cultural inequality appears a lot in the thematic of sexuality and that's why I use this in my work, because there are unwritten rules that say women can't behave in a certain way, but men can.

This abortion painting [right] is about the right to have dominion over your body. Abortion is linked to the question of sexuality. People say that women will just use this as a form of contraception; I got pregnant so I'll abort – but this isn't true, women are responsible. If a woman gets pregnant for some reason she should be able to decide. Because of the power of the evangelical churches in Brazil, this will take ages to change.

Today young girls are growing up knowing they can be what they want, including president. My generation didn't have this, I think we thought it was possible but we just didn't know it would be so soon. It's not just about having a woman in the presidency, it's about having a woman who represents our ideas, who is a feminist and wants to break taboos and win things for us. Dilma knows a lot about the economy and so on, but she's not close to the feminist movement. They used the theme of abortion against her during the election campaign to force her into an alliance with the evangelicals.

I created a graffiti project to educate women about the Lei Maria da Penha (it protects women from domestic violence) that was a great success. Because of this I won a human rights prize from a US institution called Vital Voices that was founded by Hilary Clinton when she was first lady. After this a group of us female *grafitieiras* created a network called Rede Nami (Feminist Urban Art Network) that uses graffiti to promote the rights of women.

For the Vital Voices prize there was a whole formal programming, and I opened the NY stock exchange on International Day of the Woman. Gustavo Coelho, a friend who made a film about *pixação*, said I was tricking them all: You're a 171!! (Slang from the Brazilian penal codification of fraud). How could they let a *pixadora* in among Hilary Clinton on Wall Street!"

GILVAN SAMICO

THE BRAZILIAN ARTIST WHO DRAWS THE
LINE BETWEEN ART AND ENGRAVING

by Arthur Dantas
translated by Julia Duarte

"Time runs slow for the artist. Engraving takes patience and craft. Samico is not virtuous, 'I am not skilled', he often says. Instead, he works empirically, on the basis of error and accuracy. But when the work is completed, we are certain that it will be flawless, a work of art of breathtaking beauty. Samico balances, in defined doses, imagination and detachment, fantasy and technique." – Frederico Morais, in Gilvan Samico: Works from 1980 to 1994.

It is said that the Pernambucan artist Gilvan Samico, 85, does not like talking. Like his art, his conversation is direct and frank. From his home-studio in Olinda, just steps away from the Monastery of St. Benedict and overlooking the city of Recife, he talks to me by phone.

Samico attributes luck to all the artistic achievements of a career in which destiny really has been a faithful and generous partner. "Back in Afogados [a neighbourhood of Recife], I used to live with my aunt and her two children. One day, I found a notebook in her house with a woman's head, a movie star, which she had drawn. I looked and thought: how could someone copy it so well that I recognized it was a movie star?"

The young Samico had discovered a whole new world that would unfold before him. His family, without any intellectual or artistic pretension ("there wasn't even a book at home"), begrudgingly began to encourage the talents of their child. One day his father took him to the house of the artist Hélio Feijó, who looked at his early drawings, still reproducing what was in the magazines and said: "Instead of copying magazine covers, copy what you see, what's in front of you!" It was then that Samico started drawing trees and animals like goats, birds, snakes, frogs. This was an artist primarily interested in his own land.

The artist and former art dealer Giuseppe Baccaro says that the process of engraving is difficult, almost ascetic. Engravers are often elusive types, with no special effects in life or in art. It's a theory that's seen in Brazilian artists of the genre like Goeldi, Abramo, Gruber, Roberto Magalhães and Gilvan Samico, to name a few.

Samico is not just "anyone" in Brazilian art: he has works at the Museum of Modern Art in New York and has participated in two Venice biennials, where he has won awards. But these are nothing new in a career in which Samico started as a painter before moving into engraving. He made the first of these in 1953. "It was not my choice. Abelardo da Hora thought it was easy to make an outline of wood and plaster on top of glass. When dried, it was polished already. But the plaster is brittle, a horrible material to engrave with. At home, I made a couple of pieces using wood engravings and this was my experience until I moved to São Paulo."

The Masters, Goeldi and Lívio Abramo

In 1957 Samico decided to try his luck in São Paulo. "There was a lot more going on there, there were museums of art, it was a big city, with many more attractions for artists." With recommendations from experienced artist friends like Aloísio Magalhães and Francisco Brennand, he decided to study with Livio Abramo in São Paulo, who would, in turn, recommend that Samico study under Oswaldo Goeldi in Rio de Janeiro. This first phase of Samico's work is consistent with the great work of Abramo and Goeldi, featuring expressionist engravings in which the cut would often simulate lines of a pencil drawing, evident in the piece *Três Mulheres e a Lua* (1959).

Samico was very shy and learned more from listening than producing in his classes. He rarely showed any of his engravings to his teachers, focusing instead on what they said, how they judged his fellow students' work. Once, Lívio Abramo was intrigued as to why Samico always worked in the shadows, in the corners. "When I was in front of an easel and someone walked behind me, I would stop", said Samico.

The most curious thing, however, was a physical limitation that caused Samico to ultimately opt for engraving. As his city apartment was very small and there was a newborn daughter, the artist had to opt for the less space-intrusive choice of engraving. It was a moment of destiny for the artist, who would work on his engravings in his spare time, following a strict daily routine. Soon his work began to be noticed by art galleries.

Like a Cordel Tale

In 1965, after seven years away from Pernambuco, the good son returned to his homeland, though exchanging his hometown of Recife for the nearby Olinda, where he still lives today. Olinda would not be the only change in the artist's life: a conversation with the

O Enigma, 1989

writer and defender of popular northeastern culture, Ariano Suassuna, would change his life. "I was not satisfied with the engravings I was making. They were very dark and had no indication that I was an artist from Brazil. I said that to Ariano [and] he told me: 'Samico, why don't you take a dip into the world of *cordel*?' That was like a kick from a mule to me."

Samico started researching the covers of the traditional northeastern *cordels*. He studied them carefully and came to a logical conclusion: more than the pictures themselves, the solution was to concentrate on the texts, to confer graphically the most recurrent images of the *cordelista* [the writer of the cordel stories]. In the 60s magazine Senhor, Samico would clearly define the change of direction in his work: "I stripped excesses from my engravings. The concern to enrich them with different textures was replaced by the concern to enrich them with invention". Thus, instead of creating a language similar to the popular engravers, he found his own, unique and original path.

It was a time of vain nationalist intellectuals, of artistic movements and manifestos, of mobilization in favour of Brazilian popular culture, continuing the policies of the Vargas era that had swung in that direction. In Pernambuco, Suassuna started working with artists around these principles, leading to the birth of the Armorial Movement, which in turn revalued northeastern popular culture, creating a studied Brazilian art from popular roots. Besides Suassuna, other artists and organizations such as Francisco Brennand, Raimundo Carrero, the Northeast Armorial Ballet, the Armorial Chamber Orchestra, the Orchestra Romançal and Quintet Armorial were involved in the movement. Samico, who found his own artistic ideas perfectly in line with the ambitions of the group also participated. He explains, however, that it was an armorial *avant la lettre*. "I don't conform to the ideas of the Armorial Movement: I was already armorial without even knowing it!"

Far From Reason

His work since then has become more "Brazilian". Instead of spying on the European expressionism happening on the other side of the ocean, Samico returned to the figurativism of popular engravers and looked to purify his work through economy of strokes, perspectives and colours. He turned his engraving inside out, revealing light where there was darkness, deepening the volume of the images and creating definitive black lines. He abandoned any pretension towards perspective, removed excesses and went to work with designs that included a maximum of three characters or subjects.

The procedure transformed everything and brought to light his unique plan, with no sense of depth or perspective and keeping just the minimum of details. "I reduced the engraving to a figure in linear form, some black areas, and a slight stroke to animate. It had no hint of sky, cloud, anything resembling a naturalistic space."

With his exposure at MoMA in New York) and at two Venice biennials, as well a plethora of group and solo exhibitions around the world, Samico claims that his only frustration is not being recognized as a painter. "It's a little thing that happens with some artists that, using more than one technique, are the most recognized in one, at the expense of others. I would like to have the prestige I have, not only as an engraver but also as a painter. I may not be able to show my paintings, but I put colour in my engravings."

A Árvore da Vida e o Infinito Azul, 2006

Gilvan's work has an extreme accuracy. The exhibition *Samico – Drawing the Engraving*, which took place between August and September 2004 in the state Pinacoteca, is proof of the absolute zeal with which he treats his creations; there are some works in his catalogue which come accompanied by reproductions of the many stages of 'study' for the final piece. It's a somewhat disturbing process. Now in his 80s, Samico says, not without a dose of his quirky humour, that he prefers to work less, "I can't change my ways [even though] engraving tortures me." Thus, for more than ten years Samico has produced only one work per year, limiting pressings to 120 copies for his fans and collectors.

A few days after the interview, my appreciation for Samico and his work increases, I think about going to Olinda to give him a hug and thank him for a life devoted to recreating the world as we know it. I call to solve some small bureaucracies and take the opportunity to thank him once more for the pleasure of sharing a few words with me. I mean I was afraid, because of his reputation as a man of few words. "Yeah, I invented a legend that I was walking down the street distracted and hit my head on a post and since then I can't stop speaking," laughs Samico. Maybe the post of his personal fiction is the same one that our head hits when confronted with his engravings.

DERLON ALMEIDA

FUSING THE OLD AND NEW – THE BRAZILIAN STREET ARTIST WHOSE WORK CONTINUES THE TRADITIONS OF NORTHEASTERN BRAZIL

words by Russell Slater
photos by Derlon Almeida

Derlon Almeida has become a well-known figure in contemporary Brazilian art thanks to his fusion of northeastern stories and mythology with street art. In 2013 he had his debut exhibition in London, *From Manguetown: The Urban Art of Derlon*, a sign that his work is now being discovered by an international audience. The exposure is well-deserved for an artist who has created his own visual identity that is both personal and evocative of the northeastern Brazil that he grew up in. The process to find his artistic voice involved a lot of research and practice. As with all artists, this started at a young age, as Derlon explains:

"I showed my first artistic traits in childhood. When I was small I already had the habit of drawing and making art. But it was in adolescence that I took the important step to find my way as an artist and I began to create something more concrete that would hold up for the future. That was when I began doing graffiti, inspired by the art I would see in the streets of Recife."

The switch to creating graffiti was important for Derlon to find an environment in which he could express himself, but it was still necessary to develop his style:

"My art began to change, to create this aesthetic that I am developing today, when I was already well into the world of graffiti. I had made friends with artists, learnt techniques, made some designs on the streets. Carrying on from this I began to feel the need to create a visual identity, like I saw in many artists who used it to create a strong ability to communicate. So I started researching and studying to find an aesthetic which was characteristic of my work and from where I could evolve. In my research I encountered the art of engraving [known as *xilogravura* in Portuguese], which is extremely popular in the northeast of Brazil. I was really impressed with the communicative power of this art. It was easy to understand and it had a strong visual impact. I saw that I could combine this aesthetic with the technique of graffiti, allowing me to create a form of contemporary art that united two artistic languages."

The popularity of woodcut engravings in Brazil stems from their use on the covers of *literatura de cordel* [see p. 189 for more on cordel], where the engraving would depict the main characters of the often humorous or mythological nature of the *cordel*. Many of these artists would focus on creating art just for these small *cordel* pamphlets. Derlon saw its fusion with street art as the possibility of expanding the canvas: "I imagined them being made on a grand scale, leaving paper behind and making them as a piece of graffiti or a mural. I was certain that the result would be incredible, so I started researching more into the universe of these artists, learning more about woodcutting, getting to know them and also absorbing what was in my day-to-day life and selecting what best suited the dialogue in my work. As Recife has a huge cultural wealth with lots of diversity it was natural that this would be represented in my work. Eventually,

105.B.
MUDAMOS PARA
A RUA DO RUZARIO
Nº 88 BAIRO DO
SOCORRO CONTINUO
CONSERTANDO
CALÇADOS
RES ETC CELULAR
ZÉ MARIA
O BOM DE
BOLA

SUSPENSÃO
FREIO
PONTA HOMOCINETICA
MECANICA EM GERAL
18
BAR DO GALILEU GALISTEU
COMIDA CASEIRA

after my research was complete, I was ready to show my work to the public, the mix of street art with engraving."

It was through this intense research that Derlon learnt about many of the figures that often feature in his art. "These characters and icons were influences that I learned from the works of many engravers. From there I went deeper into researching these references, to get inside stories, myths and legends that would add to my poetic imagination. Along with this there are other references, like pop art, that were a big part of my research." Derlon says that other key influences include "the engravers Samico and J. Borges; the muralist Diego Rivera; the conceptual artist Paul Bruscky; and the street art of Os Gêmeos, Shepard, Fairey and Speto."

One of the strong elements about Derlon's work is the opportunity for his art to be involved in urban interventions (see photos on previous page for examples of this) due to its scale and its link with traditional Brazilian culture which is especially appealing to public institutions and government initiatives. This is one way in which Derlon, who is increasingly in demand for art installations, is able to retain his identity as a street artist.

Yet, though Derlon's art could help preserve Recife's folkloric culture, this was never its intention: "[I used folkloric imagery] not through a desire to preserve the culture but by enjoying what I could absorb simply out of interest and using it to strengthen my work, while also contributing to the overall culture of Recife, redeeming its values and working in a more universal context."

It seems quite apt that my conversation with Derlon should swing round to Recife. The city and its cultural traditions are clearly a big influence on Derlon's work, something which he sees in all the art it produces: "The great cultural wealth of the city means that what the artists makes is also rich in culture." Without it, Derlon's work would not even exist: "If I had not been born in Recife and experienced everything I have there, then I wouldn't be here today with the work that you know."

sau
da
de

Saudade by Mateus Acioli

BRAZIL'S NEW LITERARY ENCOUNTERS

WITH THE RISE OF LITERATURE FESTIVALS AND MARGINAL AUTHORS HAS BRAZIL FINALLY FOUND THE SOLUTION TO ITS ILLITERACY PROBLEM?

by Joanna Blyth

While Brazilian music, cinema and sport have been making waves outside of the country for some time, Brazilian literature remains largely unread outside the country's borders, with relatively few works translated for English readers. However, in recent years there has been an explosion of literary activity in Brazil, with exciting new events and festivals emerging across the country every year.

At last count, Brazil was able to boast an impressive 200 separate literary fairs and festivals. Chief among these is the São Paulo Book Biennial, which has the largest number of contributing authors and is one of the most important events for those involved with the commercial side of the Brazilian literary scene; a meeting point in bustling São Paulo for the country's major publishing houses, book-sellers and distributors. It is no wonder that it attracts upwards of 800,000 visitors over its 11-day duration.

As notable as the São Paulo Biennial is, in the past few years there has been an increasing focus on the emergence of smaller, independent literary events, which aim to bring books into the lives of those who may otherwise remain marginalized from the world of writing. This increase in literary fairs and festivals has caught the attention of the Brazilian media recently, and there is growing enthusiasm for the prospect of turning the country into a nation of avid readers and making literature an integral part of life for people from all parts of the country's diverse population.

The recent explosion of literary events is due in no small part to the support of the National Library Foundation (Fundação Biblioteca Nacional FBN) which encourages investments in smaller events by offering tax waivers.

Literature In The Favelas

The support of FBN can be seen in the rise of smaller and less commercially focused events that have been gaining in popularity and momentum every year, surely a good sign of things to come, even if the lion's share of the festivals still seem to be taking place in the states of Rio de Janeiro and São Paulo. One of the most successful of these new events is FLUPP, the literary festival of the UPPs (UPP stands for Unit of Police Protection, the official name for Rio's pacified favelas), which is hosted by the Morro dos Prazeres Favela in Rio, where a constant police presence aims to keep the peace. Taking place over four days each November, this alternative book festival aims to bring the pleasure of literature to diverse sections of society, with an emphasis on creating artistic links between the favelas and the wider community through focusing on new and upcoming talent from the favelas themselves.

Julio Ludemir is the man whose idea for a festival that would showcase the work of marginalized Brazilian writers eventually evolved into FLUPP. Ludemir wanted to dispel the stereotype that favela residents were uncultured, interested only in football and capoeira: "we discovered that there is as much of an appetite for culture in these areas as there is for new mobile phones and televisions", he said. Though illiteracy rates in Brazil are still very high (14.1 million Brazilians above 15 years of age cannot read or write) Ludemir hopes that FLUPP can dispel stereotypes of those living in the favelas.

After the first FLUPP in 2012, the organizers published a book of 43 stories and poems, written by residents from several of Rio's favelas. These aspiring writers – whose varied stories showed that violence is just one element of their lives – met through the initiative FLUPP Pensa (FLUPP Think) which aims to inspire and encourage a new generation of peripheral talent, by hosting workshops leading up to the festival. Following this success the organizers of FLUPP will be publishing three books in 2013, aiming to show the talent of the favelas and that there is more to favela life than just violence.

FLIP Arrives On The Green Coast

Surprisingly it was only in 2003 that Brazil saw its first literary festival when Festa Literária Internacional de Paraty (FLIP), was launched. Hosted in Paraty, a sleepy and picturesque colonial town on the Green Coast, FLIP has become the most important annual literary event in the country since its launch and attracts authors of international renown each year along with tens of thousands of visitors. The festival was launched by Liz Calder, the British founder of Bloomsbury publishing, who fell in love with Brazil while working there as a model and journalist in the 1960s. Her Brazilian ambitions however were simply unattainable dreams until Bloomsbury picked up the monumentally successful Harry Potter franchise, allowing her the financial freedom to focus her attention on projects abroad.

When the first FLIP was hosted in the summer of 2003, Calder and her team expected a crowd of just a few hundred people: "I remember the first event, we had a room for 300 people and I was nervous about filling it." Ten years later, FLIP is one of the most eagerly anticipated literary events in Brazil, regularly drawing crowds of over 30,000 people to a town with a population of just 24,000. Each year 40 authors, 20 from Brazil and 20 from outside of the country, are invited to take part in talks, signings and other events. In the past FLIP has hosted writers as well-known as Ian McEwan, Jonathan Franzen and Salman Rushdie alongside home-grown talent like Ariano Suassuna, Ruy Castro and Lygia Fagundes Telles.

The Rise of Marginal Literature

FLIP 2013 saw the appearance of Brazilian poet Sérgio Vaz. In 2000 Vaz formed Cooperifa, a hub for poets and writers from poor backgrounds, which quickly gained significance and became a launch-pad for literature from São Paulo's margins. His role as founder and main conspirator at Cooperifa, in addition to the books of poetry he has been releasing since the late 80s, have seen Vaz become an important part of *literatura marginal*, the name for the group of writers from Brazil's poorer neighbourhoods (especially those on the outskirts of São Paulo) who, despite lack of formal education, are making a name for themselves on the Brazilian literary map.

With no university education to speak of, Vaz has worked hard to challenge the preconception that formal training is necessary to produce poetry and to raise a voice from the peripheries of Brazil, writing about such issues as police brutality, racism and corruption in the slums, bringing a fresh literary perspective to these aspects of Brazilian life. His writing is paving the way for others from marginalized areas of Brazil to speak about their experiences directly through literature, and his appearance at FLIP shows that these writers are beginning to be embraced by traditional literature circles.

Another poet who is making an impact is Ferréz, also a figurehead of *literatura marginal*. Ferréz has made a name for himself with his striking and often graphic works of literature which reflect the realities of young people living in the favelas in which he grew up. In 2013 Ferréz appeared at FlipSide festival in the UK, an event run by the team behind FLIP in Paraty which aims to strengthen literary links between Brazil and Britain as well as showcasing the best in both countries' literary talents. To have writers like Ferréz appearing alongside Ian McEwan and writers from Brazil's literary elite such as Adriana Lisboa shows the increasing importance of marginal literature in Brazil and potentially overseas too.

Even with such progress, it is obvious that the literary festival scene in Brazil has a long way to go before it can be considered truly inclusive of talent from every corner of Brazil, and this is something writers like Ferréz are eager to see change. "I don't see great efforts by these fairs in putting marginal literature on the map, the authors have to keep fighting in the streets, schools and *saraus*", says Ferréz. "There is a lot of prejudice, especially from the elite authors, who live on the richer side of town and have their own future for Brazilian literature, but we have advanced in the opposite direction, proving that the literature that comes from the streets is authentic, it is vital to the periphery and does not need to ask permission from anyone."

The difficulties encountered by writers and readers from the periphery was the subject of a recent discussion at the São Paulo biennial between Vaz, Ferréz and Ludemir, where the three writers criticized the habits of traditional publishers and authors, accusing them of ignoring readers from Brazil's poorer areas. "We have a lot of people reading, but the people who are reading don't interest the authors or publishers because they live on the periphery. No author wants to go to the periphery to launch a book, speak in public or talk to students, but they will fight to go to FLIP or the Bienal do Livro (Book Biennial)," said Ludemir.

Getting Literature to the Masses

Talking about how to combat illiteracy at the same event, Sérgio Vaz highlighted the necessity of making reading an everyday activity for Brazilian children, sparking early imagination and interest in the world of literature. This can be best achieved, he argued, by promoting literature which is written by people from different walks of life and which also touches upon themes that speak directly to traditionally marginalized groups, those outside of the Brazilian mainstream. With the launch of initiatives such as FLUPP Pensa and Cooperifa, as well as the inclusion of peripheral writers in major festivals like FLIP and FlipSide, it is clear that this process has begun, and that marginal literature is starting to reach a wider audience.

The other challenge that remains is how to spread literary activity more evenly throughout the country. Although the majority of festivals remain in the southeast, support for new festivals has grown and there is excitement about the prospect of more regional events. Jorge Teles of the FBN said that the aim of festivals in Brazil is to bring books closer to readers in order to create a dialogue between literature and citizens, something which can only be achieved by the continued diversification of festivals through the inclusion of more peripheral writers and the creation of more events outside of the major cities. Sérgio Vaz has stated that one of his aims when establishing Cooperifa in 2000 was to bring people together though art in order to share their experiences and encourage debate. This way of thinking should be a driving force behind Brazil's numerous literary festivals for many years to come, showing that there is plenty of room for talent representing all the different facets of modern Brazilian society. If Vaz is right, that will mark the point that Brazil becomes a nation of avid readers. With the country heading in that direction, we will soon find out.

GOOD, AVERAGE OR BAD?

LITERARY EVOLUTION IN BRAZIL

by Luiz Bras
translated by Eloise Stevens

The number of literary events and prizes, of new authors, publishers and readers, and of novels, short stories and poems being published has increased recently in Brazil, but is this significant? *The Cultural Vacuum (or the Imbecilization of Brazil)*, an article published in the magazine Carta Capital in September 2013, confirms the scepticism of hundreds of cultural critics, both of the press and of universities. According to the article, despite the growing economy, and the fact that a good number of Brazilians have finally been lifted out of poverty, Brazilian literature – or our culture, in general – is experiencing one of its worst phases in history.

The time has come to hear what a great number of protagonists have to say on the subject. I asked well-known writers, publishers, critics, teachers and journalists of Brazilian culture the question:

"In light of the number of published books and the quality of contemporary Brazilian prose and poetry, in your opinion, is Brazilian literature going through a good, an average or a bad phase?"

Here are some of the replies:

Marcelino Freire

I read an interview with the Portuguese novelist António Lobo Antunes in which he was asked "Do you not think that there are a lot of people writing these days?" To which he replied, "It would be worse if these people were painting. Just imagine the stench that would waft through the air! Or if they were making music. Who would be able to tolerate all that noise?"

Let people write, goddamit! It is by writing that one learns to write. I like to see people producing, taking risks, writing blogs, creating their own publishing houses, their own movements. We thus have more material to read, we have a greater choice; nowadays, it is not just the big publishing houses who dictate what is worth reading and doing. People have released their letters, freed their lines, ran around crying out their own paragraphs. They are no longer waiting, "*salve, salve*, Hallelujah!" Often in national literary columns you can find young people sharing the same page as revered household names. This plurality takes literature out of its academic cocoon and puts it on the street, onto new battle lines. When Granta compiled a list of the best new Brazilian writers, a spin-off, Granja, was published in Brazil. And this is the way it has to be. It's new and pulsing and alive.

I like literature to arrive with force, ready to fight, without delay. For example, one of our country's great recent achievements is the literature emerging from the suburbs of São Paulo. There, dozens of *saraus* (see p. 190 for more on this) are taking place all the time, with names such as Sérgio Vaz, Alessandro Buzo and Sacolinha in attendance. Why is this? Our literature has been bubbling for a while. The cauldron is boiling and I hold great hopes for it. Vibrant prose and poetry are erupting from the mix. And it is due to this diversity that we can choose to read a writer that may not be an asshole. Writers caked in literary prizes? Take a hike. We are no longer trapped in the age of the tubercolic author, locked in an asylum. Attitudes are different. Writers are invited to literary festivals, they travel nationally and abroad. Those ahead of the game spread the word not just on the page, but on street corners as well. In short, we are going through a good literary phase. It was bad a few years ago, when it was solely in the hands of the boutique literates. As the writers at the Cooperifa *sarau* say: "Let's make some noise." Not with rock, but with poetry because "Silence is a prayer." Long live literature!

Marcelino Freire is the author of Amar é Crime (Edith, 2010)

Cintia Moscovich

By having an optimistic outlook and disregarding the incredible amount of awful, truly dire literature being produced, I can say that the current climate is reasonably good. If we compare our current production to what it was two decades ago, it is easy to see that the number of people writing and publishing has doubled, if not tripled or even quadrupled. The list of national authors is increasing at the rate of inflation and literary fairs throughout the world are paying homage to Brazil. Even if not all of them are good, at least literature and the very act of writing have come to be viewed as a bit more normal. And best of all: literature is finally exempt from having to narrate with a tinge of local colour, making it more cosmopolitan.

Risking a slightly broader analysis, I would say that with the emergence and the urgency of the new middle class, literature has also come to be consumed, even as a sort of fetish, as a symbol of a necessary and desired intellectual prosperity. As such, at least on the surface, young (and also older) authors have another motive to write. Our literature's current good phase though owes itself to the increase in the number of readers or, at least, to the investment in the incentive to read.

Cintia Moscovich is the author of Essa Coisa Brilhante Que é a Chuva (Record, 2012)

Santiago Nazarian

I think the most interesting thing about contemporary Brazilian literature is its variety. Not just in the diversity of themes in so-called high literature, but also in genres such as fantasy, crime fiction and erotic fiction. Of course, this sort of literature is not yet prestigious, the literary classes still hold prejudices against it, but readers are embracing these works more and more.

Previously, the reader of fantasy, for example, would only seek out foreign works. Today the media, the most widely reaching newspapers and even the literary supplements are giving more coverage to these works and to Brazilian writers. And literary events are growing with different kinds of authors and audience members.

In any case, I still think that it needs to grow a lot, considering the size of the country. It remains very difficult for an author to survive,

21ST-CENTURY BRAZILIAN AUTHORS

Brazilian writer Luiz Ruffato picks some of the leading lights of contemporary Brazilian literature.

Starting with *Angu de Sangue*, his collection of short stories, **Marcelino Freire** (Sertânia, 1967) has dealt with marginalized characters using a rhythmic prose influenced by the poetry of the northeastern religious litany and imbuing situations of violence and cruelty with black humour (*BaléRalé, Contos Negreiros, Rasif – Mar Que Arrebenta* and *Amar é Crime*). Black humour is also the hallmark of **Evandro Ferreira Affonso** (Araxá, 1945), but in an opposing manner. He creates a mismatch between the triviality of his plots and the pompous erudition with which the facts are narrated. This can be seen in the titles of his books *Grogotó!, Araã!, Erefuê, Zaratempô!* and *Catâmbrias!* – which all use slang expressions – and even in *Minha Mãe Se Matou Sem Dizer Adeus* or *O Mendigo Que Sabia De Cor Os Adágios De Erasmo De Rotterdam*, two novels with more conventional narratives.

Sérgio Rodrigues (Muriaé, 1962) likes to shuffle between genres. He debuted with *O Homem Que Matou O Escritor*, a collection of pseudo-political short stories, following it with the sci-fi novel *As Sementes De Flowersville* and *Elza, A Garota*, a pseudo-journalistic piece about a real character murdered in 1930 at the behest of the Communist Party.

Miguel Sanches Neto (Bela Vista do Paraíso, 1965) also experiments with different forms of narrative. In *Chove Sobre Minha Infância* he creates a painful fictionalized autobiography, a device which he repeated in *Chá Das Cinco Com O Vampiro*. He also flirted with history in *Um Amor Anarquista* and *A Máquina De Madeira*, and a police story in *A Primeira Mulher*. Sanches Neto has also published two books of short stories, *Hóspede Secreto* and *Então Você Quer Ser Escritor?*

Joca Reiners Terron (Cuiabá, 1968) established in 2001 an independent publisher to launch his novel *Não Há Nada Lá*. After that, he published two books of short stories, *Hotel Hell* and *Sonho Interrompido Por Guilhotina*, and the novels *Curva De Rio Sujo*, *Do Fundo Do Poço Se Vê A Lua* and *A Tristeza Extraordinária Do Leopardo-das-neves*, as well as a hybrid book combining text and illustrations, *Guia De Ruas Sem Saída*. Coming from fine arts, **Nuno Ramos** (São Paulo, 1960) brought an experimental boldness in his use of language to express astonishment of a fluid reality (*O Pão Do Corvo*, *Ó*, *O Mau Vidraceiro*). **José Castello** (Rio de Janeiro, 1951) used real characters (the *curitibano* poet Paulo Leminski in *Fantasma*, his own father in *Ribamar*) to build pseudo-biographies that try to capture the spirit of a time, creating emotion and a rigorous narrative from elements of their lives. With a writing style imbued with melancholy, **Ronaldo Cagiano** (Cataguases, 1961) made Brasília the protagonist of several of his short stories in *Dezembro Indigesto*, *Concerto Para Arranha-céus* and *Dicionário De Pequenas Solidões*.

and even remain, if he or she is not part of the official canon, the literature of prestige. I often say that in Brazil, either you are a serious writer or an awful writer. If you don't don your academic hat, you end up being excluded from the cliques, you end up not being invited to many things – and the writer depends on invitations, both to events and to write columns and other articles, to survive.

Therefore, I think literature is in a good phase – it has been producing, people have been discussing, there are more ways to be published and more space in the media for it. But, for me, it is still far from ideal. I don't have much more to say... Obviously for me, I've seen much better phases...

Santiago Nazarian is author of Garotos Malditos (Record, 2012)

Ronaldo Bressane

Man, you know that I'm optimistic. I think that Brazilian literature is going through a magical phase, with all the ambiguity the word holds.

Never has so much Brazilian literature been published, both in prose and in verse. Writers have surged in the 70s and 80s fully formed, followed by the generations of the 90s, the noughties and the 10s, that have promoted a renovation on various levels. We have left behind the system addicted to the Rosa-Drummond-Clarice of the 60s and 70s for a multiplication of talents of different forms; there are few isolated and unreachable geniuses and more great, brilliant, interesting authors.

We also have new and diverse circuits of literature: both online (blogs, websites, social networks) and offline (fairs, festivals, literary evenings), and it seems that our publishing market has finally matured, with publishers associating themselves with foreign giants and becoming more and more capitalized and printing millions of copies; the level of quality of our publications already stands on an equal playing field as those of the great foreign ones.

On the other hand, the presence of literature in the newspapers has sensitively diminished (cultural supplements have become smaller or disappeared) and there is not one literature magazine in the country in the mould of Magazine Litteraire, for example, which brings together the erudite and the commercial, and sells well at the newsagents. And although literature is being circulated more, I don't see it being in fact read and discussed in a cultural sense, or rather, directly related to the immediate reality of society (as happens with cinema or TV). The distribution of national authors is still ridiculous when compared with our Argentinian and Colombian brothers, and we are light years away from Spain, France, Germany, the US and England. We are also not widely translated abroad (although this is changing; we already have a few good contemporary authors on the shelves in German, Spanish and French bookshops).

And, to repeat Marçal Aquino's joke, of the 3,000 mediocre copies of every first edition published, certainly 1,500 of them are bought by other writers. I don't think that the average Brazilian is actually interested in contemporary literature. I have even noted this disinterest in journalists and artists, not to mention the writers themselves.

Besides this, we are also still in a stage of fetishizing literature, in which books are valued more for their aesthetic appearance than their content: "look at this beautiful edition, I need to have it!" "But will you read

Maria Valéria Rezende (Santos, 1942) and **Paulo Rodrigues** (São Paulo, 1948) recovered, in a way, the tradition of realist storytelling. The tales gathered in *Vasto Mundo* and *Modos De Apanhar Pássaros à Mão* and the novel *O Vôo Da Guará Vermelha* indicate a predilection to take characters from the bottom of the social pyramid (Brazilian rural workers, couriers, prostitutes). With courage and kindness, Valéria Rezende animates them, extracting amazingly genuine stories of love and friendship. The combination of a learned use of language with a sophisticated formal structure is what differentiates Paulo Rodrigues, obvious in his debut novel, *À Margem Da Linha*, which tells the metaphorical journey of two brothers in search of their father, and expanded upon in his second novel, *As Vozes Do Sótão*. Rodrigues has also published a collection of short stories, *Redemoinho*.

Maria José Silveira (Jaraguá, 1947) works within the universe of the historical novel, depicting the formation of Brazil in *A Mãe Da Mãe De Sua Mãe E Sua Filha*; the Goiás war in *Guerra No Coração Do Cerrado*; the recent past of the military dictatorship in *O Fantasma De Luis Buñuel*; and even stretching to a romanticized biography, as in *Eleanor Marx, Filha De Karl*. **Maria Esther Maciel** (Patos de Minas, 1963) deconstructed genres in *O Livro De Zenóbia* and *O Livro Dos Nomes*, silent vignettes that weave short, seemingly banal but revealingly intense biographies. Also using silence and gentleness are the seamless tales of **Mário Araújo** (Curitiba, 1963), *A Hora Extrema* and *Restos*, with their characters struck by epiphanic moments. **Beatriz Bracher** (São Paulo, 1961) investigates, through a sophisticated set of narrative voices, the underground of the middle class (*Azul E Dura, Não Falei, Antonio, Meu Amor*), which also motivates the work of **Mario Sabino** (São Paulo, 1962), author of *O Dia Em Que Matei Meu Pai*, one of the most translated books of contemporary Brazilian literature. Sabino also published two books of short stories, *O Antinarciso* and *A Boca Da Verdade*, and a novel, *O Vício Do Amor*.

    Lourenço Muttarelli (São Paulo, 1964) has explored strange worlds and bizarre behaviours in his novels *O Cheiro Do Ralo, Natimorto, Jesus Kid, A Arte De Produzir Efeito Sem Causa, Miguel E Os Demônios* and *Nada Me Faltará*. Just as bizarre are the characters from the short stories and first novel of **Paulo Scott** (Porto Alegre, 1966), *Ainda Orangotangos* and *Voláteis* respectively, while in *Habitante Irreal* he makes a gritty portrayal of the mistakes of the generation that lived through the "lost decade", the 1980s, with their failed political and personal projects. The country's recent history is the backdrop of the novels of **Edney Silvestre** (Valencia, RJ, 1950); *Se Eu Fechar Os Olhos Agora* and *A Felicidade É Fácil*, that, by means of a plot that flirts with a police trauma, creates a poignant portrait of the generation that was born with Vargas as president and grew up during the military dictatorship.

by Luiz Ruffato

it?" "Who needs to read? The book will look nice on my coffee table, or on the shelf." Yes, I actually heard this conversation in a posh bookshop.

Finally, if, on the one hand, I am optimistic about the production and marketing side of the argument, on the other hand, I fear that, with regard to the cultural element, we are going straight to the stage of book as an object, without going through the essential stage in which the content (the narrative, the language, the ethics, the style, the characters) is the centre of the cultural life of a society.

We are a nouveau riche country, one that has not had sufficient education, and therefore shows off what we would like to have; we give value to literature as a means of social ascension, and not as an aesthetic fruition in itself. Perhaps the children and grandchildren of the nouveau riche Brazilians will have the necessary education to reach this stage, but that depends on a true educational revolution, of which I see hide nor hair on the public or private horizons of this country.

And, if we lose the chance to embark on this revolution with the safe full, you can bet that in 20 years' time we will be as stupid and as uncultured as we were in the 70s.

Ronaldo Bressane is the author of Céu de Lúcifer (Azougue, 2003)

Rinaldo de Fernandes

Good works will always come out of a large number. Current Brazilian literary production has a curious fact – the most important authors are currently in their 80s. They are novelists and poets: Dalton Trevisan, Rubem Fonseca, Ariano Suassuna, Manoel de Barros, Lygia Fagundes Telles, Augusto de Campos and Ferreira Gullar. These are our most noteworthy writers, I believe. These are those whose lives have been canonised. Aside from them, I don't think there are any other authors that can be canonised at the moment. There is a group of well-renowned authors in their 50s and 60s, like João Gilberto Noll and Milton Hatoum. They have good reputations but they have not yet reached the level of the names mentioned above. After them, there are the up and coming names, who started off in the 90s, and who are still in search of the great work that will make them remembered by generations to come.

On the other hand, the fairs, biennials and other literary events that are currently fashionable, although they are thought of as cultural products, with a good return/ revenue in particular for the publishers, are also beneficial to the authors who are able to make an address before an audience that wants to learn more about literary subjects. These events help to propagate books, demystify the figure of the author and create a connection between the reader and the literary corpus.

Rinaldo de Fernandes is a writer and Professor of Brazilian Literature at the Federal University of Paraíba.

Paulo Scott

In regards to literary production, there is no good or special phase. Sure enough, if you look at short stories and the number of people that write short prose, it is true that the best first published works of unknown authors have proven themselves to have a significant degree of innovation and thematic density.

Yes, there is a small technological revolution, a maturing of the market due to the increased financial capacity of certain classes to acquire cultural products like books (considering that we no longer pay for music or films), and a greater security – a decrease of the inferiority complex – in the affirmation of names of a new generation of writers, which all makes for a more optimistic landscape; a promise that may or may not be fulfilled in the future.

A country that barely "discovered" Lucio Cardoso [a poet, playwright and author who had some notoriety in the Bohemian neighbourhoods of Rio de Janeiro of the 40s and 50s] now has publishing agents waging bets and starting the publicity machine to make and break new authors. I think that the literary wave at the beginning of the 21st century is most significant. It confirmed that there is a certain way to position yourself as a novelist, which can be easily duplicated. In quantitive terms, there is assuredness in the use of language and a real possibility for authors to find their voice.

In the field of poetry, however, a revolution is happening, a revolution that is modernizing national production, in line with what is currently being written abroad. The Brazilian poet, under the lens of quantity, is being more fearless.

Paulo Scott is author of Habitante Irreal (Alfaguara, 2011)

ON A STRING

A LITERATURA DE CORDEL RESEARCHER TELLS US EXACTLY WHAT ARE THESE INFAMOUS LITTLE BOOKS OF LITERATURE

by Russell Slater
interview translated by Jurema Simoes

One of the surprising themes that emerged while putting together this book was the role of *literatura de cordel*, a big influence on the artists Gilvan Samico and Derlon Almeida, on Glauber Rocha's *Deus E O Diabo Na Terra Do Sol*, as well as northeastern musicians, such as Siba, whose poetic lyrics undoubtedly show a love for *cordel*.

Antonio Barreto [pictured bottom right] was born in the interior of Bahia, later moving to the capital of Salvador, and has spent much of his life collecting and researching *literatura de cordel*. He has published 150 *cordel* titles himself and has a personal collection of over 1,000 editions. He seemed like the perfect candidate to explain to us what exactly these little books are:

"*Cordel* is a popular art created in verses that obeys rules of rhyme, rhythm and plot. It's a form of poetry that arrived in Brazil through the Portuguese around the seventh century." Explaining the name he says that "popular poets in Portugal hung their work on a string, and so Brazilian researchers decided to call it *literatura de cordel* (literature on a string)." As important as the poetry within, which always obeys a rhyming structure, and the folkloric plots, are the covers which would traditionally feature woodcut engravings by some of the northeast's finest artists.

Though Antonio is from Bahia he confesses that "the cordel is most intense in the [northeastern] states of Pernambuco, Ceará, Paraíba, Rio Grande do Norte & Sergipe."

And to give you a feel of what *cordel* poetry is like, here's Antonio's *cordel*-ised description of himself:

"If you would like to know me
No need for this enquiring face...
My name is Antonio Barreto
And the wilderness is my place...
I am substantive, masculine and singular
All entwined in one lace..."

SOIREES FOR THE SOUL

THE STORY OF BRAZIL'S UNDERGROUND POETRY JAMS

by Russell Slater

Across São Paulo groups of writers, rappers, students, intellectuals and other engaged folk are congregating to share their poetry. In the US it would be called a poetry jam. In Brazil it's a *sarau*, literally translating as soiree, but nowhere near as decadent as that sounds.

One of the earliest notable *saraus* arrived thanks to the hard work of Sérgio Vaz, whose idea of creating a place where talented people from his neighbourhood, took some time to get off the ground. Cooperifa, as it was named, started in 2000 in an abandoned factory. When they were evicted they moved to a bar called Garajão, but it was soon sold. It turned out to be third time lucky as Vaz and fellow poet Marco Pezão eventually found Bar do Zé Batidão in São Paulo and Cooperifa really came to life. The idea was simple. The stage was open, and anyone could get up there and recite their poetry, tell stories, rap, perform theatre or even visual art installations, though the main focus has always been poetry. By 2004, Cooperifa's reputation had grown considerably – partly thanks to the fact that regular attendees included popular local rappers like G.O.G., Gaspar, Cocão and Mano Brown (Racionais).

The reputation of *saraus* as hotbeds for talent from the city's peripheries grew thanks to the parallel success of two *sarau* regulars. Ferréz is a rapper, screenwriter and poet, though best known for his novels which depict the violence of his neighbourhood Capão Redondo using rhythmic prose and local slang to bring humanity to the desperate situations that his characters often find themselves in. His exposure as a columnist via Caros Amigos, a well-respected newspaper supplement, has been extremely important in bringing the *saraus* and *literatura marginal* to national attention.

The other important figure in the rise of the *saraus* is Alessandro Buzo. He set the template for self-publishing when he did exactly that in 2000 with his first novel *Ferrovia, Nua E Crua*, a politicized account of the appalling conditions of the Brás/ Calmin Viana line of the city's train network. The release of the book was crucial in making people aware of how bad the transport infrastructure had become in certain parts of the city. He has since released a wide variety of novels as well as publishing the fanzine Boletim de Kaos, collecting stories and poetry from the periphery. These days, he is best known for hosting the Buzão Circular Periférico section of the Manos e Minas program on the TV Cultura television station, one of the few programs which shows culture happening in São Paulo's poorest neighbourhoods.

The fact that many of the peripheral neighbourhoods have no libraries, cultural centres or cinemas was a big factor in their rise in popularity. Once people saw how easy it was to set-up a *sarau* and that there was a growing network of underground poets, rappers and writers, self-publishing their own novels, fanzines and music, it was no surprise that many more *saraus* set-up around São Paulo. Their role as both a community meeting point and an avenue for creativity was something that was missing from many neighbourhoods.

Sarau do Binho was one of the earliest *saraus*, starting life in 1999 on a sporadic basis – their early *saraus* were done completely by light of candle, with all electric lights turned off – before finally becoming a weekly event in 2004. Binho, who runs the *sarau*, told me that it's a space where "every form of expression is accepted and where people can show their art and share their feelings and anxieties."

Another popular *sarau* is Elo da Corrente, which started in 2007 and has already evolved to publishing, releasing an anthology of poetry from the *sarau*, as well as books focusing on single authors. Other *saraus* in São Paulo include Sarau da Brasa, Sarau do Ademar and Sarau Suburbano, which is run by Buzo in the Bixiga neighbourhood, where he also manages the Suburbano Convicto shop selling independently released books, fanzines and CDs. [Interestingly, they share the building with Bixiga 70 (read more about them on p. 33) and it's consequently become an important point of culture for the neighbourhood.] Outside of São Paulo there are few *saraus*, Nelson Maca's Sarau Bem Black in Salvador being one of the main exceptions.

If you're a fan of the Brazilian rapper/singer Criolo you shouldn't be too surprised that he is also a *sarau* regular. It's easy to imagine how his on-stage charisma, pathos and poetic lyrics would suit the nature of a poetry evening perfectly. [Criolo was incidentally the protagonist of a 2009 film, *Profissão MC*, that was written by Alessandro Buzo and followed a rapper who had to choose between a life of drugs or follow his dream of becoming a rapper]. With more wisdom in his young life than many accrue in a lifetime, Criolo's description of the *saraus* says it all:

"I see the *saraus* as an absurd revolution of soul and essence. You go there to recite your poetry and the people listen to it. It's a ritual of respect to humanity [that] refreshes your soul."

If you ever wanted an example that Brazil has an endless source of creativity, then the *saraus* are it. With their increasing profile in Brazil and the successes of Sérgio Vaz and Ferréz at infiltrating literature circles that previously stuck their nose up at the peripheries (see p. 178 for more on this), there is no doubt that the marginal are finally getting their voice heard, which is really what it was all about anyway.

A JORGE AMADO READER

THE EPITOME OF BRAZILIAN 'SOUL'

by Gina Vergel

No compendium about Brazil's many cultural treasures can be complete without a mention of the works of Jorge Amado. Considered one of Brazil's most important, and loved, writers, Amado's works have been translated into 49 languages and published in 55 countries. So, what is it about this master storyteller from Bahia that people love so much?

Jorge Amado

According to Janet Sternberg, a media and communications expert and scholar who lived, studied, and worked in Brazil for many years, Amado's storylines appealed to everyone, because its characters cut across race, class, gender, ethnicity and age. "He wrote about men and women, young and old, poor and rich, black and white and every colour in between," she said.

Amado wrote the first Brazilian book with a black main character in the 1930s. Other unlikely heroes for the time followed, from a prostitute to a black caretaker who contests a white professor's racist theories in university.

Amado hailed from Bahia, Brazil's fifth largest state, and one of the colonial centres in early Brazilian history. The Bahia region was one heavily influenced by the slave trade with Africa, perhaps with the heaviest concentration of slavery in all of Brazil.

"Jorge Amado's work is the epitome of Brazilian 'soul:' a perfect reflection of Brazil's melting-pot history and slave-trade legacy, spiked with romance, music and plenty of local colour," Sternberg said.

"Growing up in Salvador (Brazil's earliest capital city), and later going to study and work in Rio de Janeiro during that city's period as capital, Amado was exposed to all types of Brazilian culture," she said. "His career as author, journalist, and even politician, gave him access to a tremendously wide range of people and public outlets. It would be difficult to find a Brazilian who did not know at least something about Jorge Amado."

Though he died in 2001, Amado's writing has influenced, and continues to influence, many areas of Brazilian culture. His work has inspired music, films, carnival productions (who often use Amado's stories as the basis for their shows), television programmes – including various "telenovela" soap opera series – and even the culinary arts. Many of Brazil's greatest artists have built tremendous success on works related to Amado's tales and characters.

Amado was a fan of a central female character. "His sympathetic portrayals of female protagonists in particular, such as Gabriela and Flor (also Tieta and Teresa Batista, lesser known heroines), are attractive to everyone, regardless of gender, you either want to be like Amado's ladies or you want to be in love with them," Sternberg told me.

For Amado "newbies", Sternberg recommended his two most popular and enduring hits:

Gabriela, Clove and Cinnamon (Gabriela, Cravo e Canela, 1959)
Dona Flor and Her Two Husbands (Dona Flor e Seus Dois Maridos, 1966)

"Both books inspired movies and telenovelas," she said, "and, in fact, *Gabriela* was just remade as a telenovela for the third time in 2012."

"Amado's rich legacy of work has steadily provided inspiration for generation after generation of Brazil's greatest artists in all genres. Given last year's revival of the telenovela *Gabriela*, the tradition of Brazilians being in love with Jorge Amado shows no signs of slowing down, as a whole new generation of media stars and young people join the legions of Amado's older Brazilian fans," Sternberg said.

A selection of Amado's finest: *The Violent Land (Terra do Sem Fim*, 1942) - often cited by Amado as his favourite of his own novels; *Red Field (Seara Vermelha*, 1946); *Gabriela, Clove and Cinnamon* (1959); *Dona Flor and Her Two Husbands* (1966)

CONTRIBUTORS

Lulina Abduzida is a singer/songwriter from Pernambuco living in São Paulo. She has released 12 albums, including the well-received *Cristalina* in 2009 and the recently-released *Pantim*.

Katia Abreu is a journalist and cultural producer who has reported on Brazilian independent music for over 10 years.

Mateus Acioli is a graphic designer, cartoonist, aspiring sign painter and tattoo artist.

Diego Albuquerque & Rodrigo Édipo are two of the founders and creative forces behind MI (Música Independente), an independently produced magazine focused on alternative music in Pernambuco.

Debora Baldelli is a social scientist and ethnomusicologist currently doing her PhD in Music at New University of Lisbon, Portugal.

Alicia Bastos is an independent cultural producer and curator specialized in the promotion of Brazilian art abroad; and the founder of braziliality.org.

Marlon Bishop is a New York-based journalist, writer and radio producer who specializes in cultural reporting on Latin America, Africa and the Caribbean. He is a staff writer at MTV Iggy, an associate producer for Afropop Worldwide, and a frequent contributor to various public radio programs in the US.

Joanna Blyth is a recent graduate in Spanish and Latin American Studies from UCL.

Rodrigo Brandão is an MC, music promoter and ambassador for alternative rap music in Brazil. In 2013, he compiled *Daora: Underground Sounds of Urban Brasil – Hip-Hop, Beats, Afro & Dub* for Mais Um Discos.

Luiz Bras is a writer and Doctor of Letters at USP. He is the author of the novel *Sozinho No Deserto Extremo* and short story collection *Máquina Macunaíma*.

Caçapa is a musician, arranger and researcher from Pernambuco. His debut solo album *Elefantes Na Rua Nova* was released in 2011 and was well received by critics in and outside of Brazil.

Greg Caz is a New York City-based DJ well known for his "Brazilian Beat Brooklyn" party which ran weekly in Williamsburg for eight years, as well as for his series of compilations of 70s Brazilian rarities.

Tom Crookston is a writer and DJ from London.

Rob Curto is a professional accordionist, composer and founding member of the band Matuto.

Arthur Dantas has been a political activist since the age of 14 and at age 35 returned to university to study Environmental Management. He writes about culture and art.

Alfredo Del-Penho is a samba composer, performer and playwright from Rio de Janeiro.

Alexander S. Dent is an expert on *sertanejo* music, and teaches Anthropology at George Washington University.

Beto Figueiroa is a photographer from Pernambuco.

Cícero Fraga is a videomaker and copywriter from Brasília.

Julia Furlan is a writer, editor and radio producer who is equal parts Brooklynite and Paulista.

Bruna Gala is a freelance journalist, blogger and Woody Allen fan who loves good coffee and is still trying to find the perfect espresso in London.

Amaya García-Velasco is an independent researcher and music journalist based in Puerto Rico. She holds an MA in Popular Music and Culture from the University of Western Ontario in London, Canada.

Shannon Garland is an ethnomusicologist specializing in independent music production in Brazil, Chile and Argentina.

Jody Gillett is a freelance music advisor with a special focus on Brazil and UK consultant for Brasil Music Exchange.

Kariann Goldschmitt is a music scholar who specializes in Brazilian music and teaches comparative arts and music classes in South Florida.

Bruno Guaraná is a film-maker and a PhD candidate at NYU's Cinema Studies Department.

Pedro Gutierres is an illustrator, painter and musician from Porto Alegre.

Wolfram Lange is a geographer living in Rio de Janeiro. He is also a music addict, collecting sounds and presenting them on his website SoundGoods and on German public radio Funkhaus Europa.

Nick MacWilliam is a writer and editor based in Santiago, Chile. He regularly contributes to Sounds and Colours.

Demetrios Matheou is film critic for the Sunday Herald and the Independent on Sunday. He is the author of the *Faber Book of South American Cinema*.

Pablo Miyazawa is a journalist born and raised in São Paulo. He is the editor-in-chief of Rolling Stone Brasil. He's been writing about pop culture, music and videogames since 1998.

Henrik Moltke is a journalist and documentary maker. He was the co-director of *Good Copy Bad Copy*.

Leo Nikolaidis is a writer and reviewer of art and films, and film editor for the Sounds and Colours website.

Robin Perkins is a British-born, Amsterdam-based music writer, blogger, producer and DJ.

Damian Platt is the author of *Culture is Your Weapon*. He lives and works in Rio de Janeiro.

Luiz Ruffato is a short story writer, novelist and poet born in Cataguases, Minas Gerais. His publications include the novels *Eles Eram Muitos Cavalos* and *Estive Em Lisboa E Lembrei De Você*, and the *Inferno Provisório* series of books.

Lucas Santtana is a singer, composer and producer. His album *Sem Nostalgia* was chosen as the best foreign disc by the newspaper Liberation in 2011.

Greg Scruggs is currently pursuing a master's degree in Latin American and Caribbean Studies at Columbia University.

Jessica Sequeira is a writer, translator and Latin American historian at the University of Cambridge, currently working in Buenos Aires.

Sofia Serbin de Skalon is director and founder of the Argentine Film Festival, London, and specializes in film programming, publicity and event production.

Ed Siegle is a writer based in Brighton. His first novel, *Invisibles*, was published in 2011.

Russell Slater is the founder/editor of Sounds and Colours.

Eloise Stevens is a writer, radio producer and world music enthusiast from London. She has lived in Salvador and Rio de Janeiro and is perpetually trying to propel herself from one musical adventure to the next, armed with notepad and dictaphone.

José Teles is a music critic and columnist from Paraíba. He has written extensively about music from northeastern Brazil, including books on Luiz Gonzaga, *frevo* and Chico Science.

Allen Thayer is a writer and DJ from San Francisco. He is a regular contributor to Wax Poetics magazine.

Steven Totten is an Arizona-based journalist, teacher and musician who focuses on the impacts of culture in the Americas.

Gina Vergel is a writer and publicist based in New York City.

Hermano Vianna is a Brazilian anthropologist and writer who currently works in television.

Zansky is an illustrator from São Paulo with a dirty, absurd and colourful style that can be seen in many publications. He is also a member of the artistic collective BASE-V.

CD CONTENTS

1. Kassin "Calça de Ginástica"
A clear example of the "*carioca* groove" from one of Rio's most in-demand musicians and producers. Taken from his album *Sonhando Devagar*.

2. BNegão & Os Seletores de Frequência "Chega Pra Somar No Groove"
After an absence of nine years, Rio's BNegão returned to the limelight with *Sintoniza Lá*, showing that his fusion of Jorge Ben, hip-hop and rock will never grow old.

3. Orquestra Contemporânea de Olinda "No Ar"
Orquestra Contemporânea are joyous, brass-fuelled ambassadors for traditional northeastern Brazilian music. On this track, from their recent *Pra Ficar* album, they add catchy pop melodies into the mix.

4. Ex-Exus "Estejam Sempre Aqui"
Showing the more in-your-face side of Recife are Ex-Exus whose latest album *Xô* captures their own attitude-filled experimental take on 90s rock.

5. Cabruêra "Jurema"
João Pessoa's Cabruêra fused Brazil with the East on their 2010 album *Nordeste Oriental*. "Jurema" shows that this particular fusion can still be as funky as hell.

6. Sombra "Movimente-se"
Proving that Brazilian hip-hop is in rude health is São Paulo-resident Sombra's latest album, *Fantástico Mundo Popular*, an eclectic affair featuring live instrumentation and some of Sombra's finest rhymes yet.

7. OQuadro "Tá Amarrado"
One of the most relentlessly funky compositions from OQuadro's recently released debut record. When it comes to deep bass lines and passionate rapping few do it better.

8. Metá Metá "Obá Iná"
With their extended 5-person line-up, Metá-Metá are the best live band in Brazil. Pared down to the three core members of Juçara Marçal, Kiko Dinucci and Thiago França they are also capable of some of the most serene music being made anywhere.

9. Bixiga 70 "Grito de Paz"
São Paulo's Bixiga 70 show there's more to their sound than afrobeat with the first composition they wrote together, a homage to the legendary *candomblé*-inspired vocal group Os Tincoãs.

10. Alvinho Lancellotti "Alegria da Gente"
O Tempo Faz a Gente Ter Esses Encantos, the debut solo record from Lancellotti (a member of Fino Coletivo) was an unsuspected surprise of 2012, a simple, joyous slice of Rio life.

11. Gabriel Muzak "Belém Não Para"
The Amazonian style of *carimbó* is much in demand. Here, the *carioca* Gabriel Muzak turns it into an infectious, yet angular, pop art creation.

12. Dead Lover's Twisted Heart "Meu Coração"
Channelling great pop music from all over the world are Belo Horizonte's DLTH. "Meu Coração" is from their debut EP, *Lóvi*; hopefully a full-length is on the way.

13. Felipe Cordeiro "Conversa Fora"
Representing Belém and the recent surge of interest in the pop sounds of *brega* and *lambada* is Felipe Cordeiro, featured here with one of his heavier electronic compositions.

14. D MinGus "Naturalmente Punks"
An important musician in Recife's new Cena Beto, D Mingus seems to change suit with each new release. His latest, *Fricção*, is full of charming indie rock paeans such as this.

15. Chinese Cookie Poets "Viva la Raza!"
We said that the experimental music scene in Rio is thriving, and here's the proof, a two-and-a-half minute barrage of guitar, drums and bass from one of the scene's most interesting groups.

16. Passo Torto "Cidadão"
If you put Rômulo Froes, Rodrigo Campos, Kiko Dinucci and Marcelo Cabral in a room together they will make great music. "Cidadão" is the proof.

17. Siba "Qasida"
Siba seems to wilfully pursue his own musical interests, heading deeper and deeper into traditional music of the Mata Norte, yet always possessing the power to make highly listenable, personal fare such as "Qasida", taken from latest album *Avante*.

18. Alessandra Leão "Ai, Dendê"
Leão is one of the finest singers in the northeast of Brazil. Carrying on the tradition of the *manguebit* pioneers, and of her previous group Comadre Fulozinha, here she takes influence from the region's traditional music to create something personal and unique.

19. Space Night Love Dance Laser "Ivani 2000"
Sistema Criolina are a big name in Brasília, where they hold regular tropical parties and make music under all kinds of names. "Ivani 2000" is from their recent release as Space Night Love Dance Laser, a funky, laid-back number with a hint of the exotic.

20. Os Nelsons "É Só Se Jogar"
It's always nice to end on an high, and that's exactly what this is, an up-tempo fusion of pop, bass and Latin romanticism from Bahia that seems set to spiral out of control at any minute.

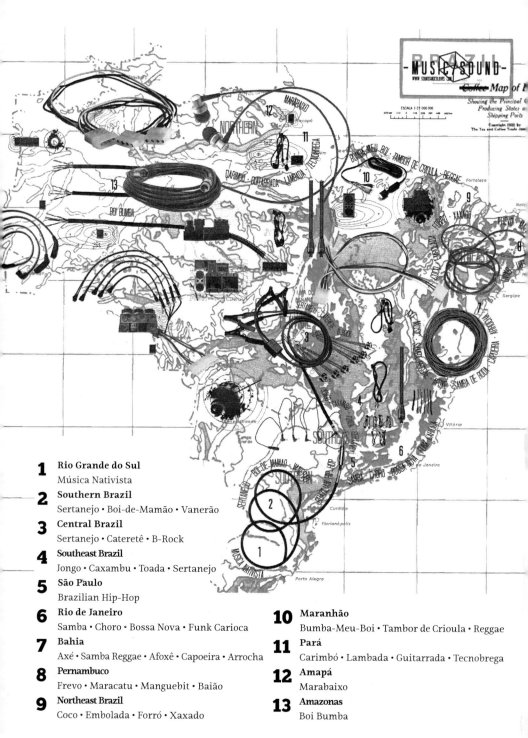

1 **Rio Grande do Sul**
Música Nativista

2 **Southern Brazil**
Sertanejo • Boi-de-Mamão • Vanerão

3 **Central Brazil**
Sertanejo • Cateretê • B-Rock

4 **Southeast Brazil**
Jongo • Caxambu • Toada • Sertanejo

5 **São Paulo**
Brazilian Hip-Hop

6 **Rio de Janeiro**
Samba • Choro • Bossa Nova • Funk Carioca

7 **Bahia**
Axé • Samba Reggae • Afoxê • Capoeira • Arrocha

8 **Pernambuco**
Frevo • Maracatu • Manguebit • Baião

9 **Northeast Brazil**
Coco • Embolada • Forró • Xaxado

10 **Maranhão**
Bumba-Meu-Boi • Tambor de Crioula • Reggae

11 **Pará**
Carimbó • Lambada • Guitarrada • Tecnobrega

12 **Amapá**
Marabaixo

13 **Amazonas**
Boi Bumba

Musical Map of Brazil by Raul Luna